THE CAMBRIDGE
COMPANION TO
DON DeLILLO

EDITED BY
JOHN N. DUVALL

CAMBRIDGE
UNIVERSITY PRESS

CAMBRIDGE UNIVERSITY PRESS
Cambridge, New York, Melbourne, Madrid, Cape Town, Singapore, São Paulo, Delhi

Cambridge University Press
The Edinburgh Building, Cambridge CB2 8RU, UK

Published in the United States of America by Cambridge University Press, New York

www.cambridge.org
Information on this title: www.cambridge.org/9780521690898

First published 2008

Printed in the United Kingdom at the University Press, Cambridge

A catalogue record for this publication is available from the British Library

Library of Congress Cataloguing in Publication data
The Cambridge companion to Don DeLillo / edited by John N. Duvall.
p.   cm.
Includes bibliographical references (p.) and index.
ISBN 978-0-521-87065-8 –
ISBN 978-0-521-69089-8 (pbk.)
1. DeLillo, Don.–Criticism and interpretation.   I. Duvall, John N. (John Noel), 1956–
PS3554.E4425Z57   2008
813'.54–dc22
2007051672

ISBN 978-0-521-87065-8 hardback
ISBN 978-0-521-69089-8 paperback

CONTENTS

NOTES ON CONTRIBUTORS

PETER BOXALL is Senior Lecturer in English at the University of Sussex. He is the author of *Don DeLillo: The Possibility of Fiction* (2006) and is currently completing a book on Samuel Beckett's influence on contemporary literature entitled *Since Beckett: Contemporary Writing in the Wake of Modernism*. He is co-editor of *The Year's Work in Critical and Cultural Theory* and the reviews editor for the journal *Textual Practice*.

JOSEPH CONTE is Professor of English at the University at Buffalo, State University of New York. He is the author of *Unending Design: The Forms of Postmodern Poetry* (1991) and *Design and Debris: A Chaotics of American Fiction* (2002). His current book project explores the relationship of compositional method and poetic texture in modern and postmodern poetry.

DAVID COWART, the author of *Don DeLillo: The Physics of Language* (2002), teaches contemporary American literature at the University of South Carolina. His other books include *Thomas Pynchon: The Art of Allusion, History and the Contemporary Novel* (1980) and *Trailing Clouds: Immigrant Fiction in Contemporary America* (2006). His current project is a book on the post-Pynchon, post-DeLillo generation of American novelists.

JOSEPH DEWEY, Associate Professor of American Literature, University of Pittsburgh at Johnstown, is the author of *In a Dark Time: The Apocalyptic Temper in the American Novel of the Nuclear Age* (1992), *Novels from Reagan's America: A New Realism* (1999), and *Understanding Richard Powers* (2002) and *Beyond Grief and Nothing: A Reading of Don DeLillo* (2006). He also co-edited *UnderWords: Perspectives on Don DeLillo's "Underworld"* (2001).

JOHN N. DUVALL is Professor of English and editor of *Modern Fiction Studies* at Purdue University. He is the author of *Faulkner's Marginal Couple: Invisible, Outlaw and Unspeakable Communities* (1990), *The Identifying Fictions of Toni Morrison: Modernist Authenticity and Postmodern Blackness* (2000), and *Don DeLillo's "Underworld"* (2002). He and Tim Engles co-edited *Approaches to Teaching DeLillo's "White Noise"* (2006).

TIM ENGLES is Associate Professor of English at Eastern Illinois University. He has co-edited *Critical Essays on Don DeLillo* (2000) and *Approaches to Teaching DeLillo's "White Noise"* (2006).

JEREMY GREEN is Associate Professor of English at the University of Colorado at Boulder. He is author of *Late Postmodernism: American Fiction at the Millennium* (2005) and is currently working on a book examining contemporary British poetry and cultural politics.

RUTH HELYER, whose research focuses on contemporary fiction and film, visual culture, and gender studies, is Senior Lecturer at the University of Teesside. In addition to her work on DeLillo, she has published essays on such contemporary novelists as Bret Easton Ellis, Zadie Smith, and Salman Rushdie.

PETER KNIGHT teaches American Studies at the University of Manchester. He is the author of *Conspiracy Culture: From the Kennedy Assassination to "The X-Files"* (2000) and *The Kennedy Assassination* (2007).

PHILIP NEL is the author of *The Avant-Garde and American Postmodernity: Small Incisive Shocks* (2002), *Dr. Seuss: American Icon* (2004), and *The Annotated Cat: Under the Hats of Seuss and His Cats* (2007). He has also co-edited (with Julia Mickenberg) a forthcoming reader, *Tales for Little Rebels: A Collection of Radical Children's Literature*. He is Associate Professor of English at Kansas State University.

PATRICK O'DONNELL is Professor of English at Michigan State University. He has written several books on modern and contemporary fiction, including *Passionate Doubts: Designs of Interpretation in Contemporary American Fiction* (1986) and *Latent Destinies: Cultural Paranoia and Contemporary U.S. Narrative* (2000), and co-edited *Intertextuality and Contemporary American Fiction* (1989). Currently he is working on two books: *The New American Novel: Reading American Fiction Since 1980* and *When Seen: Henry James Through Contemporary Film*.

STACEY OLSTER is Professor of English at the State University of New York at Stony Brook. She is the author of *Reminiscence and Re-Creation in Contemporary American Fiction* (1989) and *The Trash Phenomenon: Contemporary Literature, Popular Culture, and the Making of the American Century* (2003), and the editor of *The Cambridge Companion to John Updike* (2006).

MARK OSTEEN, Professor of English at Loyola College in Maryland, is the author of *The Economy of Ulysses: Making Both Ends Meet* (1995) and *American Magic and Dread: Don DeLillo's Dialogue with Culture* (2000). He edited the Viking Critical Library edition of DeLillo's *White Noise*, as well as a forthcoming collection of essays, *Autism and Representation*.

ABBREVIATIONS

Citations to DeLillo's novels are made parenthetically in this volume. Full publication information for these novels appears in the Select Bibliography.

A   *Americana* (1971)
BA   *The Body Artist* (2001)
C   *Cosmopolis* (2003)
EZ   *End Zone* (1972)
FM   *Falling Man* (2007)
GJS   *Great Jones Street* (1973)
L   *Libra* (1988)
M   *Mao II* (1991)
N   *The Names* (1982)
P   *Players* (1977)
RD   *Running Dog* (1978)
RS   *Ratner's Star* (1976)
U   *Underworld* (1997)
WN   *White Noise* (1985)

CHRONOLOGY OF DELILLO'S LIFE AND WORK

1916   Don DeLillo's father emigrates with his family from Italy to the USA at the age of nine, eventually becoming an auditor for a life insurance company.

1936   Don DeLillo is born on November 20 in a working-class, Italian-American, North Bronx neighborhood of New York City.

1951   Soviet Union develops the atomic bomb; DeLillo is a sophomore in high school.

1954   DeLillo graduates from Cardinal Hayes High School in the Bronx.

1958   DeLillo earns his BA in Communication Arts from Fordham University.

1959   DeLillo takes a job at Ogilvy & Mather, an advertising agency, as a copywriter.

1963   President John F. Kennedy is assassinated on November 22.

1964   DeLillo leaves Ogilvy & Mather to become a freelance writer.

1965   USA begins saturation bombing and a major troop build-up in Vietnam.

1966   DeLillo begins working on his first novel.

1971   DeLillo's first novel, *Americana*, is published.

1972   DeLillo's second novel, *End Zone*, is published.

1973   DeLillo's third novel, *Great Jones Street*, is published.

1974	Richard Nixon resigns as President of the USA on August 8.
1975	DeLillo marries Barbara Bennett; USA withdraws from Vietnam.
1976	DeLillo's fourth novel, *Ratner's Star*, is published.
1977	DeLillo's fifth novel, *Players*, is published.
1978	DeLillo's sixth novel, *Running Dog*, is published.
1979	DeLillo wins a Guggenheim Fellowship that allows him to spend the next two years in Greece, which forms the setting for his next novel, *The Names*. DeLillo publishes a short play, *The Engineer of Moonlight*.
1982	DeLillo's seventh novel, *The Names*, is published.
1985	DeLillo's eighth novel, *White Noise*, is published.
1986	*White Noise* wins the National Book Award. DeLillo's play *The Day Room* is published.
1988	DeLillo's ninth novel, *Libra* is published; it is a main selection of the Book of the Month Club.
1991	DeLillo's tenth novel, *Mao II*, is published in the USA; DeLillo completes the screenplay for *Game 6*.
1992	DeLillo's novella "Pafko at the Wall" (which becomes the Prologue to *Underworld*) is published in *Harper's Bazaar*.
1997	DeLillo's eleventh novel, *Underworld*, is published.
1999	DeLillo is awarded the Jerusalem Prize at the Jerusalem International Book Fair; DeLillo's play *Valparaiso* is published and premières at the American Repertory Theater in Cambridge, Massachusetts.
2000	The American Academy of Arts and Letters awards DeLillo the Howells Medal for *Underworld*.
2001	DeLillo's twelfth novel, *The Body Artist*, is published. DeLillo's essay "In the Ruins of the Future," on the terrorist attacks on the USA on September 11 appears in *Harper's* in December.
2003	DeLillo's thirteenth novel, *Cosmopolis*, is published.

2005   *Game 6* (directed by Michael Hoffman) premières at the Sundance Film Festival.

2006   DeLillo's play *Love-Lies-Bleeding* is published and premières in Chicago.

2007   DeLillo's fourteenth novel, *Falling Man*, is published on June 5.

JOHN N. DUVALL

Introduction: The power of history and the persistence of mystery

Since the 1985 publication of *White Noise*, winner of the National Book Award, Don DeLillo has become one of the most significant contemporary American novelists, standing in the first rank with Thomas Pynchon, Toni Morrison, Philip Roth, and John Updike. In a 2005 poll conducted by the *New York Times Book Review* that asked 125 prominent writers and critics to name the best American novel of the past 25 years, three of DeLillo's novels ranked in the top twenty: *Underworld* (1997) (runner-up to Toni Morrison's 1987 *Beloved*), *White Noise*, and *Libra* (1988).[1]

The recognition of DeLillo's achievement has not been limited to America. In 1999 DeLillo received the Jerusalem Prize at the Jerusalem International Book Fair. The award, given every two years since 1963, honors a writer whose body of work expresses the theme of the individual's freedom in society. The first American recipient of the award, DeLillo joined an international group of previous winners that includes such distinguished novelists, playwrights, and philosophers as Bertrand Russell, Simone de Beauvoir, Jorge Luis Borges, Eugene Ionesco, V. S. Naipaul, Milan Kundera, and Mario Vargas Llosa. In selecting DeLillo, the jury characterized his work as "an unrelenting struggle against even the most sophisticated forms of repression of individual and public freedom during the last half century."[2]

The author of fourteen novels, DeLillo has become a fixture on college course syllabi and is often selected to represent the American postmodern novel in undergraduate literature surveys.[3] Given DeLillo's undeniable significance to contemporary American fiction, this volume seeks to provide the reader with an overview of DeLillo's achievement as a novelist, taking up the author's poetics and themes, as well as providing more in-depth coverage of his best-known and most frequently taught novels.[4]

One reason, though by far the least significant, that DeLillo has garnered the following he has is that his fiction seems to anticipate and to comment on cultural trends and tendencies, the full significance of which emerge only after his novels are published. When *White Noise* with its Airborne Toxic

Event appeared in 1985, just weeks after the chemical spill in Bhopal, India, a number of readers took the novel to be an uncanny commentary on the environmental disaster in India, despite the fact that the novel was in press well before the accident occurred.[5] More chillingly, DeLillo's speculations on terrorists and the cultural role of terrorism in such novels as *Players* (1977) and *Mao II* (1991), it is retrospectively clear, provided us with a frame of reference for beginning to process the post-9/11 world years before the terrorist attack on America. But mere topicality is insufficient to explain why DeLillo's works will be read long after the fiction of Michael Crichton has been forgotten.

What makes DeLillo one of the most important American novelists since 1970 is his fiction's repeated invitation to think historically. For the influential Marxist critic Fredric Jameson, it is precisely historical thinking that is no longer possible in an age of multinational capitalism. In particular, Jameson sees a severely diminished role for aesthetics to ground an oppositional politics that might challenge consumer society. Indeed, for Jameson, all aesthetic production now is nothing more than a form of commodity production.[6] In simpler terms, what this means is that the amount of time between the emergence of a new aesthetic form (such as hip hop) and its appropriation by Madison Avenue to sell everything from fast food to running shoes has been so radically reduced that the ability of a new aesthetic form to establish a critical purchase on the social order has been thoroughly undercut.

In an age in which advertising has largely abandoned words in favor of the image, DeLillo, who still works with that old-fashioned word-assemblage called the novel, has a rare gift for historicizing our present, a gift that empowers engaged readers to think historically themselves. In other words, DeLillo teases out the ways in which our contemporary world bears the traces of such crucial events from the mid twentieth century as the rise of Adolf Hitler's fascism, the assassination of President John F. Kennedy, and Cold War brinksmanship. In his most important novels, then, DeLillo explores the ways in which contemporary American personal identity (as fragmented as it may be) is related to larger social and cultural forces forged over time. Fully aware that the twentieth century is the first to have been thoroughly documented on film, DeLillo shows us nothing less than how America became postmodern.

In this history such media forms as radio, television, film, and the internet must be reckoned with as social forces. In *White Noise* we see how the pressures of advertising and capital make it so difficult to think historically when the very structures of thought seem to have been coopted by the logic of television genres. Living in a culture of simulation, Jack Gladney, a professor of Hitler Studies interested only in Nazi aesthetics, has lost sight of the horrors of the Nazi past, which makes him equally oblivious to the horrors of his intensely media-driven, aestheticized present. In *Libra* DeLillo explores a transitional moment in American national consciousness. The assassination of JFK ends a certain kind of political innocence, but more importantly, DeLillo recognizes the event as a turning point in which the effects of the media (ranging from the Zapruder film of the shooting to the televised images of Jack Ruby killing Lee Harvey Oswald) serve as a fundamental mutation in Americans' lived relationship to the world; like Hitler and Elvis Presley, Lee Harvey Oswald (as well as his victim, John Fitzgerald Kennedy) becomes absorbed in the celebrity-making apparatus of media culture. In *Underworld* DeLillo gives us an anatomy of the emergence of paranoia as a constitutive feature of American identity during the Cold-War period. In his big novel DeLillo also shows us that how we "won" the Cold War was at least as much the work of American media and consumer culture as it was US nuclear tonnage. Major novels such as these are precisely why the Jerusalem Prize judges praised DeLillo for his fiction's moral focus. What they recognized is that DeLillo's fiction creates the possibility of wrestling a bit of freedom from necessity by so thoroughly diagnosing what constrains us.

Frank Lentricchia perhaps said it best when he identified DeLillo as one of those "writers who conceive their vocation as an act of cultural criticism."[7] In this regard DeLillo stands in a long tradition of American novelists from Herman Melville and Mark Twain to Morrison and Pynchon who are critical of home as found. DeLillo's critique, especially in his early fiction, often proceeds with satire and dark humor, tools favored by Melville, Twain, and Pynchon, to frontally attack those aspects of postmodernity that would turn individuals into so many iterations of Madison Avenue's dream of America.

Although his focus remains steadfastly on American postmodernity, in mature works such as *Libra*, *Mao II*, and *Underworld*, DeLillo's social critique often proceeds from a form that Linda Hutcheon has termed "historigraphic metafiction." For Hutcheon, the postmodern novel blends the reflexivity of metafiction (fiction that calls attention to itself as fiction or fiction that thematizes its own fictional production) with an explicit questioning of what counts as official history. Historiographic metafiction intentionally and self-consciously blurs the boundary between history and fiction, exploring the gaps and absences in the historical archive. For Hutcheon, the contemporary novel's blend of history and fiction creates an art with the potential to comment critically on the culture of which it is nevertheless inescapably a part.[8]

DeLillo's final significance may lie in the way that, while he recognizes the power of history, he insists on the novel as a counterforce to the wound of history through the persistence of mystery. Beyond the play of plots and plotlessness, determinism and chance, there lurks in DeLillo's writing the possibility – never overtly confirmed – of spiritual transcendence. A particular example from *Underworld*, I believe, is representative. In one of Lenny Bruce's night-club monologues, DeLillo has the beat comic begin an off-color story about a girl who can blow smoke rings from her vagina, but in mid-story Bruce loses interest and begins instead to tell a decidedly unfunny story that the reader only later recognizes as that of Esmeralda, a girl not yet born when Bruce is speaking but whose tragic death forms part of the Epilogue of the novel. Through a power of his art that exceeds his volition or any possibility of his knowing, then, Bruce begins an uncanny critique of the social forces that enable Esmeralda's violent end, forces that another of DeLillo's outsider artists, Ismael Muñoz, must engage later in the novel, again through his art.

For DeLillo, then, these ambiguous moments of possible transcendence are frequently linked to artistic production. Despite his anxiety about the role of the novelist in an age of the sound bite and the rapid image burn, DeLillo, it seems, wants us to imagine that, beyond the realm of media simulation, there is still a possibility for the artist to effect change. Thus the productive tension of DeLillo's fiction resides in the juxtaposition of this subject matter, which often resonates with Jameson's pessimistic view that contemporary art has been coopted by advertising, and DeLillo's poetics, which resonate more with Hutcheon's belief that the postmodern novel can still enable social critique. With pessimism of the intellect but optimism of the spirit, DeLillo continues to write novels that probe American postmodernity.

There is a general consensus that DeLillo writes about American postmodernity – what it feels like to live in a postindustrial nation at a time when media forms absorb increasingly more of our daily attention, so much so that these forms cease to feel like mediations of the real and are simply experienced as the real itself. But how he chooses to address his subject matter is more contested. The issue of DeLillo's poetics is addressed in Part I: in chapter 1 Philip Nel makes the case for seeing DeLillo in a direct line of descent from the modernists; in chapter 2, however, Peter Knight surveys the theoretical underpinnings of postmodernism to make the case that DeLillo is appropriately seen as a postmodern novelist.

Nel starts with DeLillo's own resistance to being identified as a postmodernist and considers resonances between DeLillo's fiction and that of James Joyce, Virginia Woolf, Malcolm Lowry, and John Dos Passos. For Nel, it is finally the richness of DeLillo's language (a topic explored in greater depth in David Cowart's chapter) and the novelist's heroic sense of the role of the artist (see also Mark Osteen's chapter) that make DeLillo a contemporary incarnation of modernism. For Knight, however, it is precisely DeLillo's acknowledgment of his debt to modernism that helps us understand his work as postmodern. To be an artist working in the wake of modernism is to be aware of the canonization and commodification of all the great modernist individual styles in art museums and literature anthologies, and Knight points out how often DeLillo's characters are aware of the weight of previous representation. At the same time, DeLillo's fiction is highly conscious of the problematic role of the artist in consumer culture. The great modernist hope to achieve an oppositional position vis à vis the market has diminished in an age when just about every aspect of modernist aesthetics has been coopted by Madison Avenue to sell all manner of consumer goods. Knight focuses our attention on the ways that DeLillo's fiction portrays the role of the media in a culture of simulation wherein representations of representations of representations create a regressive maze in which any notion of reality becomes obsolete or meaningless. In short, representation becomes the Real. Knight concludes by considering the extent to which DeLillo's fiction creates a critical purchase on postmodern simulation.

Part II examines DeLillo's early fiction. Throughout the 1970s, DeLillo explored the potential of a variety of fictional genres. However, to call *End Zone* (1972) a sports novel, *Ratner's Star* (1976) science fiction, or *Players* and *Running Dog* (1978) thrillers would be as reductive as identifying *White Noise* as an academic novel. In his first six novels, DeLillo consistently undercuts the reader's expectations of genre fiction by intellectualizing genre (though never simply producing the novel of ideas) so that these works convey his suspicions, disappointments, and occasional anger regarding American corporate capitalism.

DeLillo's first novel, *Americana* (1971), follows the episodic adventures of a young television executive, David Bell, who walks away from his job in order to travel the US in search of himself; this early exploration of American national identity forms a cornerstone for DeLillo's subsequent fiction. DeLillo's early focus on the entertainment industry is developed in his third novel, *Great Jones Street* (1973), in which rock guitarist Bucky Wunderlick discovers just how sinister the machinery of fame can be. In chapter 3, "DeLillo and media culture," Peter Boxall takes up DeLillo's first and third novels in order to think through DeLillo's relationship to both high and media culture. For Boxall, the early thinking of Samuel Beckett on the possibility of a writing that would attempt to eliminate language provides a crucial purchase for understanding DeLillo's relation to an aesthetic silence. While acknowledging the differences between Beckett's ultraminimalism and DeLillo's expansive prose, Boxall nevertheless finds a current of ascetic withdrawal in DeLillo's depiction of photography and film in *Americana* and of music and silence in *Great Jones Street*.

While *Americana* is written in a realist mode, the same cannot be said for DeLillo's second and fourth novels, *End Zone* and *Ratner's Star*, both of which are more akin to the high postmodernism of such white male writers as John Barth, Robert Coover, and Donald Barthelme. Both novels deploy allegorical elements as part of their satirical social critique. *End Zone*, by far the more approachable of the two, imagines a world in which football players at Logos College in Texas articulate various philosophical positions as part of the novel's larger mediation on the congruence of the terminology of football and nuclear war. *Ratner's Star* employs the trappings of science fiction, yet its dense and difficult foray through the history of mathematics and its representation of abstracted scientific projects yields a critique of the myth of progress. In chapter 4 Joseph Dewey explores the ways in which DeLillo's only two coming-of-age narratives allegorize apocalyptic intimations in American culture. For Dewey, the educations of Gary Harkness and Billy Twillig (of *End Zone* and *Ratner's Star* respectively) are largely failed ones since both register only the secular and never the sacred implications of apocalypse.

In chapter 5 Tim Engles explores a third main current from DeLillo's 1970s fiction, a refiguration of the genre of the political thriller. Novels such as *Players* and *Running Dog* employ plot elements of the thriller not simply to reproduce the genre but rather to critique the structuring of American identity and to subtly engage the political realities of post-Vietnam American politics. In the former, Lyle Wynant's involvement with a terrorist organization planning to blow up the New York Stock Exchange grows out of his extramarital affair; the novel suggests the extent to which by the 1970s secret agency had become a feature of late Cold War American identity. In the latter, the search by reporters and intelligence agents for a pornographic film that Hitler purportedly made in the final days of World War II becomes a way for DeLillo to register latent fascist urges in American culture.

Despite the undeniable power and promise of his fiction from the 1970s, had DeLillo stopped writing then he would not occupy the eminent place that he holds in contemporary literature. Intimations of DeLillo's greatness may be found in *The Names* (1982), a novel set in Greece in which an American risk analyst and unwitting tool of the CIA, James Axton, stumbles onto the existence of an ancient death cult that selects its victims by matching their initials with the name of the place where the cult then murders them. While continuing to use elements of the thriller, *The Names* is in fact about language and the possibility of meaning.

Part III explores the three novels most crucial to the making of DeLillo's reputation – *White Noise*, *Libra*, and *Underworld*. In chapter 6 Stacey Olster examines *White Noise* and its representation of a thoroughly postmodern, dehistoricized America in which Hitler and Elvis can become nearly interchangeable figures in a culture of celebrity. After tracing resonances between the novel's portrayal of simulacra and the theories of Jameson, Guy Debord, and Jean Baudrillard, Olster turns to the centrality of the television in the Gladney household. The television, which almost becomes a character in *White Noise*, typifies the way in which all contemporary media forms underscore the social imperative to consume. Despite DeLillo's depiction of postmodern media culture, Olster registers the ways in which he resists despairing over such conditions and finds that it is novel writing itself that serves as DeLillo's challenge to media culture.

Libra, then, takes up a moment that DeLillo sees as crucial to the history of the twentieth century, the assassination of President Kennedy. Jeremy Green in chapter 7 examines the way DeLillo negotiates the either/or logic that surrounds the event: either we accept the official lone gunman story of the Warren Commission Report or we wander in the multiple possibilities of conspiracy theory. For Green, DeLillo attempts to negotiate both possibilities in his novel by alternating chapters that provide a fairly straightforward biography of Oswald with chapters focusing on the plots of various government and anti-Castro agents to stage an act that would signal their displeasure to Kennedy in the wake of the failure of the US-backed invasion of Cuba. The third and metafictional strain of the novel mediates the other two. Nicholas Branch's role doubles DeLillo's, for Branch, a CIA analyst, has been charged with writing a report that makes sense of the assassination. Supplied by a CIA archivist with ever more pieces of textual evidence, Branch helps underscore the elements of chance and coincidence that frustrate the urge to construct a fully unified narrative of the assassination.

In *Underworld* DeLillo reflects on the history of the Cold War and its effects on American national identity. Without denying that DeLillo effectively uses the Cold War as a backdrop, Patrick O'Donnell explores in chapter 8 the ways in which *Underworld* fictionalizes postmodern subjectivity, characterized by a reversal of the classical relation between subject and object. In a contemporary world in which the human subject can no longer be assumed but rather is seen from various theoretical perspectives as a cultural product constructed from without, the connections between and among various events and spectacles are never sure. This undecidability, O'Donnell claims, can elicit paranoid alienation and/or an almost blissful acceptance of the schizophrenic cultural flow. In mapping postmodern identity DeLillo represents the contradictions and complexity of contemporary American life.

Part IV, "Issues and themes," takes up matters that transverse DeLillo's fictional worlds. The section begins in chapter 9 with Ruth Helyer's consideration of DeLillo's representation of masculinity. For Helyer, DeLillo does not model a facile, alternative masculinity; rather, he presents the reader with a number of male characters who are self-conscious and insecure about their performance of masculinity. Surveying DeLillo's fiction, Helyer looks at how DeLillo portrays men in various facets of their lives – at work, with family, sexual desire, sports, violence, and an awareness of mortality – as they try to fulfill their traditional roles, even as those roles become increasingly underscored as precisely that – enacted roles and not biological essences.

Throughout his career, DeLillo has frequently made artists central figures in his work. In chapter 10 Mark Osteen takes up DeLillo's recurring portrayal of the artist. Focusing on *Great Jones Street*, *Mao II*, and *The Body Artist* (2001), three novels that span various stages of DeLillo's career, Osteen takes seriously the author's claim regarding his desire for privacy. Echoing Joyce, DeLillo once invoked "silence, cunning, exile" as a reason for his desire not to talk about his work. For Osteen, it is precisely DeLillo's reference to Joyce that gives us access to DeLillo's take on the labyrinth of commodification. As DeLillo's depiction of the rock star Bucky Wunderlick in *Great Jones Street* and the novelist Bill Gray in *Mao II* illustrates, silence and exile themselves may become commodified. Silence and exile are tools that speak to the need for artistic detachment; however, for Osteen, it is finally DeLillo's sense of a cunning collaboration with an audience that provides a path out of the labyrinth and defines the artist's role in society.

Segueing from Osteen's sense of the artist's role, David Cowart turns our attention in chapter 11 to DeLillo's relation to his art's medium, language. Arguing for the thematic centrality of language in all DeLillo's works, Cowart pays particular attention to *The Names* and *The Body Artist*. The contemporary novelist, as Cowart sees it, is strangely and adversarially positioned between media culture's degradation of language and the post-structuralist critique of referentiality. Challenged on two fronts, DeLillo, like the best postmodern novelists, creates virtuoso performances that affirm the value of language as a medium. In a novel such as *The Names*, with its centuries-old death cult and various sites of faith, DeLillo's affirmation of language seems to point toward a spiritual force at odds with the skepticism of his characters.

Cowart's emphasis on the almost theological nature of DeLillo's language finds its complement in chapter 12, "DeLillo and mystery," in which John McClure explores recurring intimations of spirituality in DeLillo's fiction.

Without denying DeLillo's significance as a chronicler of postmodernity, McClure invites us to consider the variety of mystery in the novelist's fiction. DeLillo's appropriation of the popular genre of detective fiction clearly plays with mystery in a secular sense, but for McClure, these moments of secular mystery often give way to another order of mystery that opens the possibility of transcendence. In short, McClure charts the movement from the forensic to the sacramental. Given DeLillo's Roman Catholic upbringing, McClure shows us how one might see DeLillo in a Catholic tradition of American literature. Ranging over *Players*, *The Names*, *White Noise*, and *Underworld*, McClure identifies recurring moments of implied spiritual-communal possibility.

The volume concludes with Joseph Conte's consideration of DeLillo's fiction in the aftermath of the terrorist attacks on America on September 11, 2001. In "Writing amid the ruins: 9/11 and *Cosmopolis*," Conte considers DeLillo's recent novel in the context of DeLillo's essay on 9/11, "In the Ruins of the Future," as well as of DeLillo's earlier depictions both of terrorism and of the World Trade Center. *Cosmopolis* (2003) takes up a liminal historical moment, attempting to read the preconditions of 9/11 in the self-destructive pilgrimage through Manhattan of 28-year-old billionaire asset manager Eric Packer. Focusing on one day in April 2000, DeLillo shows the unraveling of the 1990s through Eric's downward spiral. Aware that DeLillo has previously focused on key moments in America's recent history, Conte sees *Cosmopolis* as a fictional meditation on why America's role in managing cyber-capital made it such an inviting target and helped usher in a new Age of Terror.

Because the chapters in this volume were all finished in 2006, the authors were not able to address DeLillo's most recent novel, *Falling Man*, which was published in June 2007. *Falling Man*, which examines the psychological trauma experienced by New Yorkers in the aftermath of the terrorist attacks of 9/11, once again underscores DeLillo's longstanding concern with the role of the artist in contemporary society. The Falling Man of the title refers to a performance artist who stages falls at various locations in the city that leave him suspended in mid-air. These enigmatic and macabre pieces, which recall the people who leaped from the World Trade Center towers rather than burn to death, illustrate the power of an art that operates outside of mainstream media channels to speak to the collective pain of New Yorkers. *Falling Man*'s deeper meditation on the relation of aesthetics and politics, however, occurs through the arguments of Nina Bartos, a retired professor of art history, and her lover Martin Ridnour, an international art dealer. In the 1960s, however, Ridnour (then known as Ernst Hechinger) was a member of a radical group, Kommune One, that protested against the West German state. The arguments of these two recall those of Bill Gray, a famous novelist, and George Haddad in *Mao II*. Haddad, a spokesman for a terrorist group in Lebanon, who sympathizes "with their aims if not their means" (*M* 128) sees a link between the novelist and the terrorist since "through history, it's the novelist who has felt affinity for the violent man who lives in the dark" and asks, "Where are your sympathies? With the colonial police, the occupier, the rich landlord, the corrupt government, the militaristic state? Or with the terrorist?" (*M* 130). Like Haddad, Ridnour sympathizes with the urge (if not the methods) of Islamic terrorists to seek alternatives to "the narcissistic heart of the West" (*FM* 113). As a New Yorker, DeLillo feels the pain and anger of the 9/11 attacks acutely, but he is too much of a novelist not to be able to imagine that there are people in the world who do not wish to mirror American values, especially when these "values" appear to mean nothing more than getting a good deal on consumer goods.

Notes

1. *New York Times Book Review*, May 21, 2006, pp. 16–19. DeLillo was one of only three writers to have more than one of their novels receive multiple nominations.
2. 19*th* *Jerusalem International Book Fair Home Page*, May 20, 1999, <www.jerusalembookfair.com/page6.html>.
3. DeLillo is also reputed to be the co-author of *Amazons* (New York: Holt, Rinehart, and Winston, 1980). Written under the pseudonym Cleo Birdwell, the novel is a racy fictional memoir of the first woman to play in the National Hockey League. DeLillo, however, does not publicly acknowledge his authorship of this novel.
4. DeLillo is also the author of four short plays and two more substantial plays, *Valparaiso* (1999) and *Love-Lies-Bleeding* (2005). However, since DeLillo's reputation and awards derive from his work as a novelist, the *Companion* makes his fiction its focus.
5. Mark Osteen, "Introduction," in Osteen, ed., *White Noise: Text and Criticism* (New York: Viking, 1998), p. vii.
6. Fredric Jameson, *Postmodernism, or, The Cultural Logic of Late Capitalism* (Durham: Duke University Press, 1991, pp. 16–25).
7. Frank Lentricchia, "The American Writer as Bad Citizen," in Lentricchia, ed., *Introducing Don DeLillo* (Durham: Duke University Press, 1991), p. 2.
8. Linda Hutcheon, *The Politics of Postmodernism* (London: Routledge, 1989), pp. 47–92.

PART I

Aesthetic and cultural influences

I

PHILIP NEL

DeLillo and modernism

Although celebrated as a great postmodernist, Don DeLillo resists the label.[1] As he told an interviewer in 1998:

> Post-modern seems to mean different things in ... different disciplines. In architecture and art it means one or two different things. In fiction it seems to mean another. When people say *White Noise* is post-modern, I don't really complain. I don't say it myself. But I don't see *Underworld* as post-modern. Maybe it's the last modernist gasp. I don't know.[2]

Reluctant to classify his work, DeLillo nonetheless admits an affinity to modernism. He has a point. Because DeLillo seeks the epic in the mundane, embraces a modernist avant-garde, writes a tightly controlled prose, and densely layers his allusive novels, modernism may be at least as important as postmodernism for understanding DeLillo's achievement.

For the richness of his language and the scope of his literary ambition, James Joyce looms largest in DeLillo's imagination. As he said in 1993, "it was through Joyce that I learned to see something in language that carried a radiance, something that made me feel the beauty and fervor of words, the sense that a word has a life and a history."[3] Although Joycean turns of phrase recur throughout his work, DeLillo's earliest novels make the most conspicuous allusions. In *Americana* (1971), for example, several major characters demonstrate detailed knowledge of either *Ulysses* (1922) or *Finnegans Wake* (1939). Radio personality Warren Beasley says of his fiancée that he plans to "fly her to old Dub and pretend she's Molly Bloom" (*A* 95). During a broadcast, Beasley mentions "Mollycuddling my bloomless bride" and confesses, "I've got the Stephen Dedalus Blues and it's a long way to Leopoldville" (*A* 232, 234). Inverting Stephen's remark that history "is a nightmare from which I am trying to awake,"[4] Beasley adds, "We have awakened from the nightmare of history" (*A* 234). Recalling his college years, *Americana*'s protagonist David Bell says, "I wanted to be known as Kinch. This is Stephen Dedalus' nickname in *Ulysses*, which I was reading at the time" (*A* 143). During their time at college, Bell and his friend Ken Wild "committed the usual collegiate blasphemies of word and deed, using as our text the gleeful God-baiting of Buck Mulligan in the first few pages of *Ulysses*. That was our sacred scroll and we regretted that there had been no gray Jesuits to darken our childhoods" (*A* 145). Alluding to *Finnegans Wake*, Sullivan says that her Uncle Malcolm "hated my father like plague, like incense. Brothers they were, stem and stern, Shem and Shaun, tight Dublin and tighter Belfast" (*A* 321). *Americana*'s multiple and wide-ranging references suggest that DeLillo may be modeling his own knowledge of Joyce or even aspiring to be heir to Joyce. By *Ratner's Star* (1976), DeLillo is offering subtler allusions, as when Elux Troxl speaks in *Wake*ian portmanteau words, like "extemporarily" (a combination of "extempore," "extemporaneously," and "temporarily"), "partitionage" ("partition," "patronage"), and "disaffectuates" ("disaffected," "effectuates") (*RS* 148–9). More confident in his craft, DeLillo is using Joycean language instead of quoting Joyce.

As did both Joyce and Virginia Woolf, DeLillo explores the extraordinary significance of ordinary lives – what, in describing *White Noise* (1985), he calls "a kind of radiance in dailiness."[5] *White Noise* finds beauty in the quotidian when Jack Gladney regards his family's "brightly colored food" or watches "the coffee bubble up through the center tube and perforated basket into the small pale globe" (*WN* 7, 103), but *The Body Artist* (2001) best embodies DeLillo's sense of modernist poetics. With gustatory language echoing *Ulysses*'s fourth chapter, *The Body Artist*'s opening scene finds delight in the sounds and flavors of breakfast. Where Joyce's Bloom likes "grilled mutton kidneys which gave to his palate a fine tang of faintly scented urine,"[6] DeLillo's Lauren Hartke eats soya, describing its smell as "a faint wheaty stink with feet mixed in" (*BA* 13). Lauren's husband Rey shakes the container of orange juice longer than he needs to "for its own childlike sake, for the bounce and slosh and cardboard orange aroma" (*BA* 10). Such attention to the mysteries of daily life echoes the modernist tendency to find profundity in mundane activities such as fixing breakfast (as Bloom, Lauren, and Rey do) or preparing to host a party (as Woolf's Clarissa Dalloway does).[7]

As in Joyce's *Ulysses* and Malcolm Lowry's *Under the Volcano* (1947), another of DeLillo's favorites, DeLillo seeks the epic in the everyday. "We lead more interesting lives than we think" (*L* 78), thinks CIA agent Win Everett in *Libra* (1988). Lee Harvey Oswald, the interesting life at the center of that novel, comes into focus as retired CIA analyst Nicholas Branch writes "the secret history of the assassination of President Kennedy" (*L* 15). He considers the Warren Commission Report "the megaton novel James Joyce would have written if he'd moved to Iowa City and lived to be a hundred" because "[e]verything is here" in the report (*L* 181). It is "an incredible haul of human utterance ... [so] lost to syntax and other arrangement, that it resembles a kind of mind-spatter, a poetry of lives muddied and dripping in language" (L 181). With the grisly suggestiveness of "mind-spatter" and "dripping in language," the Warren Report is not only corpus as corpse, but a way for language ("human utterance") to embody the panorama of lives and deaths connected to the assassination. When interviewer Anthony DeCurtis pointed to Everett's description of the Warren Commission Report, DeLillo explained, "I asked myself what Joyce could possibly do after *Finnegans Wake*, and this was the answer."[8] The document, DeLillo noted, is "a masterwork of trivia ranging from Jack Ruby's mother's dental records to photographs of knotted string." In other words, DeLillo makes the comparison not because *Finnegans Wake* and the Warren Report share stylistic similarities but because both harbor encyclopedic ambitions. As Branch notes in *Libra*, the Warren Report "is the Joycean Book of America, remember – the novel in which nothing is left out" (L 182). Equally significant for DeLillo, however, is the report's emphasis on the quotidian. DeLillo finds the report particularly fascinating because it includes "the testimony of dozens and dozens of people who talk not only about their connection to the assassination itself but about their jobs, their marriages, their children. This testimony provided an extraordinary window on life in the fifties and sixties."[9]

Yet, if we read *Libra* as a modernist epic, John Dos Passos's *U.S.A.* trilogy (1930–6) may be a more likely antecedent than either *Ulysses* or *Finnegans Wake*. The narratives of *U.S.A.* and *Libra* feature shifts in points of view conveyed via free indirect discourse but also via interpolated nonnovelistic texts. In this sense, Dos Passos's "Newsreel" sections prefigure DeLillo's fragmented transmissions of the Kennedy assassination (L 402–5) and passages from Oswald's "Historic Diary."[10] When Charley Anderson dies in Dos Passos's *The Big Money* (1936), the narrative swerves abruptly to song lyrics and news reports. In a sentence lacking a full stop, Charley feels that he "was dropping spinning being sucked down into" and, without pause, launches us into a "Newsreel" on the next page, where "STARS PORTEND EVIL FOR COOLIDGE," "MINERS RETAIL HORRORS OF DEATH PIT," and we hear snatches from hit songs of the 1920s like "Just Like a Butterfly (That's Caught in the Rain)" and "If You Can't Tell the World She's a Good Little Girl."[11] The pages both disorient and create provocative juxtapositions, goading us to seek links among the fragments. DeLillo performs comparable work when, moments after President Kennedy is shot, *Libra* offers on a single page the perspectives of Agent Hill on the motorcade, a radio transmission from a secret service agent (who may or may not be Hill), conspirator Ramón "Raymo" Benitez, an unnamed person unaware of the shooting, and ex-Castro supporter Frank Vasquez (*L* 402). As does *U.S.A.*, *Libra* creates a jarring effect, inviting the reader to consider the connections and disjunctions between these perspectives and the different media through which these perspectives arrive.

In its scope and its introductory claim that "U.S.A. is the speech of the people,"[12] *U.S.A.* also seems a likely antecedent for DeLillo's second modernist epic, *Underworld*, which begins, "He speaks in your voice, American" (*U* 11). That said, Catherine Morley and Mark Osteen have made convincing cases for the strong influence of *Ulysses*. As Morley notes, both Nick Shea and Leopold Bloom are "without fathers and of uncertain roots," while both "heroes constantly consider the nature of their identity, and, moreover, are forced to consider it in terms of the national identity."[13] Osteen, on the other hand, sees Albert Bronzini as DeLillo's tribute to Bloom. Each character "enjoys walks around the city," has a "voracious interest in and astute observation of people and material conditions," and "both knows and suppresses the knowledge that his wife is cuckolding him."[14]

Irrespective of its specific antecedents, *Underworld* contains many features of a modernist epic. A densely layered work with motifs that resonate on many levels, *Underworld* rewards – even requires – multiple readings. Versions of "Everything is connected" recur in *Underworld*,[15] but unlike E. M. Forster's "Only connect!"[16] DeLillo's line is not a call for interpersonal relationships. Instead, it calls attention to the novel's denseness of theme and purpose, inviting us to see how technology, business, garbage, the number 13, lucky strikes, the baseball, presidents photographed with Bobby Thomson and Ralph Branca, and other recurring motifs all fit together. As Morley says of *Underworld* and *Ulysses*, "Both novels use the mythic structure of ancient epic, on one level, to provide a framework for post-/modernity within the work of art, to limit, contain and connect divergent strands with set patterns and structures."[17]

Morley's "post-/modernity" elides an important difference between *Underworld* and its modernist influences, however. Joyce is writing about modernity, but DeLillo is writing about postmodernity, that set of historical conditions marked by a decreased emphasis on industrial production and a greater emphasis on service industries and mass culture – what Fredric Jameson calls "late capitalism." We might, then, identify DeLillo as a modernist writer who writes about postmodernity. As Frank Lentricchia puts it, "DeLillo, last of the modernists … takes for his critical object of aesthetic concern the postmodern situation."[18] With the possible exception of *Ratner's Star*, DeLillo's sole foray into Pynchonian postmodernism, Lentricchia's statement accurately characterizes the aesthetic and material concerns of DeLillo's novels.

However, how modernist techniques might deal with the "postmodern situation" requires further elucidation, as do the ways in which DeLillo's modernism may differ from earlier modernisms. After all, an epic scope and deeply interwoven themes also characterize many postmodern novels, such as William Gass's *The Tunnel* (1995), David Foster Wallace's *Infinite Jest* (1996), and Thomas Pynchon's *Gravity's Rainbow* (1973) – which also has *Underworld*'s "Everything is connected" line.[19] A sense of radiance in the everyday – characteristic of Woolf and of DeLillo's *The Body Artist* (2001) – can also be found in such postmodern works as Jeanette Winterson's *Written on the Body* (1992) and Jonathan Safran Foer's *Everything Is Illuminated* (2002). These shared characteristics highlight the frequently fuzzy boundary between modern and postmodern, but they also highlight the need to clarify further precisely which modernisms animate DeLillo's work and how those modernisms engage postmodernity.

Modernist critique of postmodernity

DeLillo complicates traditional distinctions between modern and postmodern by drawing on a high modernist aesthetic and those postmodernisms animated by a modernist avant-garde – what Paul Maltby calls "adversarial postmodernisms."[20] Juxtapositions – an avant-garde technique favored by Surrealist René Magritte and Russian filmmaker Sergei Eisenstein – give DeLillo's style its deeply oppositional impulse. Describing the imaginary lost Eisenstein film *Unterwelt*, DeLillo's *Underworld* observes that "there was an ambivalence that vitalized the crowd" (*U* 425). This description applies equally well to DeLillo's own prose, which frequently presents ambiguous juxtapositions that compel attention. *Underworld* exemplifies this method because DeLillo has structured the novel via Eisenstein's montage technique, in which, as Osteen observes, "meaning accrues through juxtaposition."[21] Introducing the *Unterwelt* film première, the narrative voice notes that this is "a movie you probably never heard of until the *Times* did a Sunday piece. But this is how the behavioral aberration, once begun, grows to lavish panic" (*U* 426–7). Juxtaposing "lavish" with "panic" initiates an unstable irony, raising the question of how one should interpret this apparently oxymoronic phrase. The characters have enjoyed the rich Art Deco Radio City Music Hall, so "lavish" seems figured positively; yet, given that hype enabled the suppressed film's screening, perhaps "panic" should also be taken seriously. Rather than resolve the question, DeLillo leaves it suspended in the air, like a subtler version of *White Noise*'s (1985) airborne toxic event.

DeLillo then amplifies the tension by figuring the Rockettes in visually contrary ways: as masculine and feminine; as dancers, soldiers, and sadomasochists;

as American entertainment and Russian propaganda. They wear "West Point gray and came out saluting" yet also have "plumed dress hats and fringed titties and faces buttered a Christmassy pink" and are "wearing bondage collars," thus complicating the image further. As avant-garde artist Klara Sax asks, "How do we know it's really the Rockettes and not a troupe of female impersonators?" (U 428). Intensifying the question, DeLillo's narrator briefly switches to second person and asks, "[I]sn't it unlikely that the real Rockettes would be wearing slave collars and doing routines with such pulsing sexual rhythm? In fact ... it's probably what they do all the time. You don't know for sure, do you?" The narrator concludes that, even if these are "the real Rockettes," they are "three dozen women in close order cadet formation, or women done up like men and not the reverse – but it's a cross-dressing event either way" (U 428). Although it may be tricky to pin down the precise political argument of these ironic juxtapositions, they are unsettling. As the narrator observes a few pages later, "You saw things differently now. If there was a politics of montage, it was more immediate here" (U 443).[22]

The ambiguous effects of DeLillo's juxtapositions bring to mind Paul Cantor's claim that "DeLillo wavers between criticizing postmodernism and practicing it."[23] That is, if, as Jameson has argued, one characteristic of postmodernism is its absence of political engagement with postmodernity, then the uncertain goals of DeLillo's critique leave it vulnerable to the charge of representing a depthless postmodern. However, DeLillo's reliance on modernist juxtapositions at least complicates such a claim and, at most, refutes it. Borrowing from Linda Hutcheon's insightful Irony's Edge (1994), we might instead value DeLillo's ironies for their ability to disrupt rigid categories. In the previous paragraph's example, the "cross-dressing" Rockettes highlight gender as a social construct by unsettling the traditional dichotomy between masculine and feminine. In White Noise DeLillo's juxtapositions tend to be comically disconcerting, as when "The smoke alarm went off in the hallway upstairs, either to let us know the battery had just died or because the house was on fire. We finished our lunch in silence" (WN 8). With his casual use of the word "or," Gladney places the dead battery and the burning house side by side, as if neither meaning were more important than the other. Gladney creates a similarly off-kilter effect when, after asking "Who will die first?" he adds, "This question comes up from time to time, like where are the car keys" – as if death and car keys were of the same order of significance. Another of White Noise's many ironic juxtapositions, "live Muzak" (WN 84), shakes one's habits of perception because it is both impossible, as muzak is prerecorded, and possible, because some live music sounds like muzak. As Hutcheon writes, "irony's doubleness can act as a way of counteracting any tendency to assume a categorical or rigid position of 'Truth' through precisely some acknowledgement of provisionality and contingency"; it offers "an undogmatic alternative to authoritative pronouncements."[24]

At its most effective, DeLillo's montages go beyond simply countering dogmatism. In the "Triumph of Death" prologue to *Underworld*, he delivers incisive social criticism by amplifying the tension between two realities: a euphoric crowd and a scene of mass death suggestive of an atomic attack. Appropriately, this prologue was born of juxtaposition. As DeLillo explained in a 1997 essay, the October 4, 1951 *New York Times*'s dual headline inspired this section: the left side of the page reported Bobby Thomson's home run and the right side, with a headline in the same size typeface, announced the Soviets' atomic bomb.[25] In "The Triumph of Death," DeLillo uses Bruegel's painting *The Triumph of Death* (reproduced in a 1951 issue of *Life* magazine) to bring these two blasts into sharp relief. J. Edgar Hoover's imagination weaves images from Bruegel's apocalyptic picture into the scene at the game, offering visions of an atomic holocaust lingering beneath the crowd's euphoria. DeLillo's placement of Bruegel's apocalyptic landscape amid the jubilant crowd forges a connection between the hysteria that motivates anti-Communist witch hunts and the hysteria that animates crowds of people at a ball game. The unexpected analogy is subversive, relying on a modernist montage to complicate the reader's understanding of the then nascent Cold War, the beginning of a central historical narrative of postmodernity. The epitome of DeLillo's oppositional stance, this scene displays how his writing interrogates what it represents. As Leonard Wilcox eloquently says in a discussion of *White Noise*, the key difference between DeLillo's and Baudrillard's relationship to postmodernism is that, while Baudrillard finds "nothing outside the play of simulations, no real in which a radical critique of the simulational society might be grounded," DeLillo believes "that narrative can provide critical distance from and a critical perspective on the processes it depicts."[26] This difference highlights the strong modernist impulse in DeLillo's work.

DeLillo's modernist language

DeLillo shares with his modernist (and Romantic) ancestors a faith in the value and power of linguistic art. His lyrical, tightly controlled prose also helps him develop a critical distance from the worlds he examines. Both *Underworld* and T. S. Eliot's *The Waste Land* (1922) end with peace – *Underworld* with the word "Peace" and *The Waste Land* with "Shantih shantih shantih," the "Peace which passeth understanding."[27] However, where Eliot's speaker can find only fragments to shore against his ruins,

DeLillo's narrator finds language sturdier than fragments. As Paul Gleason points out, "Eliot and DeLillo agree that waste and literature function as cultural productions that illuminate the civilizations from which they derive," but DeLillo overcomes what Gleason sees as Eliot's nihilism by positing "language and art as ways in which humanity can redeem historical experience."[28] Although Eliot's language might also be read as a source – perhaps the *only* source – of hope, DeLillo's work offers a stronger (if still qualified) faith in the vitality of words. In *The Names* (1982), an earlier exploration of the power of language, Owen Brademas explains that he has "begun to see a mysterious importance in the letters as such," finding their "beautiful shapes" to be "[s]o strange and reawakening" (N 35–6). As Arthur Saltzman writes, "Dead metaphors deaden; clichés inspire clichéd reactions that keep ad executives, political spin doctors, and probability experts comfortable. Lyricism destabilizes the system of rutted assumptions."[29]

This lyricism derives from DeLillo's ability to pare language down. During the years when he was writing *The Names*, DeLillo adopted a method that has given his prose since then its particular crispness. After finishing a paragraph, "even a three-line paragraph," DeLillo takes out a fresh piece of paper "to start the new paragraph." This method, he says, has "enabled me to see a given set of sentences more clearly. It made rewriting easier and more effective. The white space on the page helped me concentrate more deeply on what I'd written."[30] This technique has moved his style closer to that of Ernest Hemingway, another important modernist influence. Describing in an interview what he read in the summer when he was eighteen, working as a Bronx playground attendant, DeLillo quoted from the first page of *A Farewell to Arms* (1929):

> I'd look at a sentence in *Ulysses* or in *Moby-Dick* or in Hemingway – maybe I hadn't gotten to *Ulysses* at that point, it was *Portrait of the Artist* – but certainly Hemingway and the water that was clear and swiftly moving and the way the troops went marching down the road and raised dust that powdered the leaves of the trees.[31]

Even if he reread the novel between 1954 and 1993 (when the interview was conducted), DeLillo's memory is remarkably accurate. The full passage from Hemingway is as follows: "and the water was clear and swiftly moving and blue in the channels. Troops went by the house and down the road and the dust they raised powdered the leaves of the stream."[32] In addition to its economy of language, the passage highlights Hemingway's preference for "and," used five times in that thirty-three-word excerpt. As DeLillo points out, "the Hemingway sentence is what makes Hemingway. It's not the bullfights or the safaris or the wars, it's a clear, direct, and vigorous sentence. It's the simple connective – the word 'and' that strings together the segments of a long Hemingway sentence. The word 'and' is more important to Hemingway than Africa or Paris."[33] His reading of Hemingway very likely contributes to DeLillo's own preference for this conjunction. On the first page of *Underworld*'s prologue, set in 1951, DeLillo's narrator describes fourteen-year-old Cotter Martin, who has skipped school to attend the game: "He wants to be here instead, standing in the shadow of this old rust-hulk of a structure, and it's hard to blame him – this metropolis of steel and concrete and flaky paint and chopped grass and enormous Chesterfield packs aslant on the scoreboards, a couple of cigarettes jutting from each" (*U* 11). The five instances of "and" coupled with the compact language offer a late twentieth-century echo of Hemingway's style. This accumulative "and," of course, is also a strategy of epic lists, but on the pages of Hemingway and DeLillo, the conjunctions act like spaces, isolating the words between them.

An interest in simplification draws DeLillo, at times, to a version of the primitivism espoused by some modernists, a notion that allows him to explore the possibility of a primal or prelapsarian language.[34] In his first major interview, DeLillo asked Tom LeClair, "Is there something we haven't discovered about speech? Is there more? Maybe this is why there's so much babbling in my books. Babbling can be frustrated speech, or it can be a purer form, an alternate speech."[35] Babblers are regular characters in DeLillo novels: Wilder in *White Noise*, Tap Axton in *The Names*, "the scream lady" and Grbk in *Ratner's Star*, Bucky Wunderlick's "Mountain Tapes" and the Micklewhite boy in *Great Jones Street* (1973), and Mr. Tuttle in *The Body Artist*. After Wilder's seven-hour crying spree ends in *White Noise*, Gladney reports that his family watched Wilder

> with something like awe ... as though he'd just returned from a period of wandering in some remote and holy place, in sand barrens or snowy ranges – a place ... which we in our ordinary toil can only regard with the mingled reverence and wonder we hold in reserve for feats of the most sublime and difficult dimensions. (*WN* 79)

In a comparable scene in *The Body Artist*, when Tuttle speaks, Lauren perceives that his words "came out of him nonstop and it wasn't schizo-phrenic speech or the whoop of ripping bodies shocked by God ... It was pure chant, transparent, or was he saying something to her?" (*BA* 75). This description of "pure chant" echoes the observations of Tap Axton's narrator at the end of *The Names*: "The strange language burst out of them, like people out of breath and breathing words instead of air. But what words, what were they saying?" (*N* 335). Gladney, Lauren, and Tap all are drawn to language that appears both holy and primitive, but DeLillo never confirms that Wilder's cry, Tuttle's chant, or Tap's narrator's strange speech are anything of the kind. Their audiences want to revere these utterances as divine glossolalia but cannot provide an intelligible translation. If these babbling characters do offer any access to Truth, neither they nor we can understand what they are saying.

DeLillo is also drawn to and wary of the modernist (and Romantic) project of bridging the gap between word and world. *The Names* and *The Body Artist* in particular both explore William Carlos Williams's dictum "No ideas/but in things."[36] At the same time, these novels display DeLillo's understanding that – to paraphrase Saltzman – metaphor is inevitable but futile[37] because DeLillo recognizes that attempts to create language as direct as possible will nonetheless veer toward ambiguity. In *The Body Artist* Lauren, driving, sees "a man sitting on his porch, ahead of her, through trees and shrubs, arms spread, a broad-faced blondish man, lounging." Believing "that she saw him complete," Lauren feels that his "life flew open to her passing glance." He must be "a lazy and manipulative man, in real estate, in fairview condos by a mosquito lake … He was there, divorced and drink-haunted, emotionally distant from his kids, his sons, two sons, in school blazers" (*BA* 70). As her car passes him, Lauren realizes that "she was not looking at a seated man but at a paint can placed on a board that was balanced between two chairs. The white and yellow can was his face, the board was his arms" (*BA* 70). Lauren mistakes a paint can for a blond man because, as she realizes later, "[t]he eye … tells us a story we want to believe" (*BA* 80). With direct language suggestive of unmediated experience, DeLillo initially makes the "lounging" man seem real and then reveals the illusion, reminding us that even the most apparently literal language is always mediated, easily misled by perception.[38]

The Names provides the most dramatic evidence of DeLillo's fascination with both purely representational language and its potentially dangerous consequences. Characters in *The Names* offer theoretical speculations on and even commit terrorist acts in support of a language that binds letters to things. The Ta Onómata cult derives meaning from killing people when the victim's name matches the place's name. By way of explanation, Onómata member Andahl tells narrator James Axton, "Something in our method finds a home in your unconscious mind. A recognition … We are working at a preverbal level, although we use words, of course, we use them all the time" (*N* 208). "We are here to carry out the pattern," he says. "Abecedarian. This is what we are" (*N* 209). The novel, however, highlights the hazards in seeing – as Axton puts it – "how far men will go to satisfy a pattern" (*N* 80). Although DeLillo evidently enjoys creating succinct, resonant words, he simultaneously recognizes the impossibility of ever arriving at a pure, organic connection between word and world. Where cultists believe that such a connection would be ideal, DeLillo relishes the paradoxes of metaphor.

DeLillo also embraces the epiphany, that classic modernist feature. In the famous "tundish" conversation from *A Portrait of the Artist as a young Man* (1916), Stephen Dedalus's recognition of the Irish word for "funnel" sparks an awareness of how his language separates him from the English.[39] In this scene, as in DeLillo's novels, language is at the root of a character's epiphany. When in *White Noise* his daughter Steffie utters "*Toyota Celica*," Gladney says, "The utterance was beautiful and mysterious, gold shot with looming wonder." Although he does question its profundity, adding, "She was only repeating some TV voice," Gladney concludes by saying, "Whatever its source, the utterance struck me with the impact of a moment of splendid transcendence" (WN 155). *White Noise*'s layers of ironies may make us reluctant to read the tone as sincere. However, most of the passage – including its ending – seems to take seriously the idea of transcendence. Reinforcing the evident sincerity of this passage, DeLillo in an interview specifically links "*Toyota Celica*" to "pure chant." As he puts it:

> Years ago somebody decided ... that the most beautiful phrase in the English language was *cellar door*. If you concentrate on the sound, if you dissociate the words from the object they denote, and you say the words over and over, they become a sort of higher Esperanto. This is how *Toyota Celica* began its life. It was pure chant at the beginning. Then they had to find an object to accommodate the words.[40]

As Anne Longmuir writes, the "*Toyota Celica*" scene "should be regarded as a genuine epiphany in the modernist tradition."[41]

The artist as hero

Lentricchia has noted that an emphasis on the role of the artist as hero places DeLillo's work squarely in the modernist tradition, too.[42] Although his essay focuses on *White Noise*, this claim could be extended to the entire DeLillo oeuvre. DeLillo's artists are visionaries whose "sneak attacks on the dominant culture" (U 444) – to borrow *Underworld*'s description of the *Unterwelt* première – may not fully succeed but do at least invite readers to adopt a critical perspective toward their society. In *Americana*, David Bell (who, as producer and narrator, is an artist) takes on this role, aided by the "strange, different, curious, remarkable" artist Sullivan (A 8), who at one point Bell thinks of as the only one who could save him. In *Great Jones Street* reclusive rock star Bucky Wunderlick is the artist hero, striving with limited success to resist his own commodification. In *Underworld* there are many disruptive artists, including Eisenstein, Lenny Bruce, Klara Sax, and graffiti artist Moonman 157 (Ismael Muñoz), who sees his work as "the art that can't stand still, it climbs right across your eyeballs" (*U* 441). Less aggressive in his description of art's role, novelist Bill Gray in *Mao II* (1991) says that "a writer creates a character as a way to reveal consciousness, to increase the flow of meaning. This is how we reply to power and beat back our fear. By extending the pitch of consciousness and human possibility" (*M* 200). None of these artists fully achieves their goals, but DeLillo values their efforts against the systems in which they are enmeshed.

DeLillo's artist-characters, and DeLillo himself, hope to maintain that critical role by placing themselves at a distance from the culture. As DeLillo told Ann Arensberg in 1988, the writer "stands outside society, independent of affiliation and independent of influence. The writer . . . automatically takes a stand against his or her government . . . American writers ought to stand and live in the margins, and be more dangerous. Writers in repressive societies are considered dangerous. That's why so many of them are in jail."[43] As if to emphasize this point, *Mao II* has the poet Jean-Claude Julien held hostage by a terrorist group. Gray, who is being recruited to secure Julien's release, defines the role of the writer in terms similar to DeLillo's. Through writing, authors "reply to power and beat back . . . fear," Gray says (*M* 200).

Although one should be wary of too closely identifying an author with his character, Gray often seems to be a stand-in for his creator. DeLillo has both denied that Gray is based on him and admitted that he has long joked that he'd like "to change [his] name to Bill Gray and disappear."[44] While Gray's reclusiveness makes him more like Pynchon or J. D. Salinger, both Gray and DeLillo speak the same language – often verbatim. In a 1991 interview DeLillo repeated one of Gray's speeches word for word without acknowledging he was doing so.[45] *The Rushdie Defense Pamphlet*, which DeLillo co-wrote with Paul Auster, borrows a phrase from Gray when it says, "the principle of free expression, the democratic shout, is far less audible than it was five years ago."[46] In *Mao II*, a novel inspired partly by the fatwa calling for Rushdie's execution, Gray says, "Do you know why I believe in the novel? It's a democratic shout" (*M* 159). Although not all modernists would agree to that definition of the novel, the language does tie Gray's beliefs to DeLillo's and affirms his affiliation with adherents of a politically engaged modernism.

So, is DeLillo America's last modernist? As a modernist-influenced chronicler of postmodernity, DeLillo is difficult to periodize. He has said that the Kennedy assassination, which he defines as a postmodern media event, defined him as a writer and yet describes the Warren Report as a Joycean novel. He shares modernists' formal (and formalist) fixations but writes about postmodern concerns. He sees the artist as heroic but tempers that belief with doubt. Any attempt to identity his poetics – either as modernist or postmodernist – must always take into account the competing impulses in DeLillo's fiction. Asked how he reacts to his novels being characterized as postmodern, DeLillo replied, "I don't react. But I'd prefer not to be labeled. I'm a novelist, period."[47]

Notes

Special thanks to Anne Longmuir and Karin Westman for taking the time to talk with me about this chapter, and to Karin (again) for giving it a thorough read-through.

1. The Modern Language Association of America Bibliography lists more than fifty entries linking DeLillo to postmodernism and only one linking him to modernism.
2. Quoted in Richard Williams, "Everything Under the Bomb," *The Guardian* (January 10, 1998), <http://reports.guardian.co.uk/papers/19980109-34.html>, accessed March 15, 1998.
3. Quoted in Adam Begley, "The Art of Fiction CXXXV: Don DeLillo," in Thomas DePietro, ed., *Conversations with Don DeLillo* (Jackson: University Press of Mississippi, 2005), p. 88.
4. James Joyce, *Ulysses* (1922) (New York: Vintage, 1986), p. 28.
5. Quoted in Anthony DeCurtis, "'An Outsider in This Society': An Interview with Don DeLillo," in DePietro, ed., *Conversations*, pp. 70–1.
6. Joyce, *Ulysses*, p. 45.
7. For more on this subject, see Philip Nel, "Don DeLillo's Return to Form: The Modernist Poetics of *The Body Artist*," *Contemporary Literature* 43.4 (Winter 2002), pp. 739–41.
8. DeCurtis, "An Outsider," p. 62.
9. Ibid., p. 62.
10. Passages from Oswald's diary appear on pp. 150–6, 190, 198–9, 205, and 210.
11. John Dos Passos, *The Big Money* (New York: Signet, 1979), pp. 384–5.
12. John Dos Passos, *The 42nd Parallel* (Boston: Houghton Mifflin, 2000), p. xiv.
13. Catherine Morley, "Excavating *Underworld*, Disinterring *Ulysses*: Don DeLillo's Dialogue with James Joyce," *Comparative American Studies* 4.2 (2006), pp. 183–4.
14. Mark Osteen, *American Magic and Dread: Don DeLillo's Dialogue with Culture* (Philadelphia: University of Pennsylvania Press, 2000), pp. 276–7.
15. See, for example, pages 17, 89, 173, 185, 289, 314, 408, 465, 540–2, 575, 577, 707, and 825.
16. E. M. Forster, *Howards End* (1910) (New York: Vintage, 1989), p. 195.
17. Morley, "Excavating *Underworld*," pp. 178–9.
18. Frank Lentricchia, ed., "Introduction," *New Essays on "White Noise"* (Cambridge: Cambridge University Press, 1991), p. 14.
19. Thomas Pynchon, *Gravity's Rainbow* (1973) (New York: Penguin, 1987), p. 703.
20. Paul Maltby, *Dissident Postmodernists: Barthelme, Coover, Pynchon* (Philadelphia: University of Pennsylvania Press, 1991), p. 14 and *passim*.
21. Osteen, *American Magic*, p. 231.
22. See Philip Nel, *The Avant-Garde and American Postmodernity: Small Incisive Shocks* (Jackson and London: University Press of Mississippi, 2002), pp. 99–101.

23. Paul Cantor, "Adolf, We Hardly Knew You," in Lentricchia, ed., *New Essays on "White Noise,"* p. 60.
24. Linda Hutcheon, *Irony's Edge: The Theory and Politics of Irony* (London: Routledge, 1994), p. 51.
25. Don DeLillo, "The Power of History," *New York Times Magazine* (September 7, 1997), pp. 60–1.
26. Leonard Wilcox, "Baudrillard, DeLillo's *White Noise*, and the End of Heroic Narrative," *Contemporary Literature* 32.3 (1991), p. 363.
27. T. S. Eliot, *Selected Poems* (San Diego: Harcourt, 1964), pp. 67, 74.
28. Paul Gleason, "Don DeLillo, T. S. Eliot, and the Redemption of America's Atomic Waste Land," in Joseph Dewey, Steven G. Kellman, and Irving Malin eds., *UnderWords: Perspectives on Don DeLillo's "Underworld,"* (Newark: Associated University Presses, 2002), pp. 130, 139.
29. Arthur Saltzman, *This Mad "Instead": Governing Metaphors in Contemporary American Fiction* (Columbia: University of South Carolina Press, 2000), p. 44.
30. Quoted in Begley, "The Art of Fiction," p. 92.
31. Ibid., p. 88.
32. Ernest Hemingway, *A Farewell to Arms* (1929) (New York: Scribner's Sons, 1969), p. 3.
33. David Remnick, "Exile on Main Street: Don DeLillo's Undisclosed Underworld," in DePietro, ed., *Conversations*, p. 140.
34. For more on this subject, see Paul Maltby, "The Romantic Metaphysics of Don DeLillo," *Contemporary Literature* 37 (1996), pp. 263–5.
35. Thomas LeClair, "An Interview with Don DeLillo," in DePietro, ed., *Conversations*, p. 8.
36. Williams uses this phrase in "A Sort of Song" (*Selected Poems*, ed. Charles Tomlinson [New York: New Directions, 1985], p. 145) and repeats it in *Patterson* ([New York: New Directions, 1951] pp. 14, 18, *passim*).
37. Saltzman, *This Mad "Instead,"* p. 17.
38. See Nel, "Don DeLillo's Return to Form," pp. 742–5.
39. James Joyce, *A Portrait of the Artist as a Young Man* (1916) (New York: Viking, 1964), pp. 188–9.
40. Quoted in Begley, "The Art of Fiction," p. 97.
41. Anne Longmuir, "The Search for a Political Aesthetic in the Fiction of Don DeLillo," PhD thesis, University of Edinburgh (2003), p. 156.
42. Frank Lentricchia, "Tales of the Electronic Tribe," in Lentricchia, ed., *New Essays on "White Noise,"* p. 103.
43. Ann Arensberg, "Seven Seconds," in DePietro, ed., *Conversations*, pp. 45–6.
44. Quoted in Vince Passaro, "Dangerous Don DeLillo," in DePietro, ed., *Conversations*, p. 79.
45. "I've always seen myself in sentences. I begin to recognize myself, word by word, as I work through a sentence. The language of my books has shaped me as a man" appears in DeLillo, *Mao II*, p. 48, and in Passaro, "Dangerous Don Delillo," p. 82.
46. Don DeLillo and Paul Auster, *Salman Rushdie Defense Pamphlet*, Rushdie Defense Committee USA, February 14, 1994, <http://perival.com/delillo/rushdie_defense.html>, accessed August 3, 2006.
47. Maria Nadotti, "An Interview with Don DeLillo," in DePietro, ed., *Conversations*, p. 115.

2

PETER KNIGHT

DeLillo, postmodernism, postmodernity

The reason for the initial groundswell of interest in Don DeLillo in the mid-1980s and the reason that *White Noise* (1985) has quickly become one of the most frequently taught postwar novels is that DeLillo is seen as representing the turn to postmodernism in American literature. But the vital question is: in what sense is DeLillo a postmodern writer? Is it his detailed anthropological attention to those aspects of contemporary Western – and perhaps specifically American – life in the age of media saturation and globalized free market capitalism that is characterized by the term postmodernity? Or is it his deployment of a set of stylistic techniques that makes him an exponent of a new artistic register that goes by the name of postmodernism? Or is it a stance of opposition to contemporary economic and political trends that renders him less a gung-ho postmodernist than a determined if somewhat oblique antipostmodernist? The basic debate that has fascinated many readers of DeLillo is whether his writing is able to maintain a critical distance from the culture he describes. Put simply, is his writing a symptom, a diagnosis, or an endorsement of the condition of postmodernity?

After modernism

The critics who have examined DeLillo's recurrent interest in modernist writers such as James Joyce and William Faulkner and in artistic techniques such as cinematic montage and literary surrealism are undoubtedly correct in suggesting that he has a greater formal and spiritual affinity with the early twentieth-century avant-garde in particular and modernism in general than with other contemporary postmodernist writers.[1] But the irony is that it is the explicitness with which DeLillo acknowledges his enormous debt to modernism that ends up rendering him postmodern. One way of understanding the cultural movement of postmodernism is recognizing that it arises from artists and writers realizing (at some point in the 1960s) that the radical promise of avant-garde modernism to change the world by changing how people perceived it had come to nothing.[2] When the once-shocking paintings of the Impressionists or Pablo Picasso end up on tea towels; when the writings of Joyce, Gertrude Stein, T. S. Eliot, and Virginia Woolf end up as standard canon-fodder for first-year English majors; when the utopian architectural plans of LeCorbusier end up as the high-rise nightmares of postwar housing estates; and when the music of Igor Stravinsky becomes the sound track for a car commercial, then there really is nowhere left for aesthetic experiment to go as artists lose their special claim to authenticity, uniqueness, and resistance to the status quo. Postmodernism, on this understanding, is not so much a discovery of a new artistic style as a narrowing of the horizon of existing intellectual and aesthetic possibilities as prior ventures lose their critical purchase.

One way out of the impasse is for artists and writers to play self-reflexively with the very problem of trying to find forms of original expression after the failure of modernism or, more accurately, after the ironic success of modernism that ended up making it institutionalized and ubiquitous, the cultural wallpaper of contemporary life. If the authentic exploration of innermost feelings and ideas is no longer possible per se, the writer can draw attention to the fact rather than trying to gloss over it, by highlighting how every utterance is in part a quotation of previous sayings, in an endless chain of Chinese whispers that leads to an accelerated recycling of past styles in a process of hyperbolic intertextuality. In *White Noise*, for example, the narrator Jack Gladney ascends the hill on campus and sees "another postmodern sunset, rich in romantic imagery" (*WN* 227). The sunset is in part "postmodern" because its spectacular, lurid colors are a result not of natural, organic splendor but of the "airborne toxic event" that is affecting the weather and possibly ruining his health. But it is also self-consciously "postmodern" because it is merely a shorthand copy of endless descriptions of other sunsets that have become a literary cliché, leaving Jack to recognize the futility of trying to find an original expression for it: "Why try to describe it?" (*WN* 227). The concluding section of *White Noise*, when Jack sets out to kill the man whom he knows as Willie Mink, is likewise an ironic reworking of the ending of *Lolita* (1955), in which Humbert Humbert is caught up in the self-awareness of all the pulp-fictional clichés haunting his actions as he tries to kill his nemesis Clare Quilty: in DeLillo's doubly ironic version, Jack is self-conscious about the prior literary representation of the self-consciousness induced by the weight of prior representations.

In addition to specific literary techniques and narrative moments that address head-on the problem of coming after modernism, DeLillo's work also manifests a general awareness of the problematic role of the artist in an age of boundless consumerism. The foundation of modernism was built on the notion of "art for art's sake," a championing of the realm of pure aestheticism in the face of the life-sapping influence of the market and mass culture. This oppositional stance was slowly eroded as modernist art became just one more commodity in the marketplace. The battle lines between high art and mass entertainment were redrawn in the 1950s in the USA when cultural and political commentators began to warn that mass culture was the thin end of the wedge of totalitarianism and that only the kind of difficult, individual-centered art heralded by high modernism could save Americans from becoming the unthinking, zombified masses that bred fascism and communism.[3] DeLillo's *Mao II* (1991), for example, is an extended meditation on the traditional role of the reclusive, heroic modernist artist – a role marked out by "silence, cunning, and exile" in Joyce's famous phrase – in a postmodern age in which terrorism seems to have usurped the novel's ability to make dramatic "raids on human consciousness. What we all used to do before we were incorporated" (*M* 87). In the novel the writer Bill Gray's obsessive reclusiveness is reused as a marketing gimmick as the media's fantasized version of Gray becomes larger than life: we learn that now "Bill is at the height of his fame" (*M* 52).[4] Likewise, in *Libra* (1988) the narrator hints at the sense of futility for the contemporary novelist when a nonfictional work like the official Warren Commission Report on the Kennedy assassination outdoes any mere literary experiment – to the extent that DeLillo recreates chunks of Marguerite Oswald's inimitable testimony, like Jorge Luis Borges's fable of a writer whose lifelong work ends up being a word-for-word recreation of Cervantes's *Don Quixote* (1605).[5] Although Philip Nel is correct to argue that the quip in *Libra* – that the Warren Report was "the megaton novel James Joyce would have written if he'd moved to Iowa City and lived to be a hundred" (*L* 181) – points to DeLillo's residual fascination with the encyclopedic investigation of everyday life instigated by some modernist writers,[6] it also gestures to DeLillo's self-conscious reflection on the role of the novelist in an age when a government commission out-Joyces Joyce. In a similar fashion, *Underworld* (1997) offers Klara Sax as a model of an artist whose originality consists in recycling (first junk and then military air planes), in the same way that the novel itself constitutes a recycling of both literary antecedents and DeLillo's own oeuvre.[7]

Simulation, mediation, and the primal scene of postmodernism

In addition to DeLillo's focus on the problematic role of the writer in an age when everything seems to have already been written, his writings also engage with a more thoroughgoing shift in the relationship between art and life that theorists have characterized as distinctively postmodern. If the story of high cultural painting and writing from the mid nineteenth to the mid twentieth century is the story of a struggle to craft forms of representation that could adequately capture the ever increasing complexity of modern life and the ever increasing variety of people's perceptions of their world, then the story of the past half century is in part a complete turn away from that project of sociological and psychological realism with the recognition that art can no longer represent life itself but only other representations. A film such as *Blue Velvet* (released a year after DeLillo's *White Noise*) does not show what the 1950s were really like in a gritty exposé of the sinister underbelly of the seemingly tranquil suburbs; instead, it is a film about the clichéd 1950s of sitcoms and teen movies, a representation of other prior representations. In short, there is no longer any possibility of a direct, unmediated access to authentic emotions or events or reality: whatever we experience, the argument goes, comes to us mediated through our endless consumption of electronic entertainment.

As early as 1962, the historian Daniel Boorstin had noted a significant shift in the relationship between the news media and the real-life events they were purportedly meant to show.[8] He argued that the media – with the connivance of politicians – had begun to create "pseudo-events" such as staged photo opportunities in which public figures "spontaneously" delivered their ready-made soundbites. For Boorstin, these pseudo-events were deceptive, a breach of the trust between reality and its representation. Later theorists such as Jean Baudrillard took this argument much further, insisting that the situation had now gone way beyond Boorstin's diagnosis. According to Baudrillard, the image-obsessed media no longer reflects a basic reality or masks and perverts a basic reality (as Boorstin's argument implied). The media no longer even masks the *absence* of a basic reality. Instead, the image has come to be entirely freefloating, bearing no relation to reality whatsoever – a pure simulacrum, a copy of a copy that has no original.[9] Critics have found numerous instances of the topsy-turvy world of life imitating art in DeLillo's writing, most notably in *White Noise*, whose publication in the mid-1980s coincided with great academic interest in the ideas of Baudrillard and other theorists of postmodernism. At the heart of *White Noise* is the evacuation of Jack Gladney's family as a result of the airborne toxic event; an employee of the SIMUVAC organization (which conducts simulated evacuations) informs Jack, "We thought we could use it as a model ... a chance to use the real event in order to rehearse the simulation" (*WN* 139). In a reversal of cause and effect, the simulation becomes the original event of which reality is a mere imitation. There is also, for instance, a passing reference to a Moorish movie theater that has become a mosque, a Hollywood version coming to be taken for the real thing. Likewise, there are the nuns who fake their belief to correspond to people's sentimental fantasy of what a nun should be. Jack's children even have a sense of déjà vu of a sense of déjà vu: experiences are no longer immediate but always mediated through other, prior experiences. And in *Cosmopolis* (2003), for example, the currency trader Eric Packer repeatedly experiences a form of inverted déjà vu, in which he sees the representation of an event on screen moments before it happens, leaving him to feel that everything is always at one remove – even his own death.

But, above all, there is the scene early in *White Noise* in which Jack is taken by fellow academic Murray Jay Siskind (who teaches in the popular culture department) to "THE MOST PHOTOGRAPHED BARN IN AMERICA," the tourist equivalent of a celebrity who is famous for being famous. Murray coaches Jack through the idea that it is no longer possible to see the reality of the barn itself because all they can see is the tourist cliché, and that the point of the experience is not the barn itself but the way it is mediated through other people's reactions. He points out that people are "taking pictures of taking pictures" and that "[o]nce you've seen the signs about the barn [on the way there], it becomes impossible to see the barn." He concludes, "What was the barn like before it was photographed? ... What did it look like, how was it different from other barns, how was it similar to other barns? We can't answer these questions, because we've read the signs, seen the people snapping the pictures. We can't get outside the aura. We're part of the aura" (*WN* 12–13). Murray seems entranced by the possibility of giving in to the full drama of the irrevocable substitution of the fake for the real, but Jack's narration is deadpan, leaving readers to wonder whether the scene is sharp satire or a kind of "blank fiction" (though some critics have argued that the overall logic of the novel dictates that this scene must surely be seen as satirical).[10]

Examples of the way that individuals no longer have an unmediated access to an authentic self and perhaps no longer even have an authentic self also abound in DeLillo's writing. In the case of *White Noise*, much critical attention has focused on the handful of repetitious brand-name mantras throughout the novel: "The Airport Marriott, the Downtown Travelodge, the Sheraton Inn and Conference Center" (*WN* 15); "Dacron, Orlon, Lycra Spandex" (*WN* 52); "Leaded, unleaded, super unleaded" (*WN* 199); "MasterCard, Visa, American Express" (*WN* 100). Some critics have seen these as the disembodied voice – the white noise – of contemporary television- and ad-saturated culture, but others have argued for a more hardline interpretation, that these product-placement triads have infiltrated their way into Jack's stream of consciousness (to use a modernist phrase) in much the same way as when Jack observes his daughter Steffie sleeping he hears her mutter the phrase *"Toyota Celica"* in her dreams.[11] It is as if the innermost sanctum of individuality has been taken over by the language of advertising, so thoroughly immersed in the flow of media imagery have people become. The most extreme example of this tendency in *White Noise* is the character called Willie Mink, the man Jack attempts to kill: so completely colonized is his unconscious by the media that he randomly spouts gobbets from television, such as "Some of these playful dolphins have been equipped with radio transmitters" (*WN* 310). Mink is so far gone in mistaking the simulation for the real thing that he ducks for cover when Jack merely utters clichéd phrases from pulp thrillers, such as a "hail of bullets" (*WN* 311); on the other hand, Jack seems incapable of narrating or even experiencing the scene without ringing the changes of literary pastiche and obsessively focusing not on the act but on the act of description that has already been recounted in a thousand novels and films beforehand: "I fired the gun, the weapon, the pistol, the firearm, the automatic" (*WN* 312).

If Jack Gladney and Willie Mink are examples of media saturation taken to comic excess, DeLillo's portrait of Lee Harvey Oswald in *Libra* is deadly serious. In the novel DeLillo is ultimately less interested in who really killed Kennedy or discovering who Oswald really was than in understanding how Oswald's sense of self came to be constructed through the media. DeLillo imagines Oswald settling in to his life's work in prison after his arrest: not a traditional modernist project of self-understanding but an attempt to make sense of the person now known as Lee Harvey Oswald, the triple-monikered media version of the president's assassin. In *Libra* Oswald's sense of self has come to be channeled through media representations, not least his death, which is captured live on television. DeLillo imagines that Oswald sees himself being shot by Jack Ruby through the television cameras shooting the event, as if the only way to access his real self is not through a voyage of inner discovery but through its disembodied projection on television. Furthermore, the novel insists that Kennedy is just as much a media construct as Oswald and that other characters such as Lee's wife Marina also succumb to the allure of media fantasies. Part of the significance of Oswald's death, therefore, is that it makes visible a process that is happening to all Americans.

An important question raised by *Libra* is whether the mediation of experience through film and television is a contributing cause or an effect of the assassination. As well as discovering the pervasiveness of the media in people's lives, DeLillo explores the endless, desensitizing repetition of violent death surrounding the Kennedy assassination: "There's the shattering randomness of the event, the missing motive, the violence that people not only commit but seem to watch simultaneously from a disinterested distance."[12] The aura of an authentic, heroic, existentialist sense of self that Oswald tries to cultivate through his act of violence is eroded by the infinite and increasingly commodified repetition of the shooting. In *Libra* we see Beryl Parmenter, the wife of one of the CIA conspirators, watching the continuous reruns on television of Ruby shooting Oswald as "the horror became mechanical. They kept racking film, running shadows through the machine. It was a process that drained life from the men in the picture, sealed them in the frame. They began to seem timeless to her, identically dead" (*L* 447).

Libra suggests that in the moment of his death, Oswald's mediated detachment from himself profoundly alters the nature of the event, implicating the audience in the process as it compulsively watches him being shot over and over:

> There was something in Oswald's face, a glance at the camera before he was shot, that put him here in the audience, among the rest of us, sleepless in our homes – a glance, a way of telling us that he knows who we are and how we feel, that he has brought our perceptions and interpretations into his sense of the crime. Something in the look, the sly intelligence, exceedingly brief but far-reaching, a connection all but bleached away by glare, tells us that he is outside the moment, watching with the rest of us ... He is commenting on the documentary footage even as it is being shot. Then he himself is shot, and shot, and shot, and the look becomes another kind of knowledge. But he has made us part of his dying. (*L* 447)

The real significance of the assassination for DeLillo is the effect that endlessly watching the violent deaths of Kennedy and Oswald has on society at large, making Americans victims of the postmodern condition. Oswald's murder of Kennedy becomes the prototype of an endlessly repeated scenario, "the first of those soft white dreamy young men who plan the murder of a famous individual – a president, a presidential candidate, a rock star – as a way of organizing their loneliness and misery, making a network out of it, a web of connections." When all is said and done, "Oswald changed history not only through his involvement in the death of the president, but in prefiguring such moments of the American absurd," that long roll-call of celebrity assassinations, serial killings, and high school shootings over the last four decades.[13]

In his essay "American Blood," DeLillo argues that all the presidential assassination attempts since John F. Kennedy's have been thoroughly mediated. DeLillo looks in detail at the shooting of President Ronald Reagan by John Hinckley, a "self-created media event."[14] Hinckley, DeLillo points out, claims that he was motivated by his obsessive watching of the film *Taxi Driver* (1976), which was based on the case of Arthur Bremer, who, having watched the film *A Clockwork Orange* (1971), stalks first Richard Nixon then George Wallace. Caught up in a funhouse of representations, Hinckley shot President Reagan, an event that was, as

DeLillo describes it, "pure TV, a minicam improvisation." Part of the significance of these copy-cat shootings is that they allow us to see the Kennedy assassination in a different vein, as the early glimmerings of a trend of media obsession that has deformed the American mindscape ever since. For DeLillo, it is only in the light of subsequent events and a "condition of estrangement and helplessness, an undependable reality" that we can see the true significance of the Kennedy assassination.[15] In effect, in DeLillo's work the Kennedy assassination functions as the primal scene of postmodernism, a symbolically necessary but imagined origin of the "society of the spectacle" that America has come to inhabit.[16] In one scene in *Underworld*, it comes as little surprise to learn that the Zapruder home-movie footage of the Kennedy assassination pulls loose from its moorings as a piece of forensic evidence in the president's murder when it is shown on a continuous loop at an underground art-scene party in the 1970s. Likewise, in *Underworld* the numbing legacy of Kennedy's assassination is all too evident in the way that the amateur video of a random shooting carried out by the so-called Texas Highway Killer is endlessly repeated on television.

Given that DeLillo's work repeatedly suggests that the very nature of individual consciousness has been reconfigured by America's obsessive consumption of dehumanizing imagery, two questions present themselves: when exactly did this shift in the relationship between reality and representation occur, and does DeLillo portray it as a necessarily pessimistic falling away from a comparative golden age? As we have seen, the answer to the first question explored in *Libra* is that the Kennedy assassination marks some kind of a watershed, but it is also evident that this cultural shift was recognizable only in retrospect, as if caused by its subsequent effects. Other novels, however, suggest a different historical timeline. *Underworld*, for instance, explores how the nostalgic, historical aura of a classic baseball game is a product of the mediation of radio commentary that became so transparent that its listeners seemed unaware of the mediating effect – even when the commentary was entirely simulated.[17] And the plot of *Running Dog*, for example, revolves around the search for a mythical secret home movie of Adolf Hitler's last days in his bunker at the end of World War II, a film that turns out not to reveal some ultimate, apocalyptic truth of Nazi evil and depraved sexuality but the postmodern irony of the German dictator dressing up for an entertainment as Charlie Chaplin, whose famous parody of Hitler has come to be one of the important filters through which people see Hitler. The primal scene of the simulacrum is thus pushed back from the present to 1963, then to the 1950s, and even to the 1940s, as if this possibility of postmodern mediation has slowly been emerging – and slowly becoming visible in retrospect – during the course of the twentieth century.

Cultural logic of late capitalism

Some theorists – most notably Fredric Jameson, David Harvey and Anthony Giddens – have argued that the postmodern condition is not a philosophical proposition that you can legitimately object to or embrace or simply take a moral stance against, but is instead the entire force field of contemporary social and economic relations, as inescapable as the air we breathe.[18] One of the key features of this new world order is the spread of neoliberal (i.e., laissez-faire) capitalism into every last enclave of the globe. The claim is that capitalism has now transformed the realms of art, the unconscious, and even primitive nature itself, those precious last spaces of resistance to the voracious logic of the market that modernists explored with such fervor. According to this analysis, global market culture now cynically recuperates everything, including the resistant energies of avant-garde art and writing of earlier in the twentieth century. As we have already seen, DeLillo's novels are finely attuned to this process of the commodification of the aesthetic and the colonization of art, the unconscious and nature itself by the frenzied appetites of consumerism. In *White Noise*, for example, a rack of novels is knocked over in the supermarket and the books spill over the floor, as if fiction is just one more bar-coded item (*WN* 20). *Cosmopolis* provides DeLillo's most concentrated analysis of the "utopian glow of cyber-capital."[19] The novel's protagonist, the rogue capitalist Eric Packer, explicitly considers, for example, how the antiglobalization protests interrupting his journey attest to the market's capacity to "absorb everything around it." He also wonders if the suicide by self-immolation of a protestor might be the last sole remaining possibility for an act that is not instantly recuperated by the market, a "thing outside its reach," perhaps suggesting that the "Market was not total" (*C* 99–100). But Vija Kinski, Packer's theorist-assistant, notes that the protest is unoriginal, merely a copy of previous spectacles such as the self-immolation of a Vietnamese monk.

The real significance of Jameson's analysis of postmodernism as the "cultural logic of late capitalism" is the insight that postmodernity shapes art not just at the level of content but in its very form. This would mean that, as much as DeLillo's novels offer a partial diagnosis of the condition of postmodernity, they are also inevitably expressive symptoms of some of the profound social and economic changes that we can barely grasp at a conscious level. Jameson thus finds evidence of the cultural logic of late capitalism in, for example, the tendency of some recent culture to operate more through pastiche than parody, since parody assumes a position of ironic distance outside the system, whereas pastiche involves the mere recycling of previous styles without any clear sense of what the satirical imitation might mean. In the case of DeLillo, we could point to his rapid-fire recycling of popular and literary genres, with the mixture in *White Noise*, for example, of the campus novel, the existential drama, the disaster novel, and the domestic melodrama, none of which are ridiculed in an obvious way. At a still deeper level, we might point to the way that in DeLillo's novels many of the characters are not fully realized, autonomous individuals but are disembodied voices that often blur into one another and whose actions often seem very constrained by the narrative framework erected by the author. Perhaps the most extreme example of this tendency is in *Ratner's Star* (1976), which manipulates its characters as if they are mathematical functions within the larger equation of the plot structure. While some reviewers have regarded this merely as poor writing, we might instead read the subservience of characters to a narrative structure as a structural parallel to the way that real people are constrained by the vast contemporary social and economic forces that shape their lives and over which they have little or no control. What's important is not that actions of characters are determined by social forces (after all, late nineteenth-century naturalist writers such as Theodore Dreiser and Frank Norris had explored that possibility) but that both the constraining forces and the narrative plots that describe them are arranged as decentered networks rather than in a traditional top-down pyramid structure of power. The best example in DeLillo's oeuvre of this postmodernization of paranoid fears of control comes in *Underworld*. At the level of thematic content, the novel conducts a historical investigation of the shift from the paradoxically secure paranoia of the Cold War to the less stable insecure paranoia of postmodernity, in which it is no longer clear who or what is the enemy. In this situation fear of hidden dangers and hidden agendas is a pervasive attitude for characters living under the shadow of nuclear destruction, pollution, and other forms of unpredictable technological nightmare that create a permanent environment of risk. At the level of narrative structure, however, the novel creates a vast chain of intertextual links that ends up exceeding the simple Them/Us paranoid binary of the Cold War, sketching out new and at times barely perceptible ways of perceiving connections that global capitalism both enforces and makes possible.

Some scholars have been uneasy, though, about the idea that DeLillo's novels are merely an expression – perhaps even an unconscious expression at a deep structural level – of the all-encompassing systems of capitalist control. Even the critic who has provided the most developed analysis of DeLillo's thematic and structural interest in systems theory reads DeLillo's narrative systems as containing crucial elements of open-ended randomness that short-circuit the all-too-apparent control mechanisms.[20] The problem with the analysis of postmodernity as the encroachment of consumer capitalism into every last realm of human endeavor is that the more convincing it is, the more depressing it becomes because if true, there is nothing that can be done about it. Some theorists have taken exception to this "winner-loses" logic of post-modernism, finding unjustifiably paranoid the idea of an all-pervasive system of social and economic forces that are impossible to escape. Yet even Jameson holds out a glimmer of hope of making some kind of sense of these otherwise disorienting changes brought about by the acceleration and glo-balization of capitalism, if not by finding a safe haven of critical distance outside the endlessly linked circuit of production and consumption that spans the globe. He suggests that even if traditional forms of clear-eyed political critique are no longer available (because we are all immersed in a system that is too complex for our current perceptual apparatus to compre-hend), then certain forms of art might yield – in their deep structural form rather than their manifest content – a kind of "cognitive mapping" of our current situation.[21]

Other critics have been more sanguine about the possibility of critique. Linda Hutcheon, for one, has suggested that some forms of postmodern writing engage in a kind of "complicitous critique," using narrative strate-gies such as historiographic metafiction that self-reflexively lay bare the socially constructed character of received orthodoxies – of, say, race, sexu-ality, and national destiny – that might otherwise be taken as entirely natural and immutable.[22] On this line of thinking, although it is never possible to step outside ideology or discourse, it is nevertheless feasible to produce novels that defamiliarize particular ideologies and discourses that are most oppressive because most invisible and thereby imagine an alter-native future that is not chained to a fixed past. DeLillo's recycling of both high literature and popular fiction and his defamiliarizing of specialized languages (of, for example, advertising in *Americana* [1971], pop music in *Great Jones Street* [1973], sport in *End Zone* [1972], mathematics in *Ratner's Star*) might therefore be read not as mere blank pastiche but as a deliberate foregrounding of the way that all experience is constructed through discourse. Following DeLillo's expression of his preference for contemporary novels that "absorb and incorporate the culture without catering to it,"[23] many critics have found elements of a critique-from-within in his work, focusing, for example, on his creative use of the "physics of language" as a form of homeopathic inoculation[24] or his exploration of the transformative "magic" of literary art as a way of subduing the pervasive "American dread" of contemporary life[25] or his keeping alive the possibility of a historical counternarrative in the face of the popular perception that with the global triumph of free market capitalism we have reached the end of history.[26]

There are, finally, other ways of seeing how DeLillo's novels might open up spaces of possibility rather than merely giving in to a totalized vision of multinational capitalism. One important idea in the theoretical discussion of postmodernism has been the postmodern sublime as a moment of recognition of the seeming impossibility of realist representation because of the short-circuiting logic of the simulacrum. Jameson has given a new twist to this notion, suggesting that the traditional Romantic sublime – in which the writer experiences a sense of terror in the face of the inexpressible grandeur of Nature and the Almighty – is now replaced by the technological sublime, in which the fixation with, say, cyberspace or the mechanics of digital reproduction is a substitute for the writer's awe-struck inability to represent the impossible complexity of global capitalism and perhaps even the unfolding of history itself.[27] Evidence of the postmodern sublime might be found in the repeated moments in DeLillo's novels that exude a sense of unnamable mystery. Toward the end of *Underworld*, for example, a crowd gathers in the Bronx to gaze at a billboard that, as it is lit up by passing subway trains, miraculously seems to show the image of a young girl named Esmeralda who has recently been raped and killed in the neighborhood. What is significant about this kind of example is that it locates the source of mystery not in an uncorrupted zone outside the iron cage of capitalism but within the system itself: the moment of collective religious wonder comes not by traditional divine or artistic revelation but through the medium of advertising, the very soul of consumer capitalism.[28] Likewise the "postmodern sunset" in *White Noise* that the townsfolk find curiously mesmerizing is of course a product not of pure nature but of the frightening causal networks of pollution, risk, and industrial hazard that defy our rational powers of prediction or comprehension. Even the scene that is taken as the most emblematic moment in DeLillo's work of the thorough colonization by consumer capitalism of an individual's last space of privacy – Steffie mumbling brand names in her sleep – ends with Jack finding a strange sense of comfort:

> The utterance was beautiful and mysterious, gold-shot with looming wonder. It was like the name of an ancient power in the sky, tablet-carved in cuneiform. It made me feel that something hovered. But how could this be? A simple brand name, an ordinary car . . . Part of every child's brain noise, the substatic regions too deep to probe. Whatever its source, the utterance struck me with the impact of a moment of splendid transcendence. (*WN* 155)

It is therefore arguable that in DeLillo's novels the possibility of transcendence and the imagination of an alternative to the seeming inevitable triumph of neoliberalism is not to be found in some inaccessible and outmoded otherworldly realm but within the very technologies and discourses of contemporary life.

Conclusion

Part of the difficulty of deciding whether DeLillo is more accurately thought of as a modernist or a postmodernist is that his writings exhibit a fine-tuned awareness of what is at stake in theoretical discussions of the cultural logic of late capitalism, even to the extent of using the very terms employed by the theorists who diagnose his work. After all, the significance of the "Most Photographed Barn" episode in *White Noise* – a scene that has surely become the "Most Discussed Scene in Postmodern Fiction" – is not something that can be teased out only through the astute insights of a critic well versed in theories of postmodernism. Siskind's commentary ensures that the characters themselves (and hence readers) experience the scene through the lens of postmodern theory. This primal scene of postmodern mediation is thus itself mediated through its own built-in analysis, a short-circuiting situation that has only been exacerbated by the sudden rush of critical commentary eager to claim DeLillo as a homespun American theorist of postmodernism, a Baudrillard in a plaid shirt. As with the barn itself, it is virtually impossible to remember what reading DeLillo was like before he came to be engulfed by the aura of postmodernism.

Notes

1. See, for example, Philip Nel's chapter in this volume.
2. This idea was most famously propounded by John Barth in "The Literature of Exhaustion," *Atlantic* (Aug. 1967), pp. 29–34.
3. The classic statement of this position is Dwight Macdonald's "Masscult and Midcult" (1960) in his *Against the American Grain* (New York: Vintage, 1962).
4. For an extended discussion of the compromised role of the author, see Mark Osteen, "Becoming Incorporated: Spectacular Authorship and DeLillo's *Mao II*," *Modern Fiction Studies* 45 (1999), pp. 643–74.
5. Jorge Luis Borges, "Pierre Menard, Author of The Quixote," *Ficciones* (New York: Grove Press, 1962).
6. See Nel's chapter in this volume, pp. 14–15.
7. On DeLillo's recycling of his own work, see David Cowart, *Don DeLillo: The Physics of Language* (Athens: University of Georgia Press, 2003), pp. 181–209.
8. Daniel Boorstin, *The Image, or What Happened to the American Dream* (New York: Atheneum, 1962).
9. Jean Baudrillard, *Simulations* (New York: Semiotext[e], 1983).
10. See, for example, John Duvall's analysis of the connections made in *White Noise* between the television-saturated consumer society and fascism, in "The

(Super)Marketplace of Images: Television as Unmediated Mediation in DeLillo's *White Noise*," *Arizona Quarterly* 50.3 (1994), pp. 127–53.

11. Examples of the former position include John Frow, "The Last Things Before the Last: Notes on *White Noise*," in Frank Lentricchia, ed., *Introducing Don DeLillo* (Durham: Duke University Press, 1991), pp. 175–91. The latter argument is developed in Lentricchia, "Tales of the Electronic Tribe," in Lentricchia, ed., *New Essays on "White Noise"* (Cambridge: Cambridge University Press, 1992), pp. 87–113.

12. DeLillo quoted in Adam Begley, "The Art of Fiction CXXXV: Don DeLillo," in Thomas Depietro, ed., *Conversations with Don DeLillo* (Jackson: University Press of Mississippi, 2005), p. 102.

13. DeLillo quoted in "Oswald: Myth, Mystery, and Meaning," *PBS Frontline* forum (with DeLillo, Edward J. Epstein, and Gerald Posner), <www.pbs.org/wgbh/pages/frontline/shows/oswald/forum>.

14. Don DeLillo, "American Blood: A Journey through the Labyrinth of Dallas and JFK," *Rolling Stone* (December 8, 1983), p. 24.

15. DeLillo, "Oswald."

16. Guy Debord, *The Society of the Spectacle* (1967) (New York: Zone Books, 1994).

17. See John Duvall, "Excavating the Underworld of Race and Waste in Cold War History: Baseball, Aesthetics, and Ideology," in Hugh Ruppersburg and Tim Engles, eds., *Critical Essays on Don DeLillo* (New York: G. K. Hall, 2000), pp. 258–81.

18. See Fredric Jameson, *Postmodernism, or, The Cultural Logic of Late Capitalism* (Durham: Duke University Press, 1991); David Harvey, *The Condition of Postmodernity: An Inquiry into the Origins of Cultural Change* (Oxford: Blackwell, 1989); and Anthony Giddens, *Consequences of Modernity* (Cambridge: Polity Press, 1990).

19. Don DeLillo, "In the Ruins of the Future: Reflections on Terror and Loss in the Shadow of September," *Harper's* (December 2001), p. 33.

20. Tom LeClair, *In the Loop: Don DeLillo and the Systems Novel* (Urbana: University of Illinois Press, 1987).

21. Fredric Jameson, "Cognitive Mapping," in Cary Nelson and Lawrence Grossberg, eds., *Marxism and the Interpretation of Culture* (Basingstoke: Macmillan, 1988), pp. 347–58.

22. Linda Hutcheon, *The Politics of Postmodernism* (London: Routledge, 1989).

23. DeLillo, "Art of Fiction," p. 290.

24. Cowart, *Don DeLillo*, p. 12.

25. Mark Osteen, *American Magic and Dread: Don DeLillo's Dialogue with Culture* (Philadelphia: University of Pennsylvania Press, 2000).

26. Peter Boxall, *Don DeLillo: The Possibility of Fiction* (New York: Routledge, 2006).

27. On the idea that history itself is the hidden object of the postmodern sublime, see, for example, Peter Baker, *The Fiction of Postmodernity* (Edinburgh: Edinburgh University Press, 2000).

28. For further treatment of the idea of transcendence from within, see John McClure, "Postmodern Romance: Don DeLillo and the Age of Conspiracy," in Lentricchia, ed., *Introducing Don DeLillo*, pp. 99–115.

PART II

Early fiction

3

PETER BOXALL

DeLillo and media culture

I would like to approach Don DeLillo's relationship with media culture somewhat obliquely through Samuel Beckett's early thoughts on the aesthetic possibilities of nonexpression. On July 9, 1937, a young Beckett wrote to his friend Axel Kaun:

> More and more my own language appears to me like a veil that must be torn apart in order to get at the things (or the Nothingness) behind it ... As we cannot eliminate language all at once, we should at least leave nothing undone that might contribute to its falling into disrepute. To bore one hole after another in it, until what lurks behind it – be it something or nothing – begins to seep through; I cannot imagine a higher goal for a writer today.[1]

A certain reading of Beckett's oeuvre would suggest that these early thoughts on the goals of literature turned out to be a manifesto or a statement of intent. Beckett's works get shorter as his career progresses, in the main, working toward the extremely brief texts such as *Imagination Dead Imagine* (1965), *Ping* (1966), and *Breath* (1969). In these works Beckett appears to be abiding by his intention to come as close as possible to eliminating language. These bleached-out late works barely happen; they are works in which literature comes as close as it is perhaps conceivable to come to nonexpression and silence, works in which the nothingness that language struggles to disguise begins to "seep through."

   Don DeLillo's work would seem to have little in common with this pared aesthetics of retraction and diminishment. His work starts big and gets bigger. From the capacious ragbag of *Americana* (1971) to the engorged historical vision of *Underworld* (1997), DeLillo's fiction offers a means of absorbing and articulating an entire culture. Rather than deleting words, rather than striving for the kind of minimalism that Beckett sees as literature's highest aspiration in 1937, DeLillo uses words to make a world, to build an American edifice. Michael Ondaatje, paraphrasing Walt Whitman and anticipating the recent work of Michael Hardt and Antonio Negri, suggests in his blurb to *Underworld* that DeLillo's writing "contains multitudes," as if the teeming crowd – the crowd that Hardt and Negri think of as the agents of a new global politics – is able to find a home in DeLillo's roomy writing.[2] His is a writing that does not reject, delete, eliminate but one that absorbs, recycles, accommodates. It is large, as Whitman is large ("I am large," Whitman writes, "I contain multitudes").[3] It does not tend toward silence but toward speech; rather than failure of expression, this work tends toward a sublime articulacy.

It may be that DeLillo's relationship with media culture can be understood in terms of this accommodating spirit. While Beckett is drawn away from the messiness of the world toward the stillness and silence of the pure artwork, DeLillo's novels ring with the clamour of the marketplace. *Americana*, *End Zone* (1972), *Great Jones Street* (1973), *Mao II* (1991), *White Noise* (1985), and *Underworld* are all novels fashioned from the ready materials of the culture. They are made out of advertising slogans and rock lyrics, snippets of film and television, to the same extent that they draw on literary and philosophical traditions. In DeLillo there is a tendency for high cultural artifacts – traces of Wittgenstein, Proust, and Joyce – to merge and weave together with lines from Bob Dylan and Lenny Bruce. Hollywood film blends with the auteurist films of Ingmar Bergman, Jean-Luc Godard, and Michelangelo Antonioni; Andy Warhol sits alongside Bruegel and J. A. M. Whistler, alongside advertisements for coke and orange juice. DeLillo's work might be thought of, in his own phrase, as a "child of Godard and Coca-Cola" (*A* 269), a body of work that dramatizes, for Mark Osteen, the "collision and collusion between image and anti-image, between high culture and consumer culture."[4] In DeLillo's work, it might be argued, there is a refusal to distinguish between media culture and high culture, a refusal to discriminate, or to exclude. While the version of high culture envisaged by Beckett is one in which everything is excluded from the artwork, DeLillo's novels are works in which "nothing is left out" (*L* 25), in which "everything is connected" (*U* 825).

DeLillo's critics have generally responded in one of two ways to this perception that his work performs a merging of consumer culture with high art. The first tendency is to read him as an exemplary postmodern writer, in whom the modernist urge toward difficulty, rarefied experimentation, and cultural segregation collapses into a recognition of the inescapability of a homogenized contemporary culture. Douglas Keesey, for example, sees DeLillo's first novel, *Americana*, as a dramatization of such a collapse. David Bell, the novel's protagonist, sets out to make an avant-garde film that will allow him to escape the banality of the advertising industry for which he works, recasting his tawdry life in the shape of a sculpted filmic image. But, according to Keesey, the novel suggests how impossible such an artistic remodeling of a wasted life is under contemporary conditions. Bell's film, Keesey writes, is "insufficiently experimental, a failure of the sympathetic imagination – in short, basically another Hollywood production."[5] And if *Americana* suggests that Hollywood has no outside, that it is an image-producing machine from which there is no escape, Anthony DeCurtis reads DeLillo's rock 'n' roll novel, *Great Jones Street*, as an illustration of the impossibility of escaping from commodified media culture more generally. *Great Jones Street* tells the story of Bucky Wunderlick, a superfamous rock star who abandons his public persona in order to hide away in a shabby flat while preparing to release the Mountain Tapes – an experimental album he recorded in the isolation of his soundproof studio in the mountains. However, DeCurtis observes, Wunderlick's withdrawal does not lead to purity and experimental art but to the recognition that "it is finally impossible to withdraw." The novel demonstrates that the artwork can offer no safe haven and no retreat, that there are "no meaningful alternatives" to the market economy, that "all artists [are] objects of consumption," and that "everything is bound in the cash nexus and the exchange of commodities, outside of which there stands nothing."[6]

Against this reading of a triumphant commercial culture, however, the second critical tendency I identify sees DeLillo's work as offering a means of redeeming the culture that he depicts. Rather than dramatizing the commodification of the artwork, DeLillo is seen as a writer whose work is capable of aestheticizing the commodity. The melting together of high art and consumer culture serves not to cheapen the artwork but rather to produce a new form in which the materials of the culture themselves might be redeemed. Osteen, for example, agrees that *Americana* "interrogates the possibility of authentic political or artistic activity in a world consumed by cinematic and capitalist representations," but he comes to the conclusion not that Hollywood triumphs over the avant-garde but rather that *Americana* demonstrates "how novels (and perhaps films) can avoid becoming mere merchandise."[7] Similarly, Osteen argues that *Great Jones Street*, far from depicting the impossibility of any alternative to market forces, offers *itself* as an alternative. The novel confounds the expectations of the reader about what a rock 'n' roll novel should be and in so doing offers a form of challenge to the very idea of market-driven art. "The degree to which *Great Jones Street* resists passive consumption," Osteen argues, "is also the degree to which it defeats the sterilizing pursuit of commodities that it critically depicts." Rather than performing the abandonment of a critical aesthetic in the face of an all-consuming media culture, DeLillo's novel "becomes the 'moral form' that may enable its readers and its author to master commerce."[8]

This contradictory critical response to the relationship between high art and media culture in DeLillo's fiction, though, is complicated by a third consideration, which troubles the clean distinction between these first two positions. Everything I have said so far has been predicated on an opposition between Beckett's commitment to an art that removes elements and withdraws from the world and DeLillo's work, which leaves nothing of the world out. Both the critical tendencies I have broadly outlined are based on the supposition that DeLillo's work embraces the culture in all its forms and manifestations. But while this comprehensiveness is clearly a central and crucial aspect of DeLillo's work, it is also paradoxically the case that DeLillo's writing, and perhaps particularly his early writing, is animated by many of the ideals that Beckett lays out so enthusiastically in his letter of 1937. However vastly different DeLillo's richly idiomatic, textured, and multireferential writing is to Beckett's pale, starved fizzles of prose, DeLillo's work is driven by an investment in the possibilities of aesthetic silence, an investment that he inherits, to an extent, from Beckett. As Osteen remarks, DeLillo's first three novels are preoccupied with what the author, in reference to Bergman's remarkable film *Persona* (1966), calls the "nature of diminishing existence" (*A* 277). *Americana, End Zone,* and *Great Jones Street,* Osteen writes, "chart similar deliberate movements towards silence and oblivion."[9] DeCurtis also notes this drive in DeLillo toward silence, suggesting that Wunderlick's Mountain Tapes in *Great Jones Street* are organized around the attempt to "defeat language itself," to "elude the tyranny of language and achieve a pure, perfectly unimpeded relationship with his audience."[10] Throughout DeLillo's 1970s output, it is possible to feel the influence of a Beckettian negative aesthetic at work. Beckett's 1937 letter is echoed, for example, in *Americana,* where the novel's novelist, Brand (a forerunner of *Mao II*'s Bill Gray), speculates that "maybe I'll eliminate language itself. It may be possible to find a completely new mode" (*A* 288).

This difficult coincidence in DeLillo's fiction of expansive accommodation and ascetic, contractive withdrawal determines the relationship between his writing and the media culture that informs it. It is also through an analysis of this coincidence in early novels such as *Americana* and *Great Jones Street* that we might see through the critical contradiction that I have sketched out above. An understanding of the effect of a Beckettian inheritance on DeLillo's concatenating, hyperlinking imagination allows us to glimpse the possibility of another way of thinking about the relationship between high art and media culture. In this context DeLillo is neither a writer who gives himself up to a borderless consumer culture nor a modernist *après la lettre* who seeks to redeem a fallen culture through the alchemical operations of a miraculous art. The mingling in DeLillo of a Beckettian austerity with a (Joycean) epic catholicity suggests a new term in the relationship between high and low, between the parsimonious and the extravagant, between the speechlessness of the artwork and the articulacy of the marketplace.

"Silence and darkness": film in *Americana*

In DeLillo's first novel, *Americana*, the most powerful agent for this production of a new term in the relationship between high art and media culture is the camera. The first inkling of the force the camera exerts on DeLillo's narrative comes early in the novel as David Bell stands in the lobby of his advertising agency in New York in front of a vast, blown-up photograph of a war zone:

> In the center of the picture was a woman holding a dead child in her arms, and behind her and on either side were eight other children; some of them looked at the woman while others were smiling and waving, apparently at the camera. A young man was down on one knee in the middle of the lobby, photographing the photograph. I stood behind him for a moment and the effect was unforgettable. Time and distance were annihilated and it seemed that the children were smiling and waving at him. Such is the prestige of the camera, its almost religious authority, its hypnotic power to command reverence from subject and bystander alike, that I stood absolutely motionless until the young man snapped the picture. It was as though I feared that any small movement on my part might distract one of those bandaged children and possibly ruin the photograph. (*A* 86–7)

At this moment, many of the oppositions that the novel charts are balanced around a center marked out by the camera; the camera both sets up these oppositions and offers to transform the basis on which their opposition is founded. The photograph brings together two starkly contrasted worlds. It acts as a frame through which the victims of war might regard its perpetrators, or at least its beneficiaries. The transparent plane of the photograph is all that separates New York from Vietnam, the rich from the poor, the present from the past, the tragic from the banal. As Bell stands behind the photographer photographing the photograph, he experiences the power of the camera to "annihilate" time and distance, to bring New York and Vietnam, now and then, master and slave, victim and perpetrator, into a deeply troubling shared presence. Bell feels that he should stay still as the photographer photographs the war image because the scene that the camera has captured – the woman holding a dead child out to the camera as an offering or a judgment or a curse – is not already over but in some sense still continuing. Bell feels his body itself to be removed, to be placed as an object in a new landscape that is controlled, stilled or frozen, by the authority of the camera. New York is bent back into Vietnam. The corporate viewer, for whose pleasure this scene of hardship is laid on, is removed from his privileged position in order to become part of the scene viewed. The annihilating power of the camera effects a merging of different places and different times by revealing something shared, but unspeakable, that lies behind the differences that place us in the world. To echo Beckett's terminology, the camera tears apart the veil of a worded world to reveal to us the borderless nothingness, stripped of time and distance, that lies behind it.

This effect – whereby the camera reveals its power to uncover an empty continuity where there appears to be historical and cultural segregation – is the central discovery of *Americana*. The idea that animates David's film – the "strangest, darkest, most horrifying idea of [his] life" (*A* 125) – is that one might use this power to produce a new kind of autobiography that transfigures one's life rather than simply recording it. David is imagining here a new version of Proust's *À la recherche du temps perdu* (1913–27) that uses the annihilating power of the camera in place of the recuperative power of narrative. Throughout DeLillo's wild, loose, freewheeling novel, this idea can be felt at its heart, seeking to transform the narrative from a rough, wordy draft to a perfectly sculpted art object. As David sets off on his road trip across America, the novel reveals a nation suffering from a set of pathologies characterized by asymmetrical difference, and by what the narrator thinks of, in an obliquely Forsterian vein, as a failure to connect. The nation is broken into constituent parts that fail to arrange themselves into a recognizable whole. The Navaho, living far in the west beyond the reach of the narrative, are held against a European landscape to the east from which the first settlers arrived on the *Mayflower*, and both these ancient cultures are placed, in turn, around the culture of superficial, corporate modernity to which David belongs. He reads the incommensurability of these constituents and the national sickness to which it gives rise through his own unresolved Oedipal crisis. The narrative is soaked in a restless sexual energy, a longing for abomination, for an unspeakable sexual gratification. At the heart of the novel is the richly Proustian moment when David comes closest to consummating his relationship with his mother at his coming-of-age party, at which he is driven to a restless, bewildered distraction by the power and unreadability of his Oedipal desire. David and his mother stand in the kitchen in the midst of the party on the brink of an incestuous encounter before being interrupted by the sound of his "father's bare feet on the stairs" (*A* 197). Thrashing on his bed, tormented by baulked desire, David recounts that "I would think of something and then try to come back to it and it would be gone. I could not keep a thought going. Nothing connected" (*A* 196). It is this experience of libidinal disconnection that determines all the other such failures in the novel.

But if the novel offers such a fractured version both of America and of the state of prose fiction, it also seeks, through the power of the camera, to make of these discrete parts a new whole. David's strange, dark, and terrifying idea is that the capacity of the camera to annihilate time and distance, to bring discrete things into a shared presence, might allow him to revisit that moment of Oedipal desire and prohibition, to remove the obstacles that blocked his path, and to experience the kind of empty simultaneity that he found before that war photograph in New York, in which the camera allows one to bleed through time and space, to transcend and exceed any temporal or spatial boundary that might seek to contain and police, to divide and disconnect. David's film is composed of a number of scenes from his own life, in which he employs stand-ins to act as himself and his family members. By filming these scenes, by standing both outside the scene as director and inside the scene as a simulacrum of himself, he sets out to bend time back in on itself. And at the heart of the film is the restaging of the party scene in which he stands in a taut embrace with his mother, preparing to leap over a far edge into a sea of unchecked desire, preparing to "cry in epic joy and pain at the freeing of a single moment" (*A* 197). Where, in life, this yielding to the unspeakable was checked by paternal prohibition, in this filmic reconstruction there will be no such obstacle to connection. David stands behind the camera, watching a stage version of himself and his mother replay the scene, finding himself doubled, placed simultaneously as voyeur and transgressor. As the actor-mother looks past the reconstruction of the son, into the eye of the camera, into the eye of the son grown old, there is a reliving of that moment in New York in which time and distance fold in on themselves and the unnamable connection that exists between divided things becomes somehow palpable. "I kept shooting for two or three minutes," David writes, "lost somewhere, bent back in twenty-five watts of brown light, listening for a sound behind me" (*A* 318).

From this moment of rediscovery, this annihilation of time and distance, the novel seeks to build a transfigured America. The film works from within the novel to perform a vast merging and to produce a version of connectedness that is perhaps unspeakable in the fallen language of the culture but that dwells complete within the womb of the narrative waiting for its time to come. The film promises to spread in all directions from this central moment of reimagining, bringing all the disparate elements that have gone into the making of America into its sphere of influence. The distinctions between east and west, between advertising and the avant-garde, between Godard and Coca-Cola, between high art and consumer culture, all those distinctions that have maimed and shaped the America through which David travels, are offered a kind of reconciliation as the release of his libidinal energy produces a new artform. In allowing the camera to reveal an emptiness that lies beneath the culture, a kind of continuity that is undivided by time and language, the film offers to grant us access to a new, as yet undiscovered country, a new America free of paternal prohibition, free of the disfiguring marks of cultural difference.

It is easy to see, however, why David's film might be regarded as a failure. While the novel intimates a new America that might spring from his filmic imagination, it is clearly the case that the film remains somehow in abeyance, even as the American pathologies that the novel diagnoses remain uncured. The film – a product fashioned out of light and sound – becomes, in David's own words, a "film in silence and darkness." "Viewed in the sequence in which it was filmed," he says, "the movie becomes darker and more silent as it progresses" (A 346). Like the work of Delillo's novelist Brand, "a writer of blank pages" (A 347), David's film fails in some sense to materialize, remaining dormant and unscreenable. But I would argue that it is this silence, this darkness, this resistance to readable expression, that lends the film its power, its withheld eloquence. What the film within the novel seeks to express is itself a kind of silence, a kind of darkness – the silence and darkness that David first experiences in New York as the camera reveals its power to annihilate. The film works through its capacity to remove elements to deliver us to those latent connections that hold the culture together but that are not themselves namable in the language of the culture. It works, as in Beckett's dream of a wordless art, to allow the "nothingness" that lies behind language to "seep through." It speaks, in silence, of those connections that obtain between David and his mother, between New York and Saigon, between Europe and America. The film cannot be placed in any of the existing categories; it is neither a Hollywood product nor an avant-garde masterpiece. Rather, it inhabits some wordless place in the seams of the culture, offering, in its withdrawal, in its latency, a new way of understanding the relationship between art and the world.

"Silence endowed with acoustical properties": music and silence in *Great Jones Street*

The extent to which this silence might be thought of as a Beckettian inheritance that reconceives the relationship between high art and media culture is suggested in *Great Jones Street*. This novel, following on from *Americana*, is interested in the possibilities of a silent expression that springs from the noisiest, most rambunctious elements of the culture. The art for which Bucky

Wunderlick searches in *Great Jones Street* is one that is fashioned from "silence endowed with acoustical properties," a silence made of noise (*GJS* 166). As in *Americana*, however, the art that might transmit this silence to us remains somewhat obscured, in the case of the later novel transferred to us only through printed lyrics that, ominously, have been edited by Transparanoia, the Orwellian, Pynchonesque corporate agency handling Wunderlick's affairs. These lyrics, all that is available of Wunderlick's art, read as parodies of late Beckett. Wunderlick's hit "Pee-Pee-Maw-Maw," for example, is composed of short declarative sentences – "Least is best," "Nil nully void" (*GJS* 118) – which might be drawn directly from Beckett's late work and which uncannily predict prose that Beckett was still to compose when DeLillo wrote *Great Jones Street*. (In a 1983 prose piece *Worstward Ho*, Beckett writes, "Less best worse. No. Least best worse. Least never to be naught. Never to naught be brought. Never by naught be nulled.")[11]

Of course, this resurfacing of Beckett's excruciatingly austere work in the dodgy doggerel of an addled rock star is intended, to a degree, for comic effect. Late-Beckett rock music is an inherently unlikely idea, and it is tempting to read Wunderlick as an illustration of what would happen if Beckett were prepared for the entertainment industry, if he were to appear on television chat shows, if his work were to draw crowds of screaming fans. But while "Pee-Pee-Maw-Maw" and the "Mountain Tapes" are comic parodies of a Beckettian art distributed by Transparanoia rather than John Calder, it is nevertheless the case that this novel offers a way of bringing Beckettian silence into 1970s New York, a way of imagining how such an inheritance can help read and shape the faultlines that produce 1970s American culture. Toward the close of the novel, the wordlessness that Wunderlick strives for in his art is made manifest in his body as the terrorist organization Happy Valley Farm Commune administers a lobotomizing drug to him that attacks the speech-forming areas of the brain. While this dramatic end to the novel might, again, seem decidedly anti-Beckettian, a comic sketch of the Unnamable transplanted to an American paperback thriller, this ending does build on *Americana*'s vision of a transfigured America, of a new set of cultural possibilities that are glimpsed through the veil of wordlessness bequeathed to DeLillo by Beckett. As Wunderlick walks across a New York shorn of familiarizing words, he is granted a vision of the city from which all the distinctions that make it readable and knowable have been erased. Rather than a familiar geography, a city already settled, already carved into distinct areas, he sees a land that has not yet been written, a land that harbors a new, undiscovered potential. He sees the hump of Manhattan Island through the harbor fog as a "lone mellow promise of an island" (*GJS* 262), an unwritten novel that the gift of wordlessness has allowed him to read. It is this promise of a lyric yet to be written that the novel leaves us with, an artform still to come that can find a new accommodation between Beckett and the marketplace, between Europe and America, between high art and media culture.

DeLillo's work builds over the decades on this discovery in the early novels of the possibility of a new language won through the rigor of Beckettian silence. DeLillo's novels continue to expand, even in the shorter prose works that he has written after *Underworld*. They continue to reach for a comprehensive vision; they continue to offer us one of the most wide-ranging and inventive fictional analyses of the state of contemporary culture under the conditions produced by globalization, the mass market, and the development of transformative new media technologies. But DeLillo's work is driven, at its heart, by a continued investment in David Bell's silence and darkness, by its location of a still point that cannot be brought into expression but from which his fiction emerges and toward which it is heading. It is this silence that continues to harbor a mode of artistic production that is not namable under any of the existing cultural categories and that is endowed with acoustical properties that we are still able only faintly to hear.

Notes

1. Samuel Beckett, *Disjecta: Miscellaneous Writings and a Dramatic Fragment* (London: John Calder, 1983), pp. 171–2.
2. See Michael Hardt and Antonio Negri, *Multitude: War and Democracy in the Age of Empire* (London: Penguin, 2005).
3. Walt Whitman, "Song of Myself," in *Walt Whitman: The Complete Poems*, ed. Francis Murphy (Harmondsworth: Penguin, 1975), p. 737.
4. Mark Osteen, *American Magic and Dread: Don DeLillo's Dialogue with Culture* (Philadelphia: University of Pennsylvania Press, 2000), p. 25.
5. Douglas Keesey, *Don DeLillo* (New York: Twayne, 1993), p. 32.
6. Anthony DeCurtis, "The Product: Bucky Wunderlick, Rock 'n' Roll, and Don DeLillo's *Great Jones Street*," in Frank Lentricchia, ed., *Introducing Don DeLillo* (Durham: Duke University Press, 1991), p. 140.
7. Osteen, *American Magic and Dread*, p. 30.
8. Ibid., p. 60.
9. Ibid., p. 31.
10. DeCurtis, "The Product," p. 134.
11. Samuel Beckett, *Worstward Ho, Nohow On* (London: John Calder, 1992), p. 118.

4

JOSEPH DEWEY

DeLillo's apocalyptic satires

Small wonder Don DeLillo abandoned advertising. In 1964, five years into a promising career with Ogilvy & Mather, DeLillo quit, not to do anything as grand as write (though he had published two stories) but more because he found the premise of advertising, with its cheesy delight in surfaces, empty and incompatible with the larger perspectives that intrigued him. The son of Italian immigrants, DeLillo was raised amid the pageantries of pre-Vatican Two Catholicism and attended a Catholic prep school, where the drama of a material universe destined for purification by imminent apocalypse was as real as math or biology. Among the Jesuits at Fordham, DeLillo was enthralled by the far-reaching implications of philosophy and theology, encouraged, despite (or perhaps because of) the evident spiritual desiccation of his postwar boom culture, to approach the material universe as the abiding mystery of a created thing and, in turn, the complex circuitry of the human creature as infinitely more intriguing through its possession of something called a soul, which altered the very understanding of understanding itself.

Such conceptions, of course, put DeLillo at odds with his cultural moment. Emerging amid the Beat energy and avant-garde audacities of 1950s New York, DeLillo in his early fictions tested but could not endorse the chic existential angst of the New Wave films he admired. Such emotional thinness flatlined into glib ennui, glamorous self-destruction, and self-serving aliena-tion. Living amid the quiet panic of civil defense drills, the nerveless assem-bling of piles of nuclear weaponry, and the wonderland logic of Mutual Assured Destruction, DeLillo cast a wary eye on his culture's horizontal sense of apocalypse, a shoddy sort of cataclysm defined by a culture unin-terested in lifting its collective vision above the material realm. This hor-izontal sense of apocalypse never approached the implications of the cosmos but was bound rather by the simplest parameters of the world, locked within the cheap press of current events and forecast within the meager reach of a generation, a conflagration called down not by a righteous deity but rather by unprepossessing policy wonks working at the Pentagon. Intrigued by the frenetic trajectories of hard-bop jazz and manifestly versed in visionary literature, both Eastern and Western, DeLillo resisted the sufficiency of the horizontal vision. There is, thus, a gravitas to DeLillo's early work and none of the caustic cynicism, unearned despair, or teary nostalgia typical of apprentice works. DeLillo's sidetrack into advertising and the lengthy gestation of his first novel determined that his early fictions, such as *End Zone* (1972) and *Ratner's Star* (1976), would be the product of a writer full into his maturity, approaching forty. Such fictions thus examine not the conventional dilemmas of apprentice fictions – testing love, challenging parents, leaving home, surviving school – but nothing less than mortality itself. Given DeLillo's defiant affirmation of a cosmos validated beyond the material dimension, a universe that cannot bear to be simply what can be validated by the senses and contained by science, death is not merely a medical data-event or a simple, if catastrophic, loss of individual identity; given the vertical reach of DeLillo's sensibility, death is conceived as nothing less than a cosmic event, a complex revisiting of the apocalyptic temper that since John the Divine, chained to the rocks on Patmos, has compelled the most luminous literary expressions of Christianity.

Indeed, *End Zone* and *Ratner's Star*, despite evident differences – in heft, genre, storyline, even tone – are nearer companion texts. They bring together beginnings and endings – childhood and apocalypse. They are DeLillo's only stories about children (Gary Harkness is just past twenty, Billy Twillig fourteen), coming-of-age narratives in which adolescents edge toward revelation (pun intended). Each man-child is offered a dramatic choice: accept the difficult vulnerability implied by the apocalyptic temper or indulge naïve strategies of retreat that foretell a maturity unavailable to the fullest measure of living (documented by DeLillo's later adults). In each text the layered sublimity of mortality uneases the central character – a college football player, Gary Harkness, is haunted by his part in a ferocious tackle that killed an opposing player; a Nobel Prize-winning math prodigy, Billy Twillig, is chagrined that his adolescent body has begun its awkward concessions to maturity, which he conflates with surrender to death. Both adolescents confront events with apocalyptic implications that offer opportunities to embrace the wider perspective DeLillo values. But both choose passionless simplifications while never reaching beyond their fear of death, never tapping the consolation of apocalyptic literature. Rather, Harkness and Twillig settle for confronting catastrophe and surrendering to a panic that DeLillo, given his renunciation of the hip simplifications of the media age and his grounding in the reaching sensibility of visionary literatures, cannot endorse. DeLillo thus satirizes these faux-apocalyptics engendered by a Cold War culture that so freely appropriated the lurid Big Bang vocabulary of Christian apocalypticism but without accessing its far subtler offer of abiding hope in a dark time.

Thus, in Harkness and Twillig, DeLillo creates postmodern characters whose dilemmas – and anxieties – are decidedly medieval. Like the early fiction of Thomas Pynchon, particularly his own apocalyptic satire *The Crying of Lot 49* (1966), both *End Zone* and *Ratner's Star* are perhaps best approached as novels of idea, each with a central Everyman character who is exposed to but not educated by an assortment of flat characters (what David Cowart terms "verbal grotesques"),[1] near-allegorical figures that advocate positions at odds with DeLillo's visionary sensibility and that hence are decidedly suspect. Thus, we depart these fictions unlayered, present at last to sublimity, moved to the compelling edge of confirming that unnamed and unnamable something that validates the vertical dimension implicit in apocalyptic literature. An awareness of the unnamable is present in almost all DeLillo's main characters, from the network wunderkind David Bell in *Americana* (1971), who heads west searching for what he calls the yin-yang of the American soul to the uptown artist Alex Macklin in *Love-Lies-Bleeding* (2005), who, after multiple failed marriages and a botched suicide, abandons the gridlocked world of his Manhattan studio simply to stand amid the ancient sun-washed cave temples at Ajanta, India.

End Zone: the anxiety of apocalypse

By his own admission, Gary Harkness comes to tiny Logos College in the desolate outback of west Texas to disappear. Harkness is a shattered man-child in flight from the shock and claw of death, a psychologically damaged narrator ironically suspicious of using language to forge intimacy. Harkness shares little about a troubled adolescence that has included stints in four prestigious college football programs, each experience spiraling toward a psychotic episode before Harkness retreated to his family's home in the Adirondacks. Since his last stop, Michigan State, where he was part of a vicious tackle against an Indiana player who subsequently died, Harkness has lost both a taste for sublimity and any interest in grappling with existential dilemmas, feeling instead the heavy press of vulnerability in a world regularly prone to the bewildering thump of mortality. Seeking refuge, Harkness plays football and talks. Both are mesmerizing bob-and-weave strategies designed to avert the collision of engagement. He relishes football and delights in the discipline of interminable scrimmages in the undulating Texas heat. He finds security under the Ahab-like Coach Creed who, entowered above the practice field, methodically designs a gameworld that excludes accident and chance, the facilitators of death. Harkness thrives amid the bare options available in the backfield within the protective custody of Creed's riskless world of virtual violence. And words provide Harkness with a similarly satisfying strategy of evasion.[2] After all, "d-e-a-t-h" is hardly what scares him; that random series of glyphs and spaces actually provides comfort and simplifies the unfathomable mystery of the experience itself. Not surprisingly, Harkness, who methodically learns one new word a day, invokes an array of expressive registers as narrator. Like a master ventriloquist, he channels a stunning variety of language technologies: the miasma of military jargon and the chilling apocalyptic euphemisms of nukespeak; the pornography of motivational clichés; the sculptured eloquence of classroom lectures; the fine-spun gobbledygook of public relations (the university hires a firm to promote its resurrected football program); the cryptics of football playbooks; the harsh street talk of the locker room; and textbook passages from assorted disciplines. Even conversations among the jocks, less characters and more philosophical positions, are witty and epigrammatic, more written than spoken communication.

Even as his narrator nimbly deploys a matrix of other metaphoric systems that also suggest containment (ranging from tarot cards and crash diets to prayer and even marijuana), DeLillo satirizes such tactical retreat in an effort to guide his character to epiphanic insight.[3] In addition to the larger sense of a culture itself anticipating nuclear extermination (the subject of much classroom discussion at Logos), evidence of the scalding strike of mortality surrounds Harkness, each death an opportunity to confront what cannot be contained. The mother of Anatole Bloomberg, Harkness's roommate, is shot dead by an unidentified lunatic; the college president is killed in a freakish airplane crash; a teammate dies in a particularly gruesome car wreck; a troubled assistant coach commits suicide. But in each case, Harkness resists engagement: the news of the college president's plane crash becomes a sentence the players repeat verbatim over and over until the words become stingless and empty; when Harkness lingers about the car accident site, he is attracted erotically to the mangled legs of a dead girl in the front seat; and the assistant coach had been the subject of a game Harkness indulges in to help him fall asleep, taking strangers and filling in their lives with his imagination, a controlled exercise that ignores responsibility to engage the complication of others. Even Bloomberg, a character in full retreat from his spiritual and Jewish cutural identity, musters more engagement than Harkness; reeling from the news about his mother, Bloomberg retreats to the desert surrounding the college and there paints a single stone black as a desperate gesture of control against his oceanic grief.

Harkness himself renders death a game. On late summer evenings along the deserted campus sidewalks, the team plays Bang You're Dead, pointing "loaded" fingers at each other and then play-acting the dead-drop of being "shot." More revealing, however, is Harkness's dark joy over nuclear holocaust scenarios when he audits a ROTC course on the Strategy of War. Like Bang You're Dead, apocalyptic fantasies of vaporized cities tap an adolescent's delight in invented mayhem. By thinking the Unthinkable into the clean logic of a large-scale game (a horrific global nuclear exchange is actually rendered by Harkness as a creepy checklist of events), Harkness denies vulnerability much as he does in the backfield playing the *animé* halfback. Unlike in the biblical Revelation, within Defense Department documents the world harmlessly detonates over and over only to return to form like a halfback jumping up from a savage tackle. Death – even species-wide – is thus robbed of surprise and denied consequence, a coaxing simulation that abides by the reassuring logic of expectation and execution and the tidy Manichean simplification of us *vs.* them that define all games. As DeLillo suspects, such a secular apocalypse, enclosed and ultimately finite, is self-serving artificiality, self-important rhetoric, and, most dangerous of all, self-sustaining doom.

DeLillo, of course, understands why death lacks dimension at Logos College: what is missing is sublimity. It is only parodied. For example, students can take a course in the Untellable, where, unfamiliar with German, they are given Rainer Maria Rilke's *Ninth Elegy* (1931), which so passionately hymns the poet's ability to name the universe into reality. Ironically, however, the students struggle even to make the guttural sounds of the strange words. But it is exactly the Untellable that engages DeLillo. With sublimity removed, apocalypse becomes just another senseless, barbaric act of war. But transcendence is not an option for Harkness. Reeling from the tsunamic effect of an afternoon spent off campus playing out nuclear scenarios with his professor of military strategy, staggering back to campus across the open desert (a traditional locus for epiphany within the apocalyptic tradition), and hungering to engage the uninsulated real, he catches sight of a pile of animal waste. To Harkness, that is the grim alternative that justifies retreat into his virtual gameworld. The real world, for DeLillo's adolescent, is shit. In Harkness's screed he associates shit with death, its forbidding tincture a "whisper of inexistence" (*EZ* 89).

DeLillo is not so sure. The novel's centerpiece, the late-season showdown with rival West Centrex Biotechnical Institute, unsubtly reminds the reader of the cost of retreat. DeLillo skewers the conventional you-are-there immediacy of traditional sports writing: the game is rendered in dense pages of impenetrable playbookese, its drama forfeited as we are sealed within a forbidding fusillade-like language construct. Importantly, within this claustrophobic exercise in retreat, Harkness confronts sublimity, with DeLillo intervening to extend the reach of Harkness's narrative. Battered to the turf by a vicious hit that leaves him nearly senseless (a promising position within apocalyptic literature), Harkness sweeps his eyes hungrily across the stars ("elucidations in time, old clocks sounding their chimes down the bending universe"). Touched by sublimity, he suddenly regrets having studied astronomy, which has robbed the sky of mystery. Then the battered Harkness, Saul-like, claims, "A deep and true joy penetrated my being" (*EZ* 131). In a subsequent play Harkness (again on his knees, leveled by another hit) claims to see an unidentified figure standing above him, looking down at him intently, there on the field, a figure dressed (appropriately for apocalyptic literature) entirely in white. With allegorical suggestiveness, the figure's hand covers his mouth ("he seemed to be trying to speak" [*EZ* 141]). Thus whatever message the specter might bear goes untold. Who/what is it? Immediately Harkness is (tellingly) "buried" by a Centrex player and, as the lopsided defeat winds down, he never returns to the apparition. Mystery is thus left unexamined. In Part Three, the season over, Harkness must adjust to exile from the gameworld. Consider the pick-up game the players conduct during a freakish snowstorm. Amid the falling confusion of snow, Harkness engages football without form – no pads, no huddles, no time/space parameters, no patterned plays – just straight-ahead runs with uncontrollable skidding, jarring collisions, and the blood and pain of real violence.

But Harkness, unavailable to sublimity, is ultimately given a choice that is, finally, no choice. The novel ends on a "blank afternoon" after the Christmas break (*EZ* 230), after, that is, the season for epiphanies. The campus is windless and pale, the dead Texas sun draped in an obscuring haze, suggesting diminished illumination. During the season, Harkness had conducted an indifferent relationship with a campus misfit named Myna Corbett, an aficionado of science fiction, an overweight co-ed given to wearing mismatched outfits to escape the burden of beauty, and thus yet another artless dodger. After the Christmas break, however, Harkness meets a Corbett now twenty pounds lighter and committed to dropping twenty more, determined to stop hiding behind insulating weight and flamboyant costuming. She appears willing to engage the world, if only superficially. But Harkness cannot muster even mild enthusiasm; he rudely departs, stands by a window, stares at his thumb, and focuses for ten minutes on learning a new word – each act a self-enclosing gesture of retreat.

He then visits Taft Robinson, the team's blue-chip African American running back. He finds Robinson, his head shaved, sitting cross-legged on his bed and wearing dark glasses in a dorm room now stripped of furniture, its walls bare, save for a single patch of masking tape. Robinson reveals that he has elected not to return next season and to pass on what

Harkness sees as the guaranteed lucrative celebrity of a professional career in order, Robinson claims, to "think about things" (*EZ* 233). Embunkered, Robinson now sees the gameworld, with its faux-drama and simulated consequences, as spurious and regards his involvement within it as a prolonged self-indulgence: "I bullshit myself" (*EZ* 234). But Harkness cannot muster even the mildest enthusiasm for Robinson's strategic retreat. He yawns distractedly and moves to yet another window (this time to watch pedestrians) while wondering whether rumors of new uniforms are true, hoping that new headgear would prominently display his recently designated captainship.

As with Corbett's resolve, Robinson's unexpected retreat – monkish seclusion and engaged contemplation – tempts the reader's endorsement with its apparent appropriation of spirituality. But in such sudden retreat, with its feel of ascetic spirituality, Robinson has embraced most superficially the vertical vision (he has "read up" on Islam and eagerly awaits kneeling toward Mecca, relishing the show, unaware of its implications); he has restructured his dorm room into an exercise in hermetically sealed control akin to the very gamefield he is forsaking. The world at large is dismissed to irrelevancy. He does have a radio but only listens to it "at certain times of day for certain periods of time" as a ceremony that enhances his appreciation of his room's silence (*EZ* 239). Should we doubt the problematic nature of Robinson's retreat, he speaks of his fascination for reading accounts of Nazi atrocities, particularly against children – "the ovens, the showers, the experiments, the teeth, the lampshades, the soap" (*EZ* 240); and, as Harkness departs, Robinson rants, eyes appropriately shut, about the unacknowledged presence of African blood in Western civilization, from Abraham to Jesus, from Euclid to Bach. Much as he does with Harkness's afternoon war games that simplify the implications of nuclear weaponry and parody the luminous purification implicit in Christian apocalypticism, DeLillo astringently dismisses Robinson's narrow perception.

Corbett and Robinson are teachers in the miseducation of DeLillo's manchild, emphasizing superficial engagement or superficial retreat. Harkness finally acts with chilling immaturity and divaesque melodrama. In the closing four lines of the novel, Harkness tells us that after leaving Robinson's room he impulsively starts on a hunger strike and winds up days later in the infirmary. The fast – his own nuclear option, his private apocalypse – is his clumsy response to the premise of vulnerability. It is a disconcerting assertion of simplification, like Robinson's crash course in Islam, like Corbett's crash diet. That surrender stands as the summary gesture of an adolescent persistently unable to engage sublimity. Harkness resolves the anxiety over nuclear apocalypse by impudently pretending to claim authority over his own death, naïvely designing a playbook scenario that renders death a choice, thus diminishing the awe and dread of its necessary surprise. Like his self-exile to west Texas, his lurid fantasies about nuclear apocalypse, and his fidelity to the structured simplicities of football, Harkness's fast is ultimately a turning away from sublimity.

Ratner's Star: the apocalypse of anxiety

Compared to *End Zone*, with its episodic plot, compact design, and accessible sports metaphors, *Ratner's Star* can appear a forbidding text, with its extravagant plot, rococo design, and obscure metaphors drawn from classic mathematics. A top-flight government think-tank code named Field Experiment Number One, housed in a fifty-story cycloid-shaped facility in central Asia, is staffed by a dozen egghead researchers with goofy names who declaim tediously on equally goofy projects that render delightfully absurd the Enlightenment's pretense to understand the universe. The facility has been enlisted to decode a single transmission of 101 irregular pulses and gaps sent, apparently, from a heretofore unknown distant planet near Ratner's star. Introduced into the urgent project, like Alice into some loopy Wonderland or Gulliver among the mad Laputans (both Menippean satires DeLillo references),[4] is Billy Twillig, a Nobel Prize math whiz from the Bronx. Much as Harkness embraces Coach Creed's fetching gameworld, Billy relishes the rarified think-tank atmosphere. After all, Billy's fame rests on deriving two intricate mathematical figures – the twillig nilpotent and the stellated twilligon – so abstract that the Nobel committee itself did not understand them, and so obscure that, as Billy admits, they bear no relevance to the real world but merely testify to his ingenuity. Indeed, DeLillo imbeds within Part One an intricate recapitulation of the entire history of mathematics as, over the centuries, it offered a seductive alternative to the freewheeling mysteries of the real world.[5]

Billy's adolescent experience with that world, as with Harkness's, is rife with evidence of death. In Part One, amid the tedious esoteric conversations among the cartoonish researchers, we are given telling glimpses into Billy's childhood in a Bronx apartment along Crotona Avenue, an unsettling world of random menace (fierce summer lightning storms, domestic quarrels, sidewalk shootings, bar brawls, territorial playground squabbles, even treacherous school bus rides). Billy recalls particularly the "scream lady," a neighbor who had undergone a hysterectomy, victimized by the blind missplit of a single cell that then steadily, stupidly copied that error, metastasizing into a tumor. Now she spends summer nights wrapped in three bathrobes, given to screaming into an empty apartment, all the while scribbling wildly in black wax on pieces of paper that she would bite on and then jam into her bathrobe pockets. One night when he happens to meet her in the hallway, Billy impulsively snatches one of the bitten messages from her hand and runs up to the apartment roof to read it but finds only lines and lines of random gibberish, a message that clearly promises no decoding. As well as being isolated from his neighborhood, Billy is estranged from his own body. Unlike the elegant constructs of mathematics, the body shabbily deforms over time without laws or timetables. The obvious imperfections of his gangly adolescent body disturb Billy, who was born prematurely and spent his first days, appropriately, within the protective capsule of a hospital incubator. He abhors the hanging pall of bowel movements. He is confused over the prickly itch of sexuality. He broods over death, funerals, and the cellular holocaust of decomposition. When Billy was seven, his father, a third-rail inspector for the subway, gave Billy a tour of the system to get his genius son to respect his old man's blue-collar livelihood. The plan fails. The afternoon buried alive in the narrow tunnels of the pitch-black underworld, brushing against the "[s]creech and claw of the inexpressible" only leaves Billy terrified (RS 22), in tears, until he calms himself (recall Harkness at the window studying words) by contemplating the sensible logic of sequential prime numbers.

To Billy, "[m]athematics made sense" (RS 13). Words, prone to messy nuance, leave Billy uneasy. Thus Billy energetically attacks the challenge of decoding the transmission, exhibiting his sturdy faith in the reliability of the problem/solution structure that since Isaac Newton has been the beckoning shelter of science. Billy persists in his confidence even after meeting Henrik Endor, a celebrated astrophysicist originally summoned to decode the message but unable after weeks to crack it. Shaken by the failure of scientific inquiry, Endor has surrendered: he has dug a twelve-foot hole wherein he lives on rainwater and insect larvae. As with Harkness, Billy is thus offered a choice that is no choice: retreat into the fragile symbolic landscapes of constructed systems or surrender to the whirlwind of shoddy unpredictability that, apparently, is the world. Even when Shazar Ratner, a legendary astronomer now a desiccated centenarian kept alive in a biomembrane, imparts DeLillo's alternative to Billy, that science must concede the universe to mystery, Billy dismisses it as fuzzy-headed, offering only, "I understand you're growing a beard" (RS 230).

At the close of Part One, even as Billy begins to solve the transmission – he determines that the pulses are based on an ancient sexagesimal notation system and probably designate a time – he is reassigned to an underground facility to join a secret project, a dream team of Nobel Prize-winning scientists assembled by Robert Hopper Softly, a dwarf with preternaturally pale skin, a wide mouth, and gray eyes, who regularly ingests handfuls of pharmaceuticals and who escorts Billy to the underground facility through a lush garden, recalling Alice's White Rabbit. Softly's clandestine operation, code-named Logicon, has been set up to devise an interstellar language system based entirely on numerical symbols and radio pulses, hence without the imprecision of words. Part Two takes us into that underground world where, ironically, each of the Nobel laureates handpicked for the Logicon project comes to respect the very indeterminacy that compels the project's desolating need for control. For instance, Jean Venable, hired to write the history of Logicon, suffers from writer's block until she abandons nonfiction for the pliable competing realities of fiction; communication theorist Edna Lown comes to tap the inscrutable nuances of children's prelanguage skills; archeologist Maurice Wo, a spelunker, digs in caves for ancient artifacts only to discover, in a reversal of expectations, that the farther down he digs the more sophisticated the artifacts become; and Billy himself is enthralled while spying on Softly and Venable making love as, amid the torrid pitch, language gives way to hot babblings.

If Part One steers Billy away from the layered ambiguities of the experiential world, Part Two – like the boomerang figure that Billy's mathematical construct resembles – returns him to it. But how will DeLillo's man-child react to such opportunity? There is much promise in Part Two. Isolation gives way to community. The narrative line itself, limited by Billy's omniscience in Part One, opens into a sort of choral consciousness, a cooperative shuttling, at times paragraph to paragraph, among the Logicon scientists, their perspectives unifying into a coherent narrative line. Unlike Part One, where each scientist furiously works on individual crackpot theories, in Part Two the Logicon team actually work together, albeit indirectly, to translate the message from Ratner's star: a message, as it turns out, from Earth itself, trapped within the closed corridors of curved space and now boomeranging home millennia later. As Billy suspects, the message designates a time (28 minutes and 57 seconds after 2p.m.) that will coincide with a spectacular – and wholly unexpected – solar eclipse across central Asia.

In five dramatic pages, DeLillo recounts the slow-motion crescent of that eclipse (*RS* 429–33). Unlike *End Zone*, which borrows apocalyptic vocabulary to satirize nuclear anxiety, here we are ushered into a textual moment that unironically resonates with apocalyptic grandness: as in Revelation, here the heavens themselves betray predictability, reject expectation, and realign perception itself with a gaudy show of astronomical excess, the sheer spectacle of which mocks the cool pretenses of Enlightenment science. And DeLillo positions his man-child in the midst of it. Like Harkness during the Centrex game, Billy confronts apocalyptic sublimity. If the visionary figure in *End Zone* is mute, here we are very much given the message emphatically and sumptuously. DeLillo deploys an invitatory second person to deliver a message decidedly uncoded; he records the eclipse, this intrusion of mystery, in a florescence of words, celebrating the very medium that Billy distrusts. In five magisterial pages, the lyrical line alert with color and sound, heat and depth, DeLillo tracks the furious busyness of the quarter-slice of the planet shadowed by the shuffling penumbra of the eclipse, an exuberant world as alive (children cavort in the exhilarating suddenness of night-in-day; couples romance in spontaneous intimacy; bowed women slog across rice fields) as it is ringed by death (the impoverished struggle for sustenance in the streets; children die casually of cholera; holy men in ashrams and students in the cities struggle with the apocalyptic implications of such cosmic surprise).

It is a tantalizing revelation extended to us but not to Billy. Like the winter haze that drapes the close of *End Zone*, the eclipse for Billy and his egghead cohorts suggests only stunted illumination. The think tank, not surprisingly, freefalls into pandemonium. Softly himself flees the facility and is last seen digging feverishly into the dark security of Endor's hole, passing Endor's corpse aswarm with "vermiculate life" (*RS* 437). Just ahead of the spreading shadow of the eclipse, unavailable to the five-page magical mystery tour we have just taken, rides Billy (identified only as "a boy" [*RS* 438] indicating a stubborn immaturity), now in panicked (and absurd) flight (after all, the eclipse is harmless), awkwardly astride the narrow seat of a tricycle, pedaling away from the think tank but toward nowhere. It is a gesture of surrender as disturbing – and inexplicable – as Harkness's fast. As Billy rings the bike's tinny bell, its alarm is lost amid the harsh noises that Billy himself makes, a laughing sort of maniacal shrieking. Billy, robbed of the pleasure-prison of artificial constructs, opts out, the boy-genius flummoxed by the great eclipse. As in *End Zone*, DeLillo's apocalyptic satire reserves wisdom only for the reader. As we puzzled over the implications of the muted man in white, we now revel in the bold sweep of the unheralded eclipse; consequently, we move to that threshold where satisfaction yields to hunger, clarity concedes to mystery, expectation implodes into surprise, and deep-seated anxieties give way to the daring affirmation – appropriate to the apocalyptic temper – of the indefinable sublimity just beyond the shatter of expectation.

Conclusion

Looking back over DeLillo's fiction since *End Zone* and *Ratner's Star*, readers can position the failed apocalyptics Gary Harkness and Billy Twillig within a telling perspective. As DeLillo has matured, he has abandoned the satiric genre and forsaken cartoonish cautionary characters to address the difficult anxieties that Harkness and Billy so inelegantly dodge. These terrified children will become DeLillo's anxious adults, unavailable to sublimity and desperate for a world as unambiguous as a light switch. There is sixtyish waste management executive Nick Shay in *Underworld* (1997) settling into an expensive clarity that trims mystery and accepts as sufficient the sustained strategic containment that comes with the busyness of a daily routine and the comforts of suburban domesticity; the control freak Scott Martineau in *Mao II* (1991) fussily micromanaging the compound-retreat of recluse-novelist Bill Gray; in *Libra* (1988) the retired CIA agent Nicholas Branch, inhumed amid boxes of government evidence, struggling to disperse the cloaking shadows of Dallas; and in *The Names* (1982) archeologist Owen Brademas lavishly stroking the cuts of ancient letterings, indifferent to their message.

Each of these characters is frustrated rather than awestruck by the sheer breadth of a Christian universe that will not submit to contours, the ending of which defies rather than succumbs to measurement. They are balanced, however, by other adults in DeLillo's fiction who do engage sublimity in gestures of heroic confrontation – James Axton in *The Names* standing amid the joyful noise atop the Acropolis; Jack Gladney in *White Noise* (1985) joining the hushed congregation that nightly gathers at the overpass outside Blacksmith, mesmerized by the implications of sunsets that scatter the sky into bronze; Sister Edgar in *Underworld* glimpsing the image of a murdered child amid the shadows of a South Bronx billboard as it is swept by the headlights of a lone commuter train; in *The Body Artist* (2001) Lauren Hartke, in the wake of the gunshot suicide of her husband, relishing for the first time the tangy salt breeze from her sea cottage window, feeling the complicated, surging pulse of time itself; and the Dostoyevskyan billionaire Eric Packer in *Cosmopolis* (2003), his death by gunshot moments away, gazing into the face of his ruinously expensive watch and seeing his own tagged corpse in a morgue vault. All these are landmark moments when DeLillo's adults, exposed to the forbidding mystery of sublimity, move beyond clear sight to insight. DeLillo addresses a culture certain that death will win, a people demoralized by a century that first created death on a scale that stunned the imagination and then proceeded to render it both omnipotent and meaningless by an insanity of genocides. To such a culture, DeLillo chooses not to resist closure. With a compassion in keeping with the most eloquent apocalyptics, DeLillo encourages his reader to stand without flinching before the magnificent evidence of limitations, the unnerving, awesome beauty of mortality and vulnerability that from the Bronze Age to the nuclear age has been humanity's perplexing yet finally reassuring position within the cosmos.

Notes

1. David Cowart, *Don DeLillo: The Physics of Language* (Athens: University of Georgia Press, 2002), p. 26.
2. In 1982 DeLillo told Thomas LeClair, "It may be the case that with *End Zone* I began to suspect that language was a subject as well as an instrument in my work" ("An Interview with Don DeLillo," in Tom LeClair and Larry McCaffery, eds., *Anything Can Happen: Interviews with Contemporary American Novelists* [Urbana: University of Illinois Press, 1983], p. 81). LeClair himself reviews the language strategies that DeLillo deploys; see his *In the Loop: Don DeLillo and the Systems Novel* (Urbana: University of Illinois Press, 1987), pp. 68–74. Conversely, Neil Berman, who reads the novel primarily as a sports novel, sees language as a joyless ordering system set against the primitive joy of the game itself; see *Playful Fictions and Fictional Players: Game, Sports, and Survival in Contemporary American Fiction* (Port Washington: Kennikat, 1981), pp. 64–5.
3. David Cowart uses the language theorist Ludwig Wittgenstein (whose poster improbably enough hangs in Taft Robinson's dorm room) to explore how DeLillo uses language as a compelling expression of our hunger to know and its inevitable frustration, paralleled by Harkness's killing fast. See *Physics*, pp. 27–8.
4. Mark Osteen describes *Ratner's Star* as DeLillo's most allusive text and provides a helpful analysis of the novel's debt to a range of classic satires, including *Alice in Wonderland* and *Gulliver's Travels*. See *American Magic and Dread: Don DeLillo's Dialogue with American Culture* (Philadelphia: University of Pennsylvania Press, 2000), pp. 61–5.
5. Although many critics have cited DeLillo's use of the history of mathematics as part of his narrative structuring, Tom LeClair (*In the Loop*, pp. 124–7) provides a concise overview of this intricate strategy, including a table that maps the historic allusions, chapter to chapter, from Pythagoras to Poincaré.

5

TIM ENGLES

DeLillo and the political thriller

Despite consistently laudatory reviews, DeLillo's early fiction did not have the popular success that his work since *White Noise* (1985) has achieved. One reason why fewer readers appreciated DeLillo's early work is that it consistently thwarts readers' expectations. It does not do so gratuitously or perversely but rather as a reflection of a profoundly altered cultural landscape, a world for which he considers conventional storytelling frameworks inadequate. As DeLillo once wrote, "For me, well-behaved books with neat plots and worked-out endings seem somewhat quaint in the face of the largely incoherent reality of modern life."[1] Nevertheless, DeLillo often deploys familiar devices and conventions, both literary and cinematic. In two novels published just a year apart, *Players* (1977) and *Running Dog* (1978), he borrows heavily from a longstanding genre of popular literature and movies, the political thriller, only to rearrange and subvert the genre's conventions at every turn.

Popular since the 1950s, the political thriller has become a familiar vehicle for entertainment, thanks in large part to such bestselling novelists as Robert Ludlum, John le Carré, and Tom Clancy and to such audiovisual spectacles as the numerous James Bond films and the *Mission: Impossible* television and film series. The political thriller emerged primarily in response to the post-World War II establishment of such national intelligence organizations as the American CIA and the British MI5. In these narratives primarily white male protagonists battle threats to the national and global order against a backdrop of governmental operatives, elusive saboteurs, and alluring women, who typically function as distractions for the protagonists from their otherwise single-minded efforts. *Players* becomes this sort of story when Lyle Wynant joins a group of subversives who seek to bomb the New York Stock Exchange, and *Running Dog* also does when governmental and countergovernmental operatives join the pursuit for a film reputed to depict Adolf Hitler in a sex romp. The settings and plots of political thrillers can vary widely, but their audience expects a certain predictability. Knowing that the protagonist is likely to emerge victorious after battling odious villains and sparring with beautiful but often dangerous women, the audience can usually relax its intellectual capacities and enjoy a narrative's particular modes of suspense and excitement. DeLillo utilizes many of the thriller's conventions in *Players* and *Running Dog*, but primarily as a means to produce works that ultimately join another genre, the social or sociological novel, by subtly explicating elements within the cultural and political milieu of 1970s America.

Aestheticized violence and scripted lives

DeLillo's fifth novel, *Players*, depicts the muddled adventures of Lyle and Pammy, a married pair of white young urban professionals. Lyle works as a trader on the floor of the Stock Exchange; Pammy is a consultant at the Grief Management Council, a nebulous corporate concern located in the World Trade Center. Although both characters find themselves drawn into unusual situations, DeLillo initially follows the political thriller formula by sending the male character on a dangerous mission and by framing the female's entanglements primarily in sexual terms. On the other hand, he counters standard genre plotlines by piloting the trajectories of the male and female characters away from rather than toward each other. In Lyle's case, the shooting of a man on the Exchange floor who turns out to be carrying a bomb lures him into seeking out the perpetrators and offering to perform such a bombing himself. Pammy and Lyle are casual friends of Ethan Segal and Jack Laws, a homosexual couple, and Pammy's story consists of going to rural Maine with this couple and having an outdoor sexual encounter with Jack.

DeLillo's next novel, *Running Dog*, depicts the efforts of a wide array of interconnected characters to get their hands on a film that supposedly depicts sexual activity in Hitler's bunker during the last days of World War II. Glen Selvy is a Vietnam veteran with mercenary tendencies and robotic combat skills, and Moll Robbins is a reporter for a once-radical magazine called *Running Dog*. Initially drawn to each other, these male and female leads again split off in different directions, with Moll seeking incriminating information about a senator who collects erotic art and Selvy falling into a cat-and-mouse pursuit with two Vietnamese hitmen. Moll eventually voices some of the novel's thematic commentary on the nature of truth, while Selvy succumbs to his assassins.

A primary subversion of the political thriller genre in both novels is DeLillo's replacement of conventional excitement with repeated depictions of what amount to the opposite – detachment and boredom. Both novels do open with potentially thrilling scenarios: the brutal murder of some golfers by a band of weapons-wielding guerillas in *Players* and the stabbing to death of a man wearing a woman's dress in *Running Dog*. However, instead of structuring these narratives around such violence and then building suspense with a series of violent and/or sexual encounters, DeLillo distances both characters and readers from such excitement. The intriguing crossdresser is quickly dispatched by unknown assailants, but the rest of the chapter is taken up with a police officer's ruminations on disguises and his partner's theme-setting report of a dream he had the night before: "I'm there, but I'm not there" (*RD* 9). A similar lack of immediacy, of being in the moment, is underlined in the opening of *Players*. Violence again occurs, but only within an inflight film on an airliner. The passengers (who we later realize include the novel's main characters) find the film's midday slaughter distinctly unengaging, merely commenting ironically on the cinematic mayhem – when they even bother to notice it. This scene is one of many in which DeLillo calls attention to how thoroughly film has saturated our social environment, and to how it insidiously shapes our perceptions, behavior, and responses to reality. Indeed, DeLillo's views on film's importance throughout his career generally echo a comment by visual pop artist Andy Warhol, who figures so largely in DeLillo's later novel *Mao II* (1991): "It's the movies that have really been running things in America ever since they were invented. They show you what to do, how to do it, when to do it, how to feel about it, and how to *look* how you feel about it."[2]

 DeLillo's interest in the power of cinema is more overt in an earlier short story, "The Uniforms" (1970), which also depicts a band of guerillas assaulting a group of golfers. A closer look at this story and its specific cinematic inspiration helps to elucidate DeLillo's apparent aims in reworking thriller motifs. Regarding "The Uniforms," DeLillo has written, "I consider this piece of work a movie as much as anything else. Not my movie, however ... The movie in question is 'Weekend,' made of course by the mock-illustrious Jean-Luc Godard ... Thousands of short stories and novels have been made into movies. I simply tried to reverse the process."[3] As a member of the French New Wave in cinema, Godard also directly subverted cinematic thriller conventions, as well as those established earlier in detective and crime films.[4] These latter films, themselves often based on thriller, detective, and crime novels, had established a series of poses and styles that subsequent actors, directors, and writers, as well as ordinary people, felt compelled to repeat. In addition to Godard's *Week-end* (1967), one of the more renowned cinematic comments on this phenomenon occurs in another Godard film, *Breathless* (1960). In this revisionist thriller a killer on the run named Michel Poiccard (Jean-Paul Belmondo) repeatedly pauses to run his thumb along his upper lip; Godard underscores the cinematic source for this affectation by having Poiccard gaze in admiration at a poster of Humphrey Bogart, the prototype of thriller masculinity. When Poiccard is not eluding the authorities, he cavorts playfully, and stylishly, with Patricia Franchini (Jean Seberg), a young American student living in Paris. These two continually demonstrate their acute self-consciousness by posing and preening for each other and, in front of mirrors and reflecting windows, for themselves.

Like these Godard films, *Players* and *Running Dog* have the ostensible structure of a thriller, but their makers' interests lie elsewhere, especially in the borrowed poses, gestures, language, props, and clothing of the protagonists. Both DeLillo and Godard suggest that many forms of violence had taken on a stylish allure in the Western mind, a ritualized, aesthetic element that often supersedes its painful causes and effects. As the narrator in the *Players* prologue intones, cinema has created a "secret longing . . . in the most docile soul [for] the glamour of revolutionary violence"(*P* 8). It is this "glamour" rather than any revolutionary inclinations of his own that lures Lyle from his relatively humdrum, routine existence. In this sense, what Mark Osteen observes of *Running Dog* is true of *Players* as well: "all the characters . . . exist in a cinematic world that conflates behavior and performance . . . these performances do not produce a consistent sense of self. Instead, like film actors, these subjects create their personae by bits and pieces."[5]

In *Players*, then, DeLillo establishes film as a central thematic concern by transferring events in Godard's movie that he "made into" a short story back into the depiction of a movie in his novel's prologue. Similarly, the elusive bunker film in *Running Dog* turns out to be a depiction of Hitler imitating Charlie Chaplin – who himself had earlier imitated Hitler in *The Great Dictator* (1940). As in *White Noise*, where the teachings and identity of Jack Gladney, Professor of Hitler Studies, focus on the filmed, performative elements of Nazism rather than its fascist content and genocidal effects, DeLillo continually depicts a looping, blurred interplay between people and cinematic performance. Although the airline passengers of the *Players* prologue seem merely bored or vaguely amused by the horrors flashing before them, the novel goes on to suggest how deeply cinema, and media more generally, have shaped their conceptions of reality and of themselves. DeLillo's borrowings from the filmic thriller thus create a kind of metafiction, one that wryly acknowledges its implication in the genre even as it underscores the power of such cinematic conventions in shaping identity, behavior, and social relations.

While DeLillo's early work repeatedly foregrounds film for this purpose, his later novels explore the environment-saturating, interpellating qualities of other media. The members of the Gladney household of *White Noise* continually evince the effects of massive television exposure, while various characters in *Libra* (1988), *Mao II*, and *Underworld* (1997) demonstrate and sometimes ponder the reality-shaping qualities of print and broadcast journalism, photography, the visual arts, and more. In a society filled with such multimedia-generated "white noise," and with advertising's additional inducements to strive toward this or that mode of personhood by buying this or that product, certain roles become implicitly appropriate for various people. Attractive, white, middle-class Americans like Lyle and Pammy are steered toward an appropriate lifestyle, including lucrative corporate careers and the right products, domiciles, and relationships. DeLillo implies that while such people feel they have freedom of choice in life, the narrowness of socially proffered options can effectively reduce them to puppet-like figures, pushed and pulled to and fro by various vaguely discernible forces, their existences more like scripted performances than spontaneously experienced lives.

In both novels DeLillo depicts some characters as more sensitive than others to such societal pressures. Lyle, for instance, draws attention to the scripted nature of his own role by interspersing his clipped banter with hints that his own words, and implicitly his actions, are not quite his own; he says at one point, "Do I like cantaloupe, he asked." And at another, "I think that's interesting, said the wide-eyed young man" (*P* 33, 76). This acutely self-conscious speech tic signals Lyle's awareness that since his work and home lives follow standard, preplotted storylines, they have what amounts to a narrator and, by extension, some sort of directive author. Such utterances register as well his awareness that his life follows an expected routine and that he has become bored with this routine, as has Pammy, who repeatedly signals her own ennui in a more traditional way, by yawning. What little credit DeLillo gives to these unheroic protagonists lies in their having at least enough initiative to break out of their plotted lives in an effort to start new ones. In this way DeLillo's early analysis of American conformity prefigures his characters' direct meditations on various meanings of the word "plot" in *Libra* and *White Noise*. In the latter, protagonist Jack Gladney tries to conquer his fear of death by consciously inserting himself into another, more thriller-like plot by attempting to murder a man who has had sex with his wife, only to awaken to the clichéd silliness of this plot when confronted by the reality of his victim's blood. As with both Lyle's and Selvy's attempts to breach the confines of their predictable existences, DeLillo depicts their failure in order to expose that which hinders such floundering efforts of intelligent, educated American white men, a group whose culturally influenced inner resources provide them with little with which to create viable alternative versions of themselves.

The end game of white American masculinity

For DeLillo, then, the routine horror prefigured by the inflight film in *Players* is not so much what it depicts (violent revolutionaries slaughtering well-heeled golfers) as it is the audience's distanced reaction, both to the film's events and to its depiction of the privileged elite. They fail to see in the golfers some resemblance to themselves and thus the chance that they themselves could ever suffer such an onslaught at the hands of the aggrieved. Their yawns, laughter, and inattention thereby suggest how cinematic violence has numbed and detached audiences from an earlier, perhaps more genuine response to both cinematic and actual violence. The paradox that the ritualized modes of violence presented by the media both deaden our reactions to violence and increase our appetite for it has by now become a more familiar anxiety than it was when this novel was published. However, beyond offering this anticipatory insight, DeLillo also suggests that in the American social landscape that these privileged characters will soon rejoin, the gap between an insulated, empowered elite and a far less privileged majority has grown so wide and entrenched that the possibility of people like themselves facing any such revolutionary violence seems minimal at best. In this way DeLillo's opening encapsulation of these characters in a jet cruising high above the American quotidian also prefigures Lyle's subsequent inability to achieve actual contact or intimacy with the homeless people who repeatedly catch his attention.

A rift charged by an underlying resonance of violence and political machinations reverberates throughout *Running Dog* as well. Selvy's training and experience during the American intervention in Vietnam remain indelibly imprinted in his psyche and behavior, rendering him unable to reintegrate into the American social landscape, while his clandestine boss, Earl Mudger, spends much of his time crafting lethal weapons in his basement, unable to relinquish his nostalgia for his own glory days in Asia. While most political thrillers with characters like these portray more war-related bloodshed, DeLillo's withholding of it registers a disconnect between some of the human costs of the Vietnam conflict and the subsequent American disavowal of them. In addition, because he is really writing social novels, DeLillo withholds conventional narrative excitement, scattering his questing characters in centrifugal directions rather than the usual centripetal ones. He thereby suggests the generally decentralized drift of both the political forces that shape and guide postmodern society and the revolutionary efforts of those who attempt collective resistance.

Lyle from *Players* and Selvy from *Running Dog* are two characters who clearly animate DeLillo's depiction of this diffusion on both sides of the struggle between systems of power and those who resist them. When Lyle sets out on his pursuit of those who have attacked the Stock Exchange by seducing a new office worker who reputedly has ties to the terrorists, he does so with an excited (though perhaps self-parodic) sense that he is fulfilling "the secret dream of the white collar": "What an incredible nighttime thrill. The appeal of mazes and intricate techniques. The suggestion of a double life. 'Fantastic, sign me up, I'll do it'" (P 100). Yet, like the white male protagonists in Chuck Palahniuk's *Fight Club* (1996) and Bret Easton Ellis's *American Psycho* (1991), Lyle seems motivated less by a genuine interest in disrupting the system that has turned him into a working, consuming drone than by the rejuvenating allure of an invigorating alternative. In this sense, the quests of such protagonists reflect how the majority status of middle-class white men tends to render them less aware of their own membership of social categories and thus more inclined to heed their culture's steady (though contradictory and illusory) emphasis on individualized pursuits.[6] For this reason, and because of the diffuse quality of revolutionary behavior and belief, Lyle sees little in traditionally radical terms that could motivate his revolt; the alternative existence he does find proves no more fulfilling or spontaneous than the previous one, with plodding plotters who express no clear intentions or motives. Thus, despite his life-threatening involvement with the vaguely perverse siblings J. Kinnear and Marina Vilar, Lyle soon finds himself bored again: "He wanted to go to sleep. He couldn't understand why he wasn't more alert, interested ... It was happening around him somehow. He was slipping right through. A play. It was a little like that" (P 100). As with *White Noise*'s Jack Gladney, who registers his own role in a thriller-like setting while stalking his wife's lover with a pistol, Lyle moves from one scripted existence into another, seemingly more enlivening one, but the shift fails to awaken him because this new "play" also follows a clichéd script. Similarly, Selvy's covert quest for incriminating information on Senator Percival while ostensibly working for him is easily derailed by his other boss's decision to rub him out when Selvy reflexively destroys a planted listening device. Instead of correcting this mistake because he believes in one or the other mission, Selvy – who has also been automatized by being trained into a reflexive, virtually unthinking killing machine – instead leads his assassins into putting himself out of commission at his original training grounds in the Texas outback.

The failures of these adventurous protagonists suggest how easily such efforts to resist the interpellating forces of routinization are led astray not only by the lack of readily available modes of collective resistance with which American white men could identify, but also by the complexity and diffusion of both socio-economic power and its resistance. DeLillo's unsettled male

protagonists are repeatedly lured into pursuit of seemingly effective opportunities for revolt, only to find their enthusiasm blunted by multiplying
connections and counterconnections between shadowy figures on both
sides of an ostensible binary comprised of power versus resistance. As John
McClure notes, DeLillo's "American protagonists, hungry for romance, go
looking for some worthy cause, something to defend, and find again and
again that national institutions are complicit with the evil forces they claim to
oppose. Oppositional sources of identification are equally unsavory: the
terrorist world is a nightmare of fanatics and double agents, the Marxist
dream a dead letter."[7] Realizations of such complexities often deflate in these
newly propellant men any sense of direction and autonomy. Lyle, for
instance, after seeking out and joining those who are trying to bomb the
Stock Exchange, soon begins reporting on this group's actions to the government operatives keeping an eye on them. Selvy is initially introduced as a
representative for a US senator who hopes to buy the bunker-porn film, but
again, we soon learn that Selvy is double-dealing by spying on the senator.
Representatives for both pro- and antigovernment sides continually report
vague or conflicting reasons for their actions, which they carry out with the
same automaticity with which other characters perform their more mundane
routines. As satiric depictions of how forces in postmodern life succeed in
absorbing and neutralizing resistance, neither Lyle nor Selvy proves capable
of staying on track in his quest; in the process of becoming automatized and
individualized, they have already lost any internal motivation. This exagger-
ated state of aimlessness and lassitude prefigures a number of DeLillo's
subsequent protagonists, such as Lee Oswald in *Libra*.

Some critics have taken DeLillo to task for offering no figures who enact,
or even gesture toward, more viable modes of political resistance.[8] However,
just as we do not expect the standard thriller to portray the world in the more
conventional guises of standard literary or cinematic realism, we need not
expect verisimilitude from DeLillo's satiric depictions of our contemporary
setting nor of those who populate it. As Mark Edmundson argues, DeLillo's
characters are "brilliant hyperboles, prophetic warnings of the way culture
might be tending."[9] We can interpret Lyle as an explanation for why some
white American men who desire contact with a nonmediated reality and
who display the intelligence and wherewithal to act in resistance to that
which suppresses their more genuine interactions with it so often fail to
achieve such contact. Men like Lyle have been channeled into social roles
as hardworking, docile, and self-absorbed consumers; even when they drop
out in order to resist, their masculinized search for enlivening "thrills" is
effectively neutered by evasive, yet all-encompassing networks of power.
This emasculation is sardonically underscored near the end of *Players*,

where Lyle preps himself for some vigorous sex with Marina the terrorist, only to be confronted by the sight of her wearing a strap-on dildo. Similarly, Selvy's assassination by Mudger's Vietnamese hitmen registers more broadly the failure in that country of America's militarized "masculine thrust toward Asia."[10] Laid low by the raced and gendered impulses that have shaped their modes of resistance, Lyle and Selvy both echo and undercut earlier performances of American virility, performances in fictional narratives and in real life that were partially shaped by the ever popular political thriller.

The enlivening quest for truth

Generally, authenticity is something all four main characters in *Players* and *Running Dog* seek, a pursuit continually frustrated by the labyrinthine representations of reality overlapping one another in a media-driven culture, which itself is driven by incestuous relations between corporate and government interests and those that oppose them. The quests of Lyle and Selvy end in absurdity, offering little hope for more genuine, engaged ways to live. However, DeLillo's female characters sometimes travel further toward freedom and understanding, perhaps because DeLillo sees women as more socially conditioned to develop their sensitivity toward others.[11] In *Mao II*, for instance, a female portrait photographer expresses many of the novel's themes by sympathetically registering in her work a contemporary shift in cultural authority from novelists to terrorists; in *The Body Artist* (2001) Lauren Hartke works through her grief over the loss of her husband during her climactic performance by morphing empathetically into the guises of other people. In *Players* Pammy seeks enlivement relationally, via her sexual liaison with Jack. However, this betrayal of both Lyle and Jack's partner, Ethan, seems to bring on Jack's suicide, an act that reveals Pammy's oblivion to Jack's internal state and thus the ultimate selfishness of her seduction. On her return to Manhattan by the novel's end, she would seem to have achieved a higher degree of awareness than Lyle does of the vivid, pulsing reality around her in the city's "fibrous beauty" (*P* 207). Yet this positive depiction of her revitalized sensitivity is severely undercut by her earlier inability to react spontaneously to Jack's suicide, let alone admit responsibility for her part in it. A delayed reaction to another's sudden death is of course common, but DeLillo again drives home his point about contemporary dependence on the media to tell us how to live when Pammy, whose work at the Grief Management Council has apparently trained her all too well, can only shed tears while isolated in her apartment and watching a maudlin family drama on television. Like the dildo that confronts Lyle, television supplants genuine intimacy with representations of it. As Pammy goes on to perform a renewed appreciation for the color and life of Manhattan, she pauses beneath a flophouse marquee that reads, "TRANSIENTS," and then realizes that for a moment or two, the word makes no sense to her (*P* 207). An unwitting transient herself, in both her grieving process and her terroristic foray into Jack and Ethan's private life, Pammy is all too ready, all too soon, to move on to the next adventure.

Of the four central characters in these two revisionist thrillers, only Moll Robbins manages to get anywhere in the quest for something more genuine. As a reporter for *Running Dog*, Moll performs at times in the standard thriller role for women, as a sexually charged object (particularly in her interactions with Selvy and Senator Percival). However, like Oedipa Maas in Thomas Pynchon's earlier satiric take on the detective novel, *The Crying of Lot 49* (1966), Moll exceeds the bounds of such a role to become the most successful seeker, despite being "suspicious of quests," when she finally views the bunker film (*RD* 224).[12] Having refused Mudger's lustful advances, Moll in effect sheds the sexualized connotations of her name by refusing to become a "gun moll" for a criminally inclined male counterpart. As Moll prepares to watch the bunker film with the erotica merchant Lightborne, her reported thoughts articulate the novel's central paired thematic truths – that the truth can rarely, if ever, be found and that nevertheless, "The search itself is the reward" (*RD* 224). In this regard, the contrast between Moll's and Lightborne's estimations of the value of the film is significant. Lightborne considers the film a "disaster" because it shows Hitler's imitation of Chaplin rather than the rumored Nazi orgy; hence it has no value in the high-end pornography market. Moll, however, sees in the film "considerable value" because it offers the shock of "Hitler humanized" (*RD* 237). Despite the irretrievability of some "real" Hitler, the horrors he represents are briefly brushed aside by the bunker film's image of him seeking to comfort some doomed children with a comic performance. In this way the hunt for cash, such a common quest in political thrillers, is subordinated to a more intellectual search for meaning behind the veils of representation.

It is this search – for some tangible grasp on reality beneath the many beguiling representations of it, and thus for a more genuine existence in relation to it – that animates most of DeLillo's protagonists, from David Bell in *Americana* through to Eric Packer in *Cosmopolis* (2003). In *Players* and *Running Dog*, the only truth any characters seem able to find is some sense of why we have so much difficulty finding the truth. For Moll, and, one suspects, for DeLillo as well, this oddly mystifying truth is accompanied by the conflicting realization that the search itself is nevertheless a worthy effort as long as one maintains the faith that, as the catchphrase for the popular 1990s television thriller, *The X-Files*, puts it at the beginning of each episode, "The truth is out there."

Notes

1. Don DeLillo, letter dated October 23, 1995, to members of an email discussion group, reprinted at *Don DeLillo's America*, http://perival.com/delillo/ddwriting. html, accessed May 25, 2006.

2. Andy Warhol, *America* (New York: Harper & Row, 1985), p. 11.

3. Don DeLillo, untitled author's note in Jack Hicks, ed., *Cutting Edges: Young American Fiction for the '70s* (New York: Holt, Rinehart, and Winston, 1973), pp. 532–3.

4. See Don DeLillo, "The Uniforms," *Carolina Quarterly* 22.1 (Winter 1970), pp. 4–11. Rpt. in Hicks, ed., *Cutting Edges*, pp. 451–9.

5. Mark Osteen, *American Magic and Dread: Don DeLillo's Dialogue with Culture* (Philadelphia: University of Pennsylvania Press, 2000), p. 108.

6. See Ross Chambers, "The Unexamined," in Mike Hill, ed., *Whiteness: A Critical Reader* (New York: New York University Press, 1997), p. 192.

7. John McClure, *Late Imperial Romance* (London: Verso, 1994), p. 122.

8. For pointed criticism of the political stance expressed in DeLillo's novels, see McClure, *Late Imperial Romance*, and Vlatka Velcic, "Reshaping Ideologies: Leftists as Terrorists/Terrorists as Leftists in DeLillo's Novels," *Studies in the Novel* 36.3 (Fall 2004), pp. 405–18.

9. Mark Edmundson, "Not Flat, Not Round, Not There: Don DeLillo's Novel Characters," *Yale Review* 83.2 (April 1995), p. 123.

10. The "masculine thrust toward Asia" is historian Ronald Takaki's term for earlier American extensions of "Manifest Destiny" beyond the continental shore and toward Asia, including enforced interaction with Japan, importation of Chinese workers who were barred from citizenship, and the conquest of the Philippines. See Ronad Takaki, *Iron Cages: Race and Culture in 19th-Century America* (New York: Oxford University Press, 1990), p. 253.

11. See Erin A. Smith's summary of feminist psychoanalyst Nancy Chodorow's insights on gendered conditioning in "'Both a Woman and a Complete Professional': Women Readers and Women's Hard-Boiled Detective Fiction," in Patrocinio P. Schweickart and Elizabeth A. Flynn, eds., *Reading Sites: Social Difference and Reader Response* (New York: Modern Language Association of America Press, 2004), p. 211.

12. For a discussion of Moll Robbins as "a parodic recapitulation of [Pynchon's] Oedipa Maas," see Patrick O'Donnell, "Engendering Paranoia in Contemporary Narrative," *boundary* 2 19 (1992), p. 193.

PART III

Major novels

6

STACEY OLSTER

White Noise

President Bush: I was hoping the Prime Minister would want to come to Graceland ... This visit here shows that not only am I personally fond of the Prime Minister, but the ties between our peoples are very strong, as well.
Prime Minister Koizumi: There's Elvis song: To Dream Impossible. (Singing Elvis song.) (Laughter.) My dream came true ... Thank you very much for treating me nice, the Elvis song. (Singing Elvis song.) Thank you.[1]

The (postmodern) way we live now

The pilgrimage to Graceland that capped Junichio Koizumi's 2006 visit to the United States testified to more than just a mutual appreciation of rockabilly's favorite son, the outfitting of Air Force One with Elvis DVDs, an all-Elvis public address system, and grilled peanut butter and banana sandwiches notwithstanding. According to the *New York Times*, in fact, the trip to Graceland was "partly a reward" to the Japanese prime minister for supporting the US president on Iraq and, more recently, for reopening Japan's markets to US beef after a ban related to concerns over mad cow disease.[2] More than just a result of George Bush's desire to "treat" Koizumi "nice," then, the pilgrimage to Graceland proved that those ties between the USA and Japan that Bush found "very strong" were as much political and economic as they were (pop) cultural. This inextricable link between politics, the economy, and culture attests to the way we live now, to borrow the title of an Anthony Trollope novel. Just how that "we" has come to be constituted and whether there remain any grounds for recovering an "I" of individual subjectivity in such a climate are issues at the heart of Don DeLillo's *White Noise* (1985). They inform not only the acts of DeLillo's protagonist, a college professor forced to realize that he is just every man in any city, but also the task faced by DeLillo himself, namely, finding a critical position from which to delineate a cultural phenomenon without being wholly absorbed by it.

Unlike Trollope's 1875 work, which was inspired by "the commercial profligacy" of the late nineteenth century,[3] DeLillo's 1985 work was inspired by the profligate consumption of the late twentieth century – a time in which the sun's "corolla" is appropriated to denote a Japanese car; "[s]upranational" product names are computer-generated so as to be "universally pronounceable" (WN 233, 155); and Elvis Presley and Adolf Hitler, icons free of their historical contexts, are impressed into academic service in exchange for high tuition payments. These, of course, are some of the very features that Fredric Jameson cites in his characterization of the postmodern age, an era he defines not only with respect to specific traits – a new kind of depthlessness, a weakening of historicity, the commodification of objects and humans alike – but also as the result of two particular historical conditions: the emergence of a globalized economy in which power has shifted from nation-states to huge conglomerates, and the penetration of capital into those enclaves – notably nature and the unconscious – that formerly had resisted economic colonization. "[G]lobal, yet American," as Jameson states, postmodern culture originates as "the internal and superstructural expression of a whole new wave of American military and economic domination throughout the world" but eventuates as a universal "dominant" so that even aesthetic production – of any kind and any place – has now become a form of commodity production.[4]

Central to the maintenance of that universal dominant is the role played by new technology, particularly new electronic media. According to Jameson, in a decentered world of multinational capitalism, which strains the human capacity of people to locate themselves, it is technology that "seems to offer some privileged representational shorthand for grasping a network of power and control even more difficult for our minds and imaginations to grasp."[5] Indeed, as Guy Debord asserts, it is technology, by way of the mass media, that seems to "cause a world that is no longer directly perceptible to be *seen*," and technology, by way of the media spectacle, that seems to restore a sense of social consolidation to similarly plugged-in viewers.[6] The operative word being "seems." For the very vehicle that enables us to apprehend the world through visual images ends up replacing the history of that world with a set of consumable images, representations divorced from their referents and subject to the political whims of their manufacturer. As Debord thus recognizes, "The society that brings the spectacle into being does not dominate ... solely through the exercise of economic hegemony. It also dominates ... in its capacity *as the society of the spectacle*."[7] Or, as DeLillo bluntly puts it in *Underworld* (1997), "Whoever controls your eyeballs runs the world" (U 530).

Jean Baudrillard, the French sociologist most connected with the triumph of the simulacrum, the copy without an original, to which this loss of the real leads, has described the consequences of such an erasure: "When the real is no longer what it was, nostalgia assumes its full meaning."[8] And Jack Gladney, the narrator of *White Noise* and a character whose vocabulary is punctuated by references to God and the human soul, is a compendium of nostalgic longings. Yearning for "pre-cancerous times" (*WN* 275), he chooses to live in Blacksmith, a town "not smack in the path of history and its contaminations" (*WN* 85), and waxes eloquent over illnesses – croup, grippe, whooping cough – to which a medical facility named Autumn Harvest Farms should rightfully be devoted. Looking for "moral rigor" in an age of moral relativism, he drives to a village "Old Burying Ground," where headstones adorned with "great strong simple names" testify to individual worth in an age of mass destruction (*WN* 97). Searching for lost origins in an era filled with imitations ad infinitum, he variously invokes pueblo civilizations, Norse legends, Roman ruins, and protean gods as evidence of the "epic" qualities that still reside in the events that surround him (*WN* 127, 257, 317).

Not surprisingly, the foundational myth to which Jack most frequently returns in an age of multinational capitalism is that of American nationhood. Hence the event that opens his narration, the annual return of students to the college at which he teaches, is transformed by him into an ode to Manifest Destiny, with station wagons evoking covered wagons on their journey through the west campus, and saddles, sleeping bags, and bows and arrows taking pride of place among the students' belongings. This ode to nineteenth-century expansion, in turn, evokes an earlier seventeenth-century expansion, since the "College-on-the-Hill" in which students are joined by "the language of economic class" (*WN* 41) is deliberately framed by DeLillo to recall the theocratic "Citty vpon a Hill" in which spiritual election was a function of its Puritan settlers' visible economic prosperity.[9] As such, the spectacle that Jack witnesses each September provides what all rituals that recall a common descent grant: a sense of "communal recognition" (*WN* 3), reassuring participants that "they are a collection of the like-minded and the spiritually akin, a people, a nation" (*WN* 4).

A later spectacle to which people also respond with "a sense of awe that bordered on the religious" (*WN* 127) occurs in the aftermath of a chemical spill in Blacksmith that the media terms "[t]he airborne toxic event" (*WN* 117) and provides the most glaring repudiation of Jack's Americanist longings. Jack compares the panicked flight of cars to "wagon trains converging on the Santa Fe Trail" (*WN* 159). But the airborne toxic event is just one instance of a repudiation of American myths that has been going on since the book's beginning. When Jack unexpectedly runs into Tweedy Browner, one of his ex-wives, at an airport arrivals area, he notices a "sense of Protestant disrepair" that her WASP uniform of knee socks and penny loafers cannot disguise, further proof of that patriarchal decline already displayed by the male Browners once "the line began to pale, producing a series of aesthetes and incompetents" (*WN* 86). When waiting for their daughter Bee to disembark at a different terminal, he hears of passengers in a near-airplane crash who, no longer cushioned by economic privilege, have come scrambling from their high-priced seats into the tourist section because sitting in first class would mean being the first to strike the ground (*WN* 92). When Jack, then, later claims immunity from the airborne toxic event, stating that "[s]ociety is set up in such a way that it's the poor and the uneducated" who suffer disasters and not the middle class and intellectually gifted (*WN* 114) – a reprise, in effect, of that "Modell of Christian Charity" by which John Winthrop defended class differences as providentially ordained ("some must be rich some poore, some highe and eminent in power and dignitie; others meane and in subieccion")[10] – he misses the point of all his earlier encounters. He presumes that "[t]hese things don't happen in places like Blacksmith" but only in places with "mobile homes out in the scrubby parts of the county" (*WN* 114, 117) even though the airborne toxic event exposes how porous all borders – territorial, national, and, as Jack's exposure to Nyodene D. will force him to recognize, epithelial – now are in the postmodern world that he inhabits.

Crowd control

Shorn of all sense of national community, the characters in *White Noise* can only locate themselves collectively within the crowd and by way of those places that facilitate congregation: the evacuation center provides a "common identity" (*WN* 129), a tourist attraction promotes "collective perception" (*WN* 12), the supermarket offers "spiritual consensus" (*WN* 18). Most of these places, significantly, are not portrayed as being peculiarly American in any way – quite the contrary. Stocked with exotic products from twenty countries and staffed by people speaking languages that Jack cannot "identify much less understand" (*WN* 40), the supermarket resembles a "Persian bazaar or boom town on the Tigris" more than a lowly A & P (*WN* 169). This is as it should be since the human need to which crowds minister is portrayed as being both transglobal and transhistorical in nature, as DeLillo suggests when Jack, disregarding the acts of mass extermination by which Nazi Germany is usually distinguished, reveals the defining quality of the mass assemblies on which he places "special emphasis" when teaching his Hitler studies students (*WN* 25):

> *Death.* Many of those crowds were assembled in the name of death. They were there to attend tributes to the dead. Processions, songs, speeches, dialogues

with the dead, recitations of the names of the dead ... Crowds came to form a
shield against their own dying. To become a crowd is to keep out death. To
break off from the crowd is to risk death as an individual, to face dying alone.
Crowds came for this reason above all others. They were there to be a crowd.
(*WN* 73)

What distinguishes the crowds in the postmodern world of *White Noise*,
however, is the fact that the sense of union they instill no longer depends
on physical proximity. The Friday night gatherings with Chinese take-out
that join Jack and his wife Babette's children from various marriages into a
blended whole also join the resultant Gladney "family" to families all over
the country by way of the television shows they watch while eating. The
ATM transactions that Jack uses to check his personal holdings link him to
people all over the world by way of a "mainframe sitting in a locked room in
some distant city" (*WN* 46). And linked by technology in this manner,
interacting with what DeLillo terms the "system," it is no wonder that Jack
feels that his life is "blessed" by the automated teller machine. So much has
it "authenticated and confirmed" his "balance" – both financial and emotional – that he can note in passing a "deranged person" who is "escorted
from the bank by two armed guards" with nary a pause, having already
placed his faith in a deitific system whose very invisibility – which is to say, its
*un*locatable site – has "made it all the more impressive" (*WN* 46).

And all the more dangerous. For the ATM system is just one of many
systems in the novel through which people commune by way of screens –
movie, television, computer – that collectively produce a "new and original
historical situation," according to Jameson, in which "we are condemned to
seek History by way of our own pop images and simulacra of that history,
which itself remains forever out of reach."[11] The "movie-mad, trivia-crazed"
instructors who make up the College-on-the-Hill American environments
department, men for whom "the natural language of the culture" (*WN* 9) has
replaced Jack's early Americanist "language of economic class," revel in this
situation. When these men quiz each other about the historical event that has
most defined their generation, they do not invoke the death of a president
but the death of a movie star: "Where were you when James Dean died?"
(*WN* 68). The difference between the two is less marked than one might
think when the president whose death gives shape to their question, John
F. Kennedy, was so photogenic as to resemble a "great box-office actor," as
Norman Mailer recognized as early as 1960.[12] Likewise, when these men
gauge the past against which their rites of passage into adulthood (such as the
brushing of teeth with fingers!) have taken place, they opt for "seminal
events" like Woodstock, Altamont, and Monterey (*WN* 67) – not just rock
concerts but rock concerts made into movies. Yet with each screen

transposition (from actuality to movie to television broadcast) and repetition further distancing viewers from reality, reality becomes defined to the degree that it exists within the contours of a photographic frame. Catastrophes in India typically go unrecorded, so they might as well not have happened (WN 66). The near-airplane crash occurs over a city that has no media, so its passengers suffer their terrors "for nothing" (WN 92). And with each screen transposition further aestheticizing reality, reality becomes increasingly drained of meaning to the same degree. Jack, who is petrified of dying, can base his entire professional career on the creation of a Hitler studies program because the genocidal figure around whom he has "evolved an entire system" (WN 12) is one whose "solid" and "dependable" nature stems from the fact that, as the subject of countless media adaptations, "[w]e couldn't have television without him" (WN 89, 63). He can teach a course in Advanced Nazism because the class meets in a campus cinema and the footage he shows in it – "propaganda films, scenes shot at party congresses, outtakes from mystical epics featuring parades of gymnasts and mountaineers" (WN 25), an homage, in effect, to Leni Riefenstahl – has been edited down by him to form an eighty-minute documentary, what one might call "Hitler Lite."

The importance of this last detail cannot be underestimated in any reading of DeLillo's text for, as Susan Sontag has pointed out, the staging of the 1934 National Socialist Party Congress that is the subject of Riefenstahl's most famous work, *Triumph of the Will*, was partly determined with the making of a documentary film in mind. More than a mere transposition of history into images, then, the "radical transformation of reality" to which Riefenstahl's film, in Sontag's view, attests is one in which "the document (the image) not only is the record of reality but is one reason for which the reality has been constructed, and must eventually supersede it."[13] In DeLillo's book, of course, these coming attractions have already arrived: SIMUVAC mounts practice evacuations by using real evacuations as models (WN 139) and Jack Gladney creates the persona of J. A. K. Gladney, thus becoming "the false character that follows the name around" (WN 17). Lost in a funhouse of mirroring and seemingly infinite copies, in which it becomes impossible to distinguish between a true and false déjà vu, Jack can legitimately follow the question of "[w]hich was worse, the real condition or the self-created one" with a second query: "and did it matter?" (WN 126).

Yes, it does, DeLillo might answer, given the political ramifications to which such confusion leads. Nowhere are those consequences better suggested than in the scene in which Jack and a visiting colleague journey to "THE MOST PHOTOGRAPHED BARN IN AMERICA." Jack the nostalgist is noticeably silent throughout the scene, as befits someone who looks at fifty-year-old photographs and finds proof that his churchgoing forebears were "skeptical of something in the nature of the box camera" (*WN* 30). Fellow academic Murray Jay Siskind, however, knows better. Watching other people taking pictures of the barn, he correctly concludes that "[n]o one sees the barn," because "[o]nce you've seen the signs about the barn, it becomes impossible to see the barn" (*WN* 12). And not just the five signs that Jack and Murray count on their way to the tourist attraction or the myriad postcards available to visitors at a booth located on the site. For the cowpaths, rolling fields, and white fences that precede the men's arrival at the site – the "signs" that *we*, in the most literal sense of the word, "read" – also offer us the promise of a preindustrial and, therefore, authentic past. That DeLillo refuses to describe the barn itself and thus denies that myth of origins is moot. The "we" who, as Murray states, "can't get outside the aura" (*WN* 13), and, in the case of the tourists, even "reinforce the aura" by way of their own photographic equipment, extends to all of us who, in "agree[ing] to be part of a collective perception," acquiesce to "a kind of spiritual surrender" (WN *12*).

Except that we don't, at least no more consciously than the characters in *White Noise* consciously agree to the manner in which they delineate disaster. Unlike the victims of the first mushroom cloud, whose use of the word *"pikadan"* or "flash-boom" showed a lack of words to describe the bomb that was dropped on them at Hiroshima, the people in *White Noise* have an image arsenal at hand that they use to depict the "roiling bloated slug-shaped mass" lit by spotlights and flanked by helicopters that is the toxic cloud threatening them (*WN* 157) – the imagery of Japanese monster movies, themselves responses to the fears generated by nuclear radiation. Likewise, the passengers in the near-airplane crash have a set of film clips – from *Airport* to *Airplane!* – contained within their brains that they can use to describe themselves plummeting to earth as part of "a silver gleaming death machine" (*WN* 90), and they can envision their corpses "in some smoking field, strewn about in the grisly attitudes of death" because the experience has already been preprocessed for them as "[f]our miles of prime-time terror" (*WN* 90, 92). Such cannibalization of the mind by the media can be seen as an inevitable consequence of the process of mechanical reproduction that Walter Benjamin outlined seventy years ago. For the technological processes that liberated art from its basis in ritual and caused a withering of what he termed its religious "aura" ended in an increased exhibition of mass-produced art and the reconstitution of art's cult values by consumers who "absorb" art while in a state of "distraction." It was this form of reception that enabled mass-produced art to serve as a kind of "covert control," which, in Benjamin's formulation, would eventually lead to fascism.[14]

Living in a world of "shifting facts and attitudes" that one day "just started appearing" (*WN* 171) – a point confirmed by the hilarious data debates in which the Gladneys engage ("What is it that camels store in their humps?"; "What are the three kinds of rock?"; "How cold is space?" [*WN* 81, 176, 233]) – the characters in *White Noise* are quite willing to place themselves under the control of others. As Babette recognizes, "people need to be reassured by someone in a position of authority that a certain way to do something is the right way or the wrong way" (*WN* 171–2). It is a belief in the reassurance that rules provide, in fact, that underlies the pedagogical approach of all those in the book who instruct others, not only to affirm the importance of their subjects but ultimately to establish their own presence. Babette teaches posture to old people who think they can avoid death "by following rules of good grooming" (*WN* 27). Murray secures Elvis's "place in legend" by reminding students of the terms of the rock star "contract" that the self-destructive King (of Excess) "fulfilled" to the letter (*WN* 72). Jack, made "untouchable" by the "aura" that his own teaching generates, exits classrooms like Moses, as the crowds who gather around him part like the Red Sea (*WN* 74). *Heil Gladney!*

Screens, systems, and souls

Yet the producer of the kind of "distraction" that Benjamin found necessary for fascism to thrive and the main source of authority in DeLillo's text is not a person, but a thing: television. Always on and hence omnipresent, television provides the one "custom" and "rule" that the Gladneys ritually observe on Friday evenings when they band together in front of the set, worshipfully "silent," "totally absorbed," and "attentive to our duty" (*WN* 64). And not only the Gladneys, since television – in contrast to those tabloids that DeLillo portrays as devotional tracts – does not demand literacy as a prerequisite for congregation. As Jack's German teacher, Howard Dunlop, whom a television weather report saves from despair after his mother's death, observes, "Everyone notices the weather" (*WN* 55). All-knowing, television dispenses data – concerning everything from an artificial flipper attached by Florida surgeons (*WN* 29) to a stomach consistent with a creature's leafy diet (*WN* 95) to a quick and attractive lemon garnish for seafood (*WN* 178) to a world war fought over salt (*WN* 226) – that the Gladneys do not dispute, the inane nature of the soundbytes notwithstanding. Anthropomorphized by Jack in the early sections of the book in which he, like any good disciple, just reiterates what the "TV said,"[15] television is steadily disembodied by Jack over the course of the book to the degree that Nyodene D. exposure increases his fears of death. Its transformation into an invisible "voice at the end of the bed" (*WN* 178) and "voice next door" (*WN* 239) reaches its deitific apotheosis when Jack refers to it as simply "[t]he voice upstairs" (*WN* 226, 257).

The commandments issued by this postmodern god are easy to follow, having been reduced to one: "Consume or die," as DeLillo writes in *Underworld* (*U* 287). It is consuming, as Mark Osteen points out, that "attaches persons to the things whose reproducibility betokens immortality."[16] Hence television, conceived in DeLillo's first novel, *Americana* (1971), as an "electronic form of packaging" in which commercials are interrupted by programs (*A* 270), is ascribed in *White Noise* the same "sealed off" and "timeless" qualities as the supermarket (*WN* 38, 51, 104). Hence the triadic listings of products – "Dacron, Orlon, Lycra Spandex" (*WN* 52), "Krylon, Rust-Oleum, Red Devil" (*WN* 159), "Clorets, Velamints, Freedent" (*WN* 229) – that Jack verbally fingers like a set of rosary beads. At the same time, *White Noise* also signals the change that an intervening decade and a half has wrought in DeLillo's sensibility. In *Americana*, as its title suggests, the advertising impulse to which television ministers is portrayed as a response to the arrival of the first consumer aboard the *Mayflower* (*A* 271). The opening pages of *Underworld*, set in 1951, affirm the point in attributing to the industry an explicitly Americanist slant: "In a country that's in a hurry to make the future, the names attached to the products are an enduring reassurance," names like Johnson & Johnson, Bristol-Myers, and Quaker State serving as "the venerated emblems of the burgeoning economy, easier to identify than the names of battlefields or dead presidents" (*U* 39). In the period of *White Noise*, by contrast, it is no longer the indigenous "*Coke is it, Coke is it, Coke is it*" that serves, in DeLillo's yoking of religion and retail, as the "sacred formula" that television dispenses, as Murray claims (*WN* 51), but "*Toyota Celica*," a "language not quite of this world" (certainly not the American world) that forms the "ecstatic chant" uttered by Jack's daughter Steffie while sleeping in the evacuation center (*WN* 154–5). And Dylar, the product that lends its name to the largest part of DeLillo's book and the drug alleged, in television argot, to "speed relief" to the fear-of-death part of the human brain (*WN* 200), is developed by a research group that is funded by a "multinational giant" (*WN* 299).

That being said, the violence that can erupt "as a kind of sardonic response to the promise of consumer fulfillment,"[17] what DeLillo terms "funny violence" (*A* 364), is typically portrayed by DeLillo as a phenomenon specific to America. Television frustrates the poverty-stricken Lee Oswald in *Libra* (1988) because the life of consumer fulfillment it promises is repudiated by the life in small rooms that he and his mother have been forced to live, and the upshot (pun intended) is the purchase of two mail-order firearms. It is thus to Jack's credit in *White Noise* that he is well aware that the "sense of well-being, the security and contentment" that stuffed supermarket bags afford his securely middle-class family is "a fullness of being that is not known to people who need less, expect less" (*WN* 20). What he does not realize is that the "fullness of being" – in the most literal sense of the term – that comes from consumption offers no real protection to anyone. Dimitrios Cotsakis, Murray's rival in the internecine Elvis wars and an "enormous man" of 300 pounds, is "lost without a trace" off Malibu (*WN* 169). Orest Mercator, a "big" boy training to break the world record for sitting in a cage full of poisonous snakes (*WN* 181), is bitten within the first four minutes. Jack, a male of "substantial height, big hands, big feet" (*WN* 17), becomes a victim of toxic waste after only two and a half minutes of exposure; when he frantically searches the trash compactor for Dylar, the one consumer item he thinks might help him – if only psychologically – all he finds are banana skins, tampons, ear swabs, and flip-top rings, evidence of "the dark underside of consumer consciousness" (*WN* 259).

This discovery, however, is not nearly as unsettling as what Jack is forced to contemplate in the three scenes in which he goes to get himself medically checked after that toxic exposure, scenes that reveal to him the fraudulent nature of all those collective systems in which he has tried to subsume his individual fears. Still equating information with power, he first goes to a SIMUVAC technician at the evacuation center, whom Jack wants "on my side" because "[h]e had access to data" (*WN* 139). But when he later visits his doctor who, in turn, sends him to Autumn Harvest Farms for further consultation, Jack is told by a technician who reminds him "of the boys at the supermarket" that "[k]nowledge changes every day" and the data are "conflicting" (*WN* 277, 280). Still presuming a single connection to exist between signs and what they signify, he expects that the bracketed numbers and pulsing stars that appear on screen in response to his medical history will have a one-to-one correlation with a specific medical condition. But he later finds out that those signs transmitted by "the whole system" (*WN* 141) can mean a high level of potassium or trace amounts of Nyodene D., a "situation" or a "nebulous mass" (*WN* 138, 280), "nothing" or "a very great deal" (*WN* 260). And still thinking that he can "neutralize events" by turning them into pictures (*WN* 140), much like those climatic disasters occurring elsewhere that he watches on television, he undergoes a battery of tests – braingraphing, scanning, imaging – that turn *him* into a televised picture, only to discover that he has no directorial control over what the screens broadcast. Instead of the "impassive man, someone in line at a hardware store waiting for the girl at the register to ring up his heavy-duty rope" (*WN* 140), a man safe in the act of consumption, who stars in the teleplay that Jack envisions, the computer displays a picture of someone being consumed from the inside, someone whom death has unquestionably "entered" (*WN* 141).

Equally unsettling is the fact that the one drug that might help Jack cope with that condition is described as a "drug delivery system" that interacts with the human brain conceived as a "system of intercommunication" (*WN* 187, 189). Jack, a modernist in postmodernist clothing, responds to this prospect with outrage. Not only does it confirm the brain theories of his son Heinrich, who does not know "what's you as a person and what's some neuron that just happens to fire or just happens to misfire" (*WN* 46), it consigns to the dustbin "a whole tradition of human failings" (*WN* 200) in which man exists *a priori* to society, history, and language that can be traced at least as far back as Aristotle. "We can see more deeply, more accurately," says the Autumn Harvest Farms technician when explaining to Jack the advantages that state-of-the-art equipment affords (*WN* 277). Yet the "more accurate" fact that making Jack's body "transparent" via imaging block may reveal is that there is no "deep" quality in Jack – or anyone else for that matter – to see (*WN* 276). This, of course, is exactly what Jack has briefly considered after seeing Babette, another person of girth, "tall and fairly ample" (*WN* 5), reduced to a two-dimensional, black-and-white facsimile by the cable network that televises her posture class: "If she was not dead, was I?" (*WN* 104). But it is not until his own "death is rendered graphically, is televised so to speak," complete with a *TV Guide* printout of his body, that Jack can fully appreciate the horror that comes from viewing a person as "the sum total of [his or her] data" (*WN* 142, 141). Thinking that his talk with the Autumn Farms technician will constitute the "human part" of his examination (*WN* 276–7), Jack is forced to recognize that there may not be a "human" part of himself available to discuss.

The death to which DeLillo alludes in these scenes, and the kind of extinction with which he is most concerned, is not, then, the death of the body. After all, as Jack's doctor reminds him, when it comes to the death of the body, "you are all permanent patients, like it or not" (*WN* 260). Rather, DeLillo's main concern is with the "second kind of death" to which the burning of the Blacksmith asylum for the insane testifies (*WN* 240). The "synthetic" quality that Jack ascribes to this form of death literally derives from the odor of acrid matter emanating from the building – perhaps polystyrene, perhaps a dozen other manmade substances, all kin to the "gene-piercing" ones perhaps responsible for Heinrich's receding hairline (*WN* 22) and the asbestos and chlorine perhaps to blame for grade school children's headaches (*WN* 35). The "unnatural" element that causes the crowds gathered at the site to feel "betrayed" (*WN* 240), however, stems from the fire's destruction of an institution founded upon a depth-model of human subjectivity – "How deep a thing was madness" (*WN* 239) – that they have all their lives internalized as "natural." The death that, as Jack puts it, "entered your mouth and nose" is thus a death that can "somehow make a difference to your soul" (*WN* 240).

Ironically, the man who confronts Jack with a question about the state of his own soul – "Are you heartsick or soulsick?" (*WN* 305) – is the man in whom DeLillo portrays the utter voiding of modernist subjectivity, as Jack discovers when he enters Willie Mink's motel room near the end of the book and finds before him the postmodern condition in extremis. "[G]lobal, yet American," to recall Jameson's phrasing, Mink is a "composite" of Melanesian, Polynesian, Indonesian, Nepalese, Surinamese, and Dutch-Chinese facial features and has an accent indicative of someone who has learned English from watching American television (*WN* 307, 308). Prostrate before a set "floating in the air" and "pointing down at him" (*WN* 305), his discourse a stream of unrelated soundbytes, he is also the burning bush through which this electronic god now speaks. If, as Emile Benveniste argues, "[i]t is in and through language that man constitutes himself as a *subject*, because language alone establishes the concept of 'ego' in reality, in *its* reality,"[18] Mink's schizophrenia confirms the complete disintegration of the humanist sense of self. It is no wonder, then, that Jack describes the setting of this climactic encounter as a "white room" awash with "[w]hite noise" (*WN* 312, 310), the intensity of which is "the same at all frequencies" (*WN* 312). The state of linguistic entropy to which Mink's meaningless babble attests brings to fruition the notion of death that Jack and Babette have earlier articulated with respect to all the ambient sound that surrounds them, "[u]niform, white," and "insinuate[ing] itself into [the] mind" (*WN* 198–9).

The problem is that Jack, still searching for modernist epiphany and underlying truth, does not recognize his own implication in the scene he describes. On the contrary, he thinks that as he "approache[s] a violence, a smashing intensity," he is "moving closer to things in their actual state" and seeing "things new" (*WN* 305, 308). What Jack does not see is how much Mink is his own doppelgänger. Mink responds with "somewhat stylized" gestures to the fusillade of words with which Jack assaults him ("Falling plane," "Plunging aircraft") because, in the context of the immediate scene, he has been popping Dylar pills like Pez and is in a state of extreme suggestibility (*WN* 310, 309). Yet Jack's gestures – which, as narrator, inhere not only in what he does but in how he relates what he does – bespeak a sensibility that is no less media-colonized. Hardly "beyond words," as he claims (*WN* 312), he has in fact at his disposal only clichéd words – "cult-related frenzy" (*WN* 311), "squalid violence," "shadowy fringes of society" (*WN* 313) – to describe his B-movie plan to kill Mink, the details of which he repeats seven times in instant replay. A "white man" in a "white room" permeated by "white noise" (*WN* 310),

Jack can no longer be divorced from Mink. He has disintegrated to the point where he has become identical to Mink, the two conjoined into a "we" with their mutual shooting (*WN* 314, 315).

Given how much this climactic scene itself replays an earlier literary scene involving amorous rivals – the shooting of Clare Quilty by Humbert Humbert in *Lolita* (1955), which also ends with the commingling of doubles into a unified "we" – it necessarily raises questions about the degree of DeLillo's own complicity in the postmodern phenomenon he delineates. As John N. Duvall asks, "if [DeLillo] insists that the world is wholly mediated, what distinguishes the novel as a medium and the electronic media he criticizes?"[19] To be sure, both partake of perhaps the most culturally pervasive system of all – language – which, when it assumes the form of "state-created terminology" (*WN* 117), is consistently portrayed by DeLillo as obscuring realities that might disrupt the status quo. "Landing" attached to "crash" quiets passengers in a plummeting airplane (*WN* 91). "Black billowing cloud" reassures those in the path of a toxic air mass that "they're" – which is to say, some amorphous authority – "coming to grips with the thing" (*WN* 113). Yet, as Babette astutely realizes, "We have to use words. We can't just grunt" (*WN* 233), a point that is underscored by the portrait of her son Wilder, whose vocabulary, stalled at twenty-five words at the beginning of the book (*WN* 35–6), is found to decrease steadily as the book continues (*WN* 264). If, as the neurochemist Winnie Richards observes, an infant's brain develops in response to stimuli and America still leads the world in stimuli (*WN* 189), the exemption from mortal fear that Wilder displays comes at the expense of intellectual maturation. Being without language, simply put, means being autistic.

Yet DeLillo differentiates between the way that print and visual media employ language. In *Mao II* (1991), a novel that explicitly considers whether it is only the terrorist that has not yet been entirely absorbed by the media (a possibility that, in the post-9/11 era, the video-obsessed Osama bin Laden would seem to have answered in the negative), Brita Nilsson makes a point of looking at the captions that accompany the photographs of famines, fires, and wars that entrance her: "The words helped her locate the pictures. She needed the captions to fill the space" (*M* 174). A poet taken hostage by fundamentalists and left with only visual memories to contemplate comes to a similar conclusion: "The only way to be in the world was to write himself there" (*M* 204).

It is by affirming that act of narrative in the book's final pages, locating the "awe" that "transcends previous categories of awe" (*WN* 324) in a sky that is, in his metafictional punning, "under a spell, powerful and storied," that DeLillo "writes himself" into the world of *White Noise* (*WN* 325). Yes, the depiction of nuns practicing simulated faith while living in a town that is said to have no media would seem to confirm postmodernism's infiltration of the world's last remaining enclaves. And, yes, the concluding scene that takes place in the supermarket, where "we" – which is to say, all of us – assemble and await our passage through the terminals, is rife with intimations of an inescapable deadening of our souls (*WN* 326). But Jack refuses to talk to the doctor who wants to see how his death is "progressing" (*WN* 325). More to the point, he refuses to be inserted one more time into "the imaging block" (*WN* 325). It may not be equivalent to the "sneak attacks on the dominant culture" mounted in *Underworld* by those figures in the recovered Sergei Eisenstein film who exist "outside nationality and strict historical context" (*U* 444, 443). Nor may it constitute as thunderous a "NO!" as that invoked by Herman Melville when describing the "sovereignty in [him]self" with which Nathaniel Hawthorne faced the "visible truth," which is to say, "the absolute condition of present things as they strike the eye of the man who fears them not, though they do their worst to him."[20] Still, the fact that Jack does not have the wherewithal should not obscure the fact that he has the will. And it is in granting to Jack even that small amount of volition that we locate DeLillo's own authorial triumph.

Notes

1. Office of the Press Secretary, June 30, 2006.
2. Sheryl Gay Stolberg, "Koizumi Joins Bush in Warning North Korea Not to Fire Missile," *New York Times* (June 30, 2006), p. A6.
3. Robert Tracy, "Introduction," in Anthony Trollope, *The Way We Live Now*, ed. Robert Tracy (Indianapolis: Bobbs-Merrill, 1974), p. xxxix.
4. Fredric Jameson, *Postmodernism, or, The Cultural Logic of Late Capitalism* (Durham: Duke University Press, 1991), pp. 5, 4.
5. Ibid., pp. 37–8.
6. Guy Debord, *The Society of the Spectacle* (1967), trans. Donald Nicholson-Smith (New York: Zone, 1995), p. 17.
7. Ibid., p. 37.
8. Jean Baudrillard, *Simulacra and Simulation* (1981), trans. Sheila Faria Glaser (Ann Arbor: University of Michigan Press, 1994), p. 6.
9. For a more extended discussion of DeLillo's use of early American motifs in *White Noise*, see Laura Barrett, "'How the Dead Speak to the Living': Intertextuality and the Postmodern Sublime in *White Noise*," *Journal of Modern Literature* 25.2 (2001–2), pp. 99–102.
10. John Winthrop, "A Modell of Christian Charity" (1630), rpt. in *The Puritans*, 2 vols., vol. 1, ed. Perry Miller and Thomas H. Johnson (New York: Harper and Row, 1963), p. 195.
11. Jameson, *Postmodernism*, p. 25.

12. Norman Mailer, "Superman Comes to the Supermart," *Esquire* (November 1960), p. 122.
13. Susan Sontag, "Fascinating Fascism" (1975), rpt. in Sontag, *Under the Sign of Saturn* (New York: Anchor, 1991), p. 83.
14. Walter Benjamin, "The Work of Art in the Age of Mechanical Reproduction" (1936), rpt. in Benjamin, *Illuminations*, ed. Hannah Arendt, trans. Harry Zohn (New York: Schocken, 1969), pp. 224, 239–41.
15. See pp. 18, 29, 61, 95, 96.
16. Mark Osteen, *American Magic and Dread: Don DeLillo's Dialogue with Culture* (Philadelphia: University of Pennsylvania Press, 2000), p. 171.
17. Don DeLillo, "Matters of Fact and Fiction," interview with Anthony DeCurtis, *Rolling Stone* (November 17, 1988), p. 120.
18. Emile Benveniste, *Problems in General Linguistics* (1966), trans. Mary Elizabeth Meek (Coral Gables: University of Miami Press, 1971), p. 224. I am grateful to Linda Hutcheon for bringing this quotation to my attention in *A Poetics of Postmodernism: History, Theory, Fiction* (New York: Routledge, 1988), p. 168.
19. John N. Duvall, "The (Super)Marketplace of Images: Television as Unmediated Mediation in DeLillo's *White Noise,*" *Arizona Quarterly* 50.3 (1994), p. 148 n.3.
20. Herman Melville, letter to Nathaniel Hawthorne, [April 16?] 1851, rpt. in *Correspondence*, ed. Lynn Horth, *The Writings of Herman Melville*, 14 vols., vol. 14 (Evanston and Chicago: Northwestern University Press and The Newberry Library, 1993), p. 186.

7

JEREMY GREEN

Libra

Don DeLillo once suggested that the assassination of President John F. Kennedy made him into the writer he became – shaped, that is, the novelist who wrote *Libra* (1988), a charged historical novel about the life of Lee Harvey Oswald and the assassination of JFK. "As I was working on *Libra*," DeLillo told an interviewer, "it occurred to me that a lot of tendencies in my first eight novels seemed to be collecting around the dark center of the assassination."[1] By the time he set to work on his first direct treatment of the assassination, an essay published in *Rolling Stone* under the title "American Blood: A Journey Through the Labyrinth of Dallas and JFK," DeLillo had already written at length of violence, conspiracy, and the seductive lure of paranoia. *Libra*, which followed DeLillo's breakthrough novel *White Noise* (1985), took a little more than three years to write, a remarkably short period of time given the extensive research the book demanded, and was published in 1988, in time for the twenty-fifth anniversary of the assassination. In *Libra* DeLillo approached recent American history directly for the first time, drawing from the evidence, testimony, and analysis compiled in the aftermath of Kennedy's murder. The novel recreates the traumatic moment in Dallas, the "seven seconds that broke the back of the American century" (*L* 181), and offers, as the author's note appended to the first edition puts it, "a way of thinking about the assassination without being constrained by half-facts or overwhelmed by possibilities, by the tide of speculation that widens with the years" (*L* 458). But the novel is more than just the imaginative recreation of a particularly important and troublingly elusive historical event; it is also a speculative study of the origins of our own historical and cultural moment.

In DeLillo's novels of the 1970s, the assassination serves as a reference point for crisis and uncertainty. At the end of *Americana* (1971), for example, the protagonist, David Bell, ends his desperate odyssey through the American heartland by driving his rental car, horn blaring, through Dealey Plaza, the site of the assassination; with this gesture he links his own splintered sense of self to the rupture in American history that took place in Dallas. In *Players* (1977), DeLillo's interweaving of domestic and espionage subgenres, Lyle Wynant finds himself mixed up with a potential terrorist who claims to have known Oswald. In this instance, the assassination becomes a sly allusion, almost a joke, a well-worn reference point for paranoia and conspiracy. Similarly, DeLillo's *Running Dog* (1978), which features a senator's wife who is reading her way through the twenty-six volumes of testimony that accompanied the Warren Commission Report on the event, uses the assassination as a signifier of the paranoid sensibility. These oblique references to the shooting point to the nimbus of uncertainty and danger that emanates from the events of late 1963.

DeLillo does more than simply reinforce the hackneyed notion that the assassination of John F. Kennedy destroyed American innocence. Even before *Libra*, his writing engaged with the suspicion that has, since Dallas, infected American culture, a sense that history has been manipulated, that the real story is buried under layers of bureaucratic obfuscation or missing altogether. Such feelings, often tantamount to paranoia, grew stronger in the wake of other political assassinations (Martin Luther King, Robert Kennedy) as well as Watergate, Vietnam, and Iran-Contra. The apprehension of dark plots in high places was abundantly justified; paranoia entered the popular imagination.

Conspiracy theorists found ample fuel for their speculations in the bewildering mass of contradictions and gaps in the evidence and witness statements amassed by the Warren Commission. As DeLillo noted in 1983, even basic physical facts about the assassination, a murder committed in bright sunlight in front of more than a hundred witnesses, proved curiously elusive:

> We are not agreed on the number of gunmen, the number of shots, the origin of the shots, the time span between shots, the paths the bullets took, the number of wounds on the president's body, the size and shape of the wounds, the amount of damage to the brain, the presence of metallic fragments in the chest, the number of caskets, the number of ambulances, the number of occipital bones.[2]

Such perplexities were compounded by the confusion of motive and agency that the Warren Report at once documented and tried to contain. All this fed the current of suspicion that flowed from Dallas.

Conspiracy theorists draw together the disasters and misdeeds of the 1960s and 1970s to expose the real story about the United States, a narrative of the nation thrown off course, expropriated, manipulated by opaque forces. Oliver Stone's cinematic treatment of the notorious Garrison case, *JFK* (1991), epitomizes the paranoid fabulation of a national metanarrative. Jim Garrison, the flamboyant New Orleans District Attorney, comes to conclude that the assassination amounted to a *coup d'état* carried out on behalf of the military-industrial complex. Even as the film lays out its doomladen thesis, it celebrates Garrison's liberal conscience, suggesting that the nation's moral value, however compromised in high office, resides still in his person, in his quest for the truth about Kennedy's murder. For DeLillo, the events surrounding and following the assassination did indeed mark a transformation "in the vast strange vapor we call the nation."[3] His treatment of it steers clear of grand narratives and moralistic fervor, yet it does chart a shift in the imagined community of nationhood. After Dallas, the bond that links the plural particles of the nation will be "forged in blood,"[4] as DeLillo puts it, established through the spectacle of violent and catastrophic events. *Libra* ends with a diptych of mourning women: Marguerite Oswald, who vows at her son's graveside to pursue the meaning of his life in history, and Beryl Parmenter, the wife of one of the conspirators, who cannot tear herself away from the relentlessly rerun news footage of Jack Ruby shooting Oswald in the basement of the Dallas police building. The shock and grief of the two women symbolize the violent events of Dallas entering the stream of American consciousness and history with transformative effect.

With Oswald's murder, two days after Kennedy's, the question of his role in the assassination was left open, subject to minute scrutiny and wild conjecture, even as the Dallas Police Department and FBI hastened to close the case. When Oswald made an attempt on the life of the ultra-conservative Dallas demagogue General Edwin Walker in April 1963, he apparently acted from political conviction, a point DeLillo underscores by introducing the fictional Bobby Dupard, a disgruntled African American veteran, as Oswald's co-conspirator and getaway driver. But when Oswald participates in the assassination of President Kennedy, his motivation is much more obscure. DeLillo's Oswald admires Kennedy and even identifies with him, reading books that he knows Kennedy has read. His involvement in the assassination falls outside the usual cause-and-effect accountancy of historians. The Warren Report, committed to the idea of Oswald as the lone gunman but facing the difficulty of ascribing a motive for his actions, fell back on writing vaguely of his desire for recognition and his hostility to American society. Conspiracy theorists, by contrast, have since ascribed plausible motives to a variety of groups – anti-Castro Cubans inflamed by Kennedy's policy toward Cuba, branches of the Mafia infuriated by the administration's crusade against organized crime, and even forces within the government committed to an anticommunist agenda on which Kennedy had apparently grown weak – and have treated Oswald as a cipher, the instrument of sinister cabals.

The assassination was either the work of a loner driven to murder the President through his own disaffection and pathological need for recognition, or a plot that developed out of a desire for revenge or to attain some political end. Such, it would seem, are the mutually exclusive stories that may be told about the assassination. DeLillo, however, structures *Libra* to embrace the possibilities of both narratives. He puts the enigma of Oswald at the center of his novel but also invents a small-scale conspiracy involving renegade CIA officers, anti-Castro Cubans, and a few key players from the mob. This conspiracy, a rather haphazard and vengeful business, brings the para-political forces of the Cold War (mercenaries and ideologues from various intelligence agencies and right-wing pressure groups) into play in a political arena increasingly informed by surveillance and spectacle, the emerging lineaments of the contemporary moment. And then there is Oswald, whose impulsive, contradictory, self-consultative psyche, split into spectator and spectacle, brings elements of chance, performance, and fantasy into a murderous constellation with politics. He prefigures the violent loners, the fantasists turned killers, who will spring into the public gaze over the following decades:

> After Oswald, men in America are no longer required to lead lives of quiet desperation. You apply for a credit card, buy a handgun, travel through cities, suburbs and shopping malls, anonymous, anonymous, looking for a chance to take a shot at the first puffy empty famous face, just to let people know there is someone out there who reads the papers. (*L* 181)

The Oswald of *Libra* exemplifies this new regime, where acts of consumerism and violence overlap, where anomie and lethal intent feed off media attention.

The novel traces Oswald's peripatetic and contradictory life story from his teenage years in the Bronx and New Orleans, through service in the Marines and defection to the Soviet Union, to his shadowy existence in Louisiana and Texas, and finally to his death in police custody. This is a novel of motion and mobility, of restlessness and fleeting attachments that anticipate Oswald's subsequent haphazard attempts to project himself into history. Oswald's narrative, divided into chapters denoted by place names, alternates with dated sections covering the emergence and fragmented development of the conspiracy over the months leading up to November 22, 1963, when Kennedy comes to Dallas. The assassination occurs only when the timeline of the conspiracy intersects with Oswald's biography.

From the outset, divergent ideas of history enter the text as the various players in the assassination seek to control the plotting of events. DeLillo's main conspirators look to redress the history of the nation's dealings with

Cuba, and in particular to undo the shame of the disastrous Bay of Pigs invasion, the failure of which they blame on Kennedy. Although they tend to be tight-lipped, pragmatic operatives from the CIA and its clients in the anti-Castro movement, the plotters are driven by the desire to ensure that there will be no reconciliation between the United States and Castro. What they initially envision as a simulated presidential assassination that will send a message to both Kennedy and the country regarding Cuba's threat, however, spirals out of the plotters' control as more people (with less awareness of the original design) are brought into the scheme in order to hide the plot's source. In Baudrillardian fashion, then, the model of assassination precedes and constitutes the actual events in Dallas. Oswald, by contrast, imagines history as an impersonal metaphysical force that will at once give him a permanent identity and sweep him out of his isolation: "History means to merge. The purpose of history is to climb out of your own skin. He knew what Trotsky had written, that revolution leads us out of the dark night of the isolated self. We live forever in history, outside ego and id" (*L* 101). Although Oswald imagines finding his way into history through action and secrecy, emulating Trotsky, his attitude toward the power he imagines to be history is essentially passive, one of submission to an overwhelming force. Such passivity makes him vulnerable to the machinations of those with plots of their own to hatch. If he casts himself as Trotsky at one moment, Oswald also fantasizes that he is Herb Philbrick, the protagonist of the 1950s television show *I Led Three Lives*: "ordinary citizen, member of the Communist Party, undercover agent for the FBI" (*L* 47).

Yet the fateful movement toward the assassination refuses to conform to a neatly patterned historical narrative, one that would, in Oswald's own words, as he settles down to write his self-styled "Historic Diary," "bring a persuasion and form to events" (*L* 211). DeLillo introduces an element of historiographic self-reflection through the figure of Nicholas Branch, a retired CIA officer charged with writing a secret history of the assassination. The brief but important sections dealing with Branch – the name aptly suggests both connection and division – are set outside the doubled time scheme of the novel, placing the character in the late 1980s, fifteen years into his labor, a double for *Libra*'s author, hopelessly marooned amid his documentary sources. Branch analyzes an unstinting stream of material – files, testimony, ballistics reports, surveillance logs, Zapruder's home movie of the assassination, biographies, and even works of fiction – forwarded to him by the CIA curator, all of which he presumes he must reckon with and incorporate into the definitive history he is charged to write.

Overwhelmed by the sheer volume of information he must absorb, Branch also recognizes the inadequacy of the two favored approaches to the assassination: there is the empirical study of the "[s]ix point nine seconds of heat and light" (*L* 15), a process that depends on scientific scrutiny and technology that grows ever more sophisticated. As the novel closes, Branch, still no closer to completing his history, learns of computer models that have been constructed to understand the moments in Dealey Plaza. Such attention becomes at once bureaucratic and all-consuming – "Let's call a meeting to analyze the blur. Let's devote our lives to understanding this moment, separating the elements of each crowded second" (*L* 15) – but still fails to provide the elusive bedrock of fact on which comprehension might finally rest. Equally, Branch sardonically pinpoints the temptation to "build theories that gleam like jade idols, intriguing systems of assumption, four-faced, graceful" (15). The language here suggests that the theory-building impulse springs from the same source as religious belief and entails the worship of idols constructed by the faithful themselves onto which faith is pinned. Both scientific analysis and paranoid speculation search for a redemptive narrative that might rescue history from apparent confusion. As technology develops, it holds out the promise of an ultimate solution to the mysteries of the event, a clear picture where before there was only a blur. DeLillo offers an echo of this impulse in *Underworld* (1997), where computer fanatics, like Nick Shay's son, pore over video images of one of the Texas Highway Killer's attacks, a Zapruder film for the age of cable television. Similarly, the paranoid approach to the assassination seeks the one big story that tells all, that links together the jumbled pieces of evidence and rumor in a grand scheme, a master narrative that will convert uncertainty into knowledge through the power of suspicion.

Both approaches, whether complementary or not, promise conclusions that Branch finds misleading. His attitude to his material veers – restlessly, inconclusively – between a distrust of paranoia and its schematic formulations and a sense of something deeply mysterious and inexplicable about the events of Dallas, down to the minutiae of evidence and contingency: "Elm Street. A woman wonders why she is sitting on the grass, bloodspray all around. Tenth Street. A witness leaves her shoes on the hood of a bleeding policeman's car. A strangeness, Branch feels, that is almost holy" (*L* 15). The Warren Report, though flawed as an investigation, provides this strangeness of contingent things through its monstrous inclusiveness: "Branch thinks this is the megaton novel James Joyce would have written if he'd moved to Iowa City and lived to be a hundred" (*L* 181). The testimony and exhibits attached to the Report include everything, or so it would seem, evidence fraught with potential significance and the most prosaic piece of quotidian reality, all poured regardless into those capacious twenty-six volumes. Yet Branch, with his "sense of responsible obsession," must read as if everything has significance, a controlled hermeneutic drive that flirts unavoidably with paranoia:

> Everything belongs, everything adheres, the mutter of obscure witnesses, the photos of illegible documents and odd sad personal debris, things gathered up at a dying – old shoes, pajama tops, letters from Russia. It is all one thing, a ruined city of trivia where people feel real pain. This is the Joycean Book of America, remember – the novel in which nothing is left out. (*L* 182)

And this is the historical legacy of Dallas: a melancholy ruin and a myriad of suggestive links. Branch's labor represents the extraordinary difficulty of casting the details into a plausible historical narrative. His efforts, which will apparently reach no end, no finished work, and which entail in any case writing a history that no one will read, come to resemble a work of modernist complexity, a text that defies conventional legibility, not to mention aesthetic conventions, to pursue a principle to its logical end. Mastering the mess of this history, with all its bizarre coincidences and baffling contradictions, thwarts Branch's historiographic endeavor.

Yet DeLillo has given his readers a remarkably economical and lucid novel. *Libra* deftly sketches the outline of a plausible conspiracy, unravels the movements and contradictory impulses of Oswald, and shades in the background of America in the 1950s and 1960s with imagistic precision. If the novel does indeed offer a way to think about how the assassination happened, it does not do so by constructing a narrative that restores coherent cause and effect and cogent agency to the whole of the sprawling mess that surrounds the events in Dallas. The sections dealing with Branch, who distills the reflections of several major characters, draw attention to the elements of chance and coincidence that bedevil the idea of an organically unified narrative of the assassination. Coincidences in particular, which occur with disturbing frequency, provoke a compound of contradictory responses – skepticism and wonder – for coincidences involve random occurrences, which those of paranoid disposition cannot help but see as plotted. If the coincidence is not transmuted into the sinister operation of some concealed force, and so turned into design rather than chance, it generates a sense of the uncanny, of an order in reality that eludes comprehension. David Ferrie, a key figure in the conspiracy, opines, "We don't know what to call it, so we say coincidence. It goes deeper ... There's a hidden principle. Every process contains its own outcome" (*L* 172).

Although Ferrie's peculiar brand of superstition, with its blend of apocalyptic fervor and pseudo-science, must be treated with caution, his words gesture toward the novel's attempt to dramatize the mysterious facets of motivation and historical process that make the events of Dallas so significant for DeLillo. For this "hidden principle" is what makes the era after Dallas – our own historical moment – different from what came before Dallas. The events of Dallas transform our understanding of events and the way they affect the national sensibility. Oswald's strange career, from obscurity to notoriety, provides DeLillo with a way to chart this shift in sensibility, the movement from a restricted paranoia to a more general one, and the development of a traumatized subject position as the typical and emblematic one for public consciousness in the wake of the assassination.

In *Libra* the truly paranoid are those creatures of the Cold War who have built a worldview out of suspicion of an insidious and all-powerful communist menace. This is paranoia of a restricted and focused kind. For example, Guy Banister, the virulently right-wing detective who serves as a channel between the CIA and the anti-Castro groups based around New Orleans, maintains files of outlandish rumors – Chinese troops massing in Baja California – and harbors deep suspicion of the Kennedy White House. His paranoia constitutes an ideology, a perspective on history, and a subject position. His decline from a crack FBI operative in the glorious prewar days when he participated in the capture of John Dillinger outside the Biograph Theater in Chicago ("history with a fucking flourish" [*L* 140]) serves as an index of historical as well as personal decline. The popularity of President Kennedy marks for Banister the rise of a politics of the spectacle, a phenomenon he despises: "Banister's rage toward the administration was partly a reaction to public life itself, to men who glow in the lens barrel of a camera" (*L* 62).

More extreme still is General Edwin Walker, the ultra-right segregationist and pillar of the John Birch Society, who detects signs of decline and betrayal everywhere. Indeed, he serves as a clearing-house for the embittered:

> He sat with his back to the window, totaling figures on a scratch pad, taxes, doing his taxes, like any fool and dupe of the Real Control Apparatus. Letters from the true believers were stacked in a basket to his right. The Christian Crusade women, the John Birch men, the semiretired, the wrathful, the betrayed, the ones who keep coming up empty. They had intimate knowledge of the Control Apparatus ... The Apparatus paralyzed not only our armed forces but our individual lives, frustrating every normal American ambition, infiltrating our minds and bodies with fluoridation, with the creeping fever of trade unions and the left-wing press and the income tax, every modern sickness that saps the nation's will to resist the enemy advance. (*L* 282)

The "Real Control Apparatus" forges a devastating link between the body politic and the individual body, infecting both with an insidious disease. The effects of the disease are both ubiquitous, damaging institutions and under-mining individual systems of belief, and troublingly elusive. Indeed, the elusiveness is the condition of the infection, a sure sign of its danger:

> In the Old Senate Caucus Room they asked him to name the members of the Real Control Apparatus. This is like naming particles in the air, naming molecules or cells. The Apparatus is precisely what we can't see or name. We can't measure it, gentlemen, or take its photograph. It is the mystery we can't get hold of, the plot we can't uncover. (L 283)

General Walker's paranoia fits the classic account that the historian Richard Hofstadter elaborated in "The Paranoid Style in American Politics." Hofstadter's mid-century analysis, addressing the anticommunist excesses of the Cold War, saw paranoia as a formation of the alienated and marginal, given public voice by Joseph McCarthy and the John Birch Society.[5] Walker's correspondents are drawn from the ranks of disaffected white southerners as concerned about civil rights and integration as the threat of communism. Hostile toward multifarious social change, the paranoid in this mold projects a unified agent with malign purpose, whose very invisibility and scope are conditions of its existence.

Although he is an extreme and morbid case, situated on the cusp of political reaction and mental pathology, General Walker emerges from an anticommunism that permeates the mass culture of the late 1950s and early 1960s. In *Libra* the voice of warning is never far away. "Danger every-where," intones a radio commentary "on the need for parents to be more vigilant in checking what their children read and watch and listen to" (L 18). Mary Frances Everett, who hears these words at breakfast one morning, later applies their lesson to her six-year-old daughter, worrying about her moods, her secrecy, the fact that she listens to a particular radio station. Similarly, Oswald finds himself banished from a friend's house when the father hears him espousing communism over a game of chess. As his friend jokes, the young Oswald is a "teenage communist," one of those whom Senator Eastland, a virulent McCarthyite, seeks on his anticommunist crusade. These instances, taken from the intersection of private and public realms, historicize the restricted paranoia of anticommunism, in which the national body is conceived as being vulnerable to the depredations of the invisible menace called communism.

It is one of the telling ironies of the novel that the measures taken to safeguard the populace against communism, particularly the practice and technology of surveillance, undermine the integrity of the subjects they are intended to protect. Win Everett, a disgraced CIA officer who has an intimate knowledge of surveillance technology, muses on its troubling aspects:

Spy planes, drone aircraft, satellites with cameras that can see from three hundred miles what you can see from a hundred feet. They see and they hear. Like ancient monks, you know, who recorded knowledge, wrote it painstakingly down. These systems collect and process. All the secret knowledge of the world ... I'll tell you what it means, these orbiting sensors that can hear us in our beds. It means the end of loyalty. The more complex the systems, the less conviction in people. Conviction will be drained out of us. Devices will drain us, make us vague and pliant. (*L* 77)

Oswald presents the extreme test case for Everett's assertions. Throughout his life, he is enmeshed with the bureaucratic systems and surveillance technologies of mid-century America. These systems and technologies, material embodiments of authority and secrecy, fuel his fantasies and inform his acts, simultaneously draining him of conviction and encouraging him to seek it in performances of power. His fantasies of secrecy and power – the two are indissociable for Oswald – are linked insistently to technology.

DeLillo opens the novel with Oswald playing truant to ride the subway of New York City, a habit by which he grasps the social reality around him and imagines his special place within it. Riding the subway might seem a poor way to survey the city, but it is typical of Oswald that he finds the odd angle of perception more acute and telling than the street-level view. He is drawn to the unique viewpoint offered by the front of the first car, staring into the dark, confirmed in his isolation, understanding that "[t]here was nothing important out there, in the broad afternoon, that he could not find in purer form in these tunnels beneath the streets" (*L* 4). His vantage point allows him to glimpse things as the train hurtles down the track – sewer rats, workers on adjacent tracks, people standing on station platforms "staring nowhere, a look they'd been practicing for years" (*L* 3). Oswald finds here a deep, gratifying separateness from the lonely crowd, a narcissistic pleasure in submitting himself to the alarming and almost painful experience of riding the rails:

His body fluttered in the fastest stretches. They went so fast sometimes he thought they were on the edge of no-control. The noise was pitched to a level of pain he absorbed as a personal test. Another crazy-ass curve. There was so much iron in the sound of those curves he could almost taste it, like a toy you put in your mouth when you are little. (*L* 3)

This practice of submission and self-examination, of self-formation through submission, constitutes an instructive tableau, a frontispiece to the novel, as it were, that demonstrates Oswald's relation to the power around him. He subsequently longs to submit himself to a power – an abstraction he comes to name History – in order to emancipate himself from the practiced oblivion of the crowd.

In the subway Oswald fabricates a self at the confluence of brute power, a technological network, and access to secrets. His fantasies of power, forged in his adolescence from the raw material of popular culture, strengthen his sense of self through images of a control and authority that derives from secrecy and violence: "He lay near sleep, falling into reverie, the powerful world of Oswald-hero, guns flashing in the dark. The reverie of control, perfection of rage, perfection of desire, the fantasy of night, rain-slick streets, the heightened shadows of men in dark coats, like men in movie posters" (L 46). This *noir*ish cluster evokes what Frank Lentricchia has called one of the primal scenes of DeLillo's imagination: the man who identifies with the image on television or film, dreaming a magical passage from one order of reality to another.[6] In this case, Oswald identifies with the image of a secret world, an alternative to the everyday reality that surrounds and demeans him. The outlet for violence and control underscores the "world inside the world" (L 47) – one of the phrases DeLillo repeats over the course of the novel to limn Oswald's interiority – that constitutes the veiled self he wishes both to preserve and to surrender. From this fantasy of rage, control, and violence, it is only a small step to his identification with the struggles of historical revolutionaries and to the privileged access to history they seem to promise.

Years later, on the eve of the assassination, Oswald happens to see a double feature on late-night television: *Suddenly* (1954), a movie in which Frank Sinatra plays a combat veteran who plans to assassinate the President, and *We Were Strangers* (1949), starring John Garfield as a revolutionary in 1930s Cuba plotting to assassinate the dictator Machado. The movies are chillingly appropriate – assassins, Cuba, the President. The programming might have been arranged with Oswald in mind, or so he thinks: "Lee felt a stillness around him. He had an eerie sense that he was being watched for his reaction" (L 369). In particular, the movies tap into the secret realm of "Oswald-hero," bringing it alive on the screen: "An old scratchy film that carried his dreams. Perfection of rage, perfection of control, the fantasy of night ... Lee felt he was in the middle of his own movie" (L 370). The uncanny power of this scene – Oswald watching his reveries come to life on the small screen – derives from the channel established between his inner world and the controlling attention of an implied Other. Far from being a "zero in the system" – another of Oswald's defining refrains – he finds himself momentarily subject to a gaze of intense scrutiny.

Oswald experiences a certain paranoia, to be sure, since he imagines himself to be at the mercy of some incalculable force, one capable of arranging the television schedule to suit its purposes. But this is paranoia quite unlike that of the febrile anticommunist. Oswald's feeling of being observed allows him to identify, in mediated fashion, with a powerful Other. His lived fantasy life, his trail of aliases and new identities, entails identification with this Other, imagined or otherwise, who scrutinizes him. As with the television double bill and the subway-riding, the dynamics of identification and suspicion come to life through technologies of one sort or another. On Oswald's defection to the Soviet Union, a KGB interrogator named Alek Kirilenko comes to embody the interest, both menacing and benign, that the state takes in the "stateless" subject Lee Harvey Oswald. Oswald adopts the name Alek among the friends he makes in Minsk because "Lee" is hard for Russian speakers to pronounce. Going by Alek, Oswald identifies with state power, with the figure of authority and secrecy, no more so than when the scrutiny of the state becomes increasingly intense. As he maneuvers to repatriate himself to the United States, Oswald notes various signs indicating that he is under surveillance: a car that apparently keeps watch on his street, interception of his mail, and, most intriguing of all, "this funny little device on the wall of his flat and it's not a socket, a light switch or a thing to hang a picture from" (*L* 205). Such attention is faceless, and Oswald worries that he has had no contact with his interrogator:

> No sign of Alek. Not a word. Total silence.
> Maybe this is all Alek. It is everything Alek. It is get the goods on him. It is pin him to the wall when all I want to do is study. (*L* 205)

The switch from third to first person, a mid-sentence modulation from free indirect style to interior monologue, signifies the gap that has opened between Oswald the subject of the KGB's crude agenda and Oswald the subject of his own narrative intent (the good comrade who wants to extend his knowledge of languages and ideology). But the slippage of "he" and "I" shadows the stranger slippage between the Alek/Oswald and KGB Alek, both of whom are pinned to the wall, one as the trapped subject of surveillance and the other as the mysterious little device that is neither a socket nor a switch: "It is everything Alek."

Most important among the surveillance devices that cross Oswald's path is the U-2 spy plane. While stationed as a marine in Japan, he works in the radar bubble tracking the path of the U-2 on its secret flights. When he defects to the Soviet Union, he offers information about the U-2 in exchange for acceptance by the authorities. And it is while living in Minsk that a U-2 is shot down over Russia, perhaps as a result of the information Oswald has supplied to the KGB. Later still, Oswald works at a graphics company that develops photographs rumored to include those taken from the ubiquitous spy plane:

> The mysterious U-2. It followed him from Japan to Russia and now it was here in Dallas. He remembered how it came to earth, sweet-falling, almost feathery,

dependent on winds, sailing on winds. That was how it seemed. And the pilot's voice coming down to them in fragments, with the growl and fuzz of a blown speaker. He heard that voice sometimes on the edge of a shaky sleep. (*L* 275)

The U-2 occupies a fantasy vantage point from which all may be seen and known: it offers "a lesson in physics and ghosts" (*L* 161), at once the measure of reality – the U-2 verifies the existence of Soviet missiles on Cuban soil – and a signifier of the supernatural. A skeptical KGB interrogator ponders the startling information Oswald has provided about the U-2's flight-path: "Ninety thousand feet? Nothing flies that high. Fly to ninety thousand feet, you see the souls of the dead in rings of white light" (*L* 166). Surveillance technology becomes the focus of elements that lie "outside history"[7] – fantasies, dreams, and images of salvation.

For this reason, it is not surprising that Oswald reverts to the U-2 in his last moments. Mortally wounded by Ruby in the basement of the Dallas police headquarters, Oswald thinks of the pilot bailing from the spy plane: "It is the white nightmare of noon, high in the sky over Russia. Me-too and you-too. He is a stranger in a mask, falling" (*L* 440). In these last moments, the fear of death and the fantasy of omnipotence are yoked together. Oswald has earlier imagined the pilot of the U-2 parachuting down over the vast secret of the Soviet Union, in a position of power and utterly powerless:

> The land smells fresh. He is coming down to springtime in the Urals and he finds that this privileged vision of the earth is an inducement to truth. He wants to tell the truth. He wants to live another kind of life, outside secrecy and guilt and the pull of grave events. This is what the pilot thinks, rocking softly down to the tawny fields of a landscape so gentle and welcoming it might almost be home. (*L* 116)

This scene fuses the appeal of sensuous immediacy with the most spectacular technology of mediation. To float down onto the fields of Russia is to be invested in a secret and to assume a power represented not as coercion or violence, as so often in the novel, but as a plenitude of the self that exists beyond all lack and alienation. Ironically, this plenitude is conveyed in the language of confession: the powerful secret with which Oswald longs to identify finally takes the form of a quasi-sacramental ritual.

With his murder, carried out live on television, Oswald enters a new kind of history. In DeLillo's treatment the murder has a disturbing element of self-consciousness, as Oswald seems, however fleetingly, to acknowledge his own televisual presence: "The only thing left was the mocking pain, the picture of the twisted face on TV . . . He watched in a darkish room, someone's TV den" (*L* 440). Having, as far as possible, arrived at the symbolic place of knowledge, the place from which he is seen, he must, it seems, be divided into two, a suffering body and a spectator of that suffering, a condition in which sub-jectivity collapses. DeLillo's novel comes to an end therefore not with the conclusion of a conspiracy, "the perfect working of a scheme" (*L* 440), but with the arrival of the chaos and randomness that characterize both Oswald's and the President's deaths. The media treatment of these moments, foregrounded in DeLillo's treatment, heralds the era of traumatized public consciousness, of a public consciousness created by trauma, that he will address in *Mao II* and *Underworld*. But it is in *Libra* that the ruinous nature of this moment of history, DeLillo's moment and ours, emerges in all its most vivid and alarming detail.

Notes

1. Anthony DeCurtis, "'An Outsider in This Society': An Interview with Don DeLillo," in Thomas DePietro, ed., *Conversations with Don DeLillo* (Jackson: University Press of Mississippi, 2005), p. 48.
2. Don DeLillo, "American Blood: A Journey through the Labyrinth of Dallas and JFK," *Rolling Stone* (December 8, 1983), p. 22.
3. Ibid., p. 74.
4. Ibid.
5. Richard Hofstadter, "The Paranoid Style of American Politics," *Harper's* (November 1964), pp. 77–86.
6. Frank Lentricchia, "*Libra* as Postmodern Critique," in Lentricchia, ed., *Introducing Don DeLillo* (Durham: Duke University Press, 1991), p. 195.
7. DeCurtis, "An Outsider," p. 51.

8

PATRICK O'DONNELL

Underworld

Published in 1997, *Underworld* is widely regarded as Don DeLillo's major novel to date. In many ways it represents the culmination of DeLillo's novelistic career, though one must exercise caution in making such monumental statements about a living author who shows no signs of slowing down. We can say with certainty that *Underworld* brings together and extends themes that DeLillo has explored throughout his fiction: the relation between humans and technology; the contrast between history (and the subjects of history) conceived as a totality and history (and the subjects of history) conceived as multiple, fragmented, accidental; the excesses of consumer capitalism and its effects on individual life; the relation between language and the social order; the possibility of community amid the failure of politics; the contestation of secrecy and transparency in the contemporary world; and the world as waste and waste as art.[1]

Underworld's range and discursive multiplicity suggest that it is an example of encyclopedic narrative, comparable to Robert Burton's *Anatomy of Melancholy* (1621), Lawrence Sterne's *Tristram Shandy* (1759), Herman Melville's *Moby-Dick* (1851), or more recently, Thomas Pynchon's *Gravity's Rainbow* (1973), a novel that anatomizes the West from World War II to the Nixon era, and to which DeLillo's multilayered portrayal of American life during the Cold War is often and easily compared. To be sure, *Underworld* takes the Cold War as its backdrop. The prologue, "The Triumph of Death," published separately as "Pafko at the Wall" in the October 1992 issue of *Harper's*, is one of the most extraordinary openings in contemporary fiction. It brings together two seemingly unrelated events from October 3, 1951: the home run hit by Bobby Thomson ("the shot heard round the world") as the Giants beat the Dodgers in the dramatic finale of the 1951 National League play-offs, and the second test of an atomic device by the Soviet Union, which serves as both the symbolic and real beginning of the nuclear arms race. Throughout the novel, the threads of the Cold War are woven: in the reconstructions of Lenny Bruce's comedy routines during the Cuban Missile Crisis; in the visit of one of the novel's protagonists, Nick Shay, to a former Soviet nuclear test site now being converted to a plutonium waste dump; and in the childhood remembrances of Nick's brother, Matt, regarding the ID tags and bomb drills that took place in the Bronx Catholic school he attended ("Then Sister told them to place their dog tags out above their shirts and blouses so she could see them ... The tags were designed to help rescue workers identify children who were lost, missing, injured, maimed, mutilated, unconscious or dead in the hours following the onset of atomic war" [U 717]). Yet I want to suggest that for *Underworld* the historical era and political condition commonly labeled "the Cold War" provides but the canvas on which DeLillo constructs a textured, dense pastiche of the human subject – its articulation of desire, its relation to and flight from historical experience, and its anxiety about becoming archaic or objectified in the face of technology and rampant consumerism.

Underworld is, perhaps, the most capacious fictionalization of human subjectivity in the postmodern era available to us – a postmodernism that, in Fredric Jameson's hands, is founded on a modernity where the entangled relationships among "self," "object," and "world" have undergone a fundamental change: "in Heidegger's narrative, the object may be said to produce the subject," rather than the reverse where, classically, human selves are the makers of objects in the world and have mastery over them.[2] *Underworld* is largely about this transformation in the relation between subjects and objects; its dozens of characters and identities, scattered across the temporal and geographical terrain of America during the Cold War, become available to us by means of a series of connected objects, sites, and spectacles. Whether these connections occur randomly or as part of plots and schemes that chart the progress of history *per se* is open to question in the novel, but DeLillo consistently portrays the correlation between self and other, as well as between subject and object, as a reversible and collapsed relation in which human identity and interiority are constructed from without. This recognition and the attendant feelings of powerlessness, paranoia, and alienation or, alternatively, joyful submission to the chaotic or conspiratorial "whole" of reality are at the heart of DeLillo's fiction, especially in *Underworld*, which frames the question of the subject within the historical and national contexts of the Cold War and its aftermath. In drawing out some of the most significant patterns and juxtapositions from the encyclopedic density of the novel, we can observe how DeLillo undertakes one of the oldest tasks of the novelist: to hold up a mirror to vast contradictions and complexity of contemporary American life and thereby to elicit what constitutes identity for us, now.

The vocation of waste

One of the significant facts of contemporary American life is waste. We are surrounded by it. In disposing of it, we orchestrate the weekly domestic ritual of putting out the trash (and many a marital relation rises or falls on the distribution of this responsibility). Vast waste dumps occupy the periphery of our cities, and where to put it – particularly nuclear waste – is the source of heated local (and, increasingly, national and international) political debates. As titles such as William L. Rathje and Gullen Murphy's *Rubbish! The Archaeology of Garbage* (2001) or Elizabeth Royte's *Garbage Land: On the Secret Trail of Trash* (2006) indicate, the subdiscipline of "garbology" has come about as the result of attempts by cultural archeologists to "read" waste for traces of our social practices and collective desire. Waste is everywhere as well in *Underworld*, and as Royte's title suggests, it is one of the novel's "secrets," one of the simultaneously hidden and transparently manifest under/worlds to which the novel's title refers.[3]

If *Underworld* contains anything like a central character, it is Nick Shay. The novel traces Nick from his adolescent flirtations with a life of crime in the Bronx of the 1950s and 1960s – a juvenility that comes to an abrupt end when Nick accidentally shoots and kills a waiter who has attempted to introduce him to heroin – to his career in the waste management industry (specializing in the disposal of contaminated waste) as he engages with the problem of waste in increasingly global proportions. Early in the novel, Nick describes his occupation, his "discipline" as a waste bureaucrat:

> My firm was involved with waste. We were waste handlers, waste traders, cosmologists of waste. I traveled to the coastal lowlands of Texas and watched men in moon suits bury drums of dangerous waste in subterranean salt beds . . . It was a religious conviction in our business that these deposits of rock salt would not leak radiation. Waste is a religious thing. We entomb contaminated waste with a sense of reverence and dread . . . Waste has a solemn aura now, an aspect of untouchability. White containers of plutonium waste with yellow caution tags. Handle carefully. Even the lowest household trash is closely observed. People look at their garbage differently now, seeing every bottle and crushed carton in planetary context. (*U* 88)

For Nick, waste management is part of a global system of design and control that has both sacred and secular implications. Waste is both the fallout of our quest for empowerment in life (whether that comes about through the possession of objects and the accumulation of capital or through the demonstrations of military prowess that characterize an arms race) and, as detritus, the spoor of our mortality, the map of our progress toward death, individual and collective.[4]

Yet, as much as it may be both something to be contained and, for Nick, evidence of containment – a sign that the system is working as it partitions off dross and separates life from death ("[w]e entomb contaminated waste") – waste simultaneously signifies randomness, accident, and disorganization; it registers the breakdown of material order as well as the human attempt, through production of objects, to achieve mastery over the physical world. The flood of litter that rains down from the stands in the baseball park after the home run that ends the 1951 play-off series between the Dodgers and the Giants is described as follows:

> It is coming from all points, laundry tickets, envelopes swiped from the office, there are crushed cigarette packs and sticky wrap from ice-cream sandwiches, pages from memo pads and pocket calendars, they are throwing faded dollar bills, snapshots torn to pieces, ruffled paper swaddles for cupcakes, they are tearing up letters they've been carrying around for years pressed into their wallets, the residue of love affairs and college friendships, it is happy garbage now, the fan's intimate wish to be connected to the event, unendably, in the form of pocket litter, personal waste, a thing that carries a shadow identity – rolls of toilet tissue unbolting hysterically in streams. (*U* 44–5)

The paradoxes of waste are revealed in this passage. It is comprised of random objects, some whole, some now broken or torn apart. Objects that once held specific personal and historical significance (old letters) or economic value (faded dollar bills) are now converted into a growing, erratically spreading and accumulating pile of "happy garbage." At the same time, this random assemblage also serves as a means for identification with the mass, the crowd, and the historical event it has just witnessed. The "happy garbage" ("happy" suggests chance, happenstance, as well as celebration) signifies the loss of personal identity and the acquisition of communal identity, save that the latter is only a "shadow identity," a vestigial and momentary collectivity that evaporates as the disorganized mass of the crowd leaves the stadium and goes a thousand separate ways.

Throughout the novel, the depictions of waste, garbage, junk – the accumulated objects that society has cast off in the aftermath of use, act, or desire – suggest the relation DeLillo draws between the order of things and mortality, the eventual progression of all things toward disorder and death (the realm called the "underworld" in classical mythology). Nick observes that Klara Sax, a performance artist with whom he has had a brief affair during his youth in the Bronx, and whose current project is the painting of hundreds of B-52 bombers mothballed in a remote desert location, has had a career "marked at times by her methods of transforming and absorbing junk" (*U* 102). Brian Glassic – Nick's co-worker whose brief affair with Nick's wife,

Marian, serves as the watershed for the Shays' complete assimilation into middle-class conformity, consumerism, and bored satisfaction – integrates waste with geography by viewing a monumental dump as an "organic thing, ever growing and shifting, its shape counter-plotted by the day and hour. In a few years this would be the highest mountain on the Atlantic Coast between Boston and Miami" (U 184).

Jesse Detweiler, a "waste theorist" in Nick's firm, opines that "cities rose on garbage, inch by inch ... Garbage always got layered over or pushed to the edges ... [but] ... It pushed back. It pushed into every space available, dictating construction patterns and altering systems of ritual. And it produced rats and paranoia. People were compelled to develop an organized response" (U 287). "Garbage comes first, then we build a system to deal with it," as Detweiler puts it (U 288). Detweiler suggests that we are compelled to generate systems in order to contain the leavings of our advancement through time and that this "system-work" is fundamental to the construction of historical identity.[5] Reflecting on the omnipresence of waste in America, a building superintendent in the Bronx of the 1950s tells a group of cardplayers that "[t]his goddamn country has garbage you can eat, garbage that's better to eat than the food on the table in other countries. They have garbage here you can furnish your house and feed your kids" (U 766–7). In a historical rejoinder, Albert Bronzini, a schoolteacher who has taught both Nick and Matt Shay and who is the former husband of Klara Sax, tells the group about the "ancient Mayans": "[t]hese people did not bury their dead with gleaming jewelry and other valuable objects. They used old broken things. They put cracked vases in with the dead ... They used the dead as a convenient means of garbage disposal" (U 767). Finally, Victor Maltsev, a Russian waste engineer working with Nick and Brian on the "beating fire with fire" waste dump project in which the contaminated byproducts of nuclear power plants would be destroyed by exploding underground nuclear bombs, says of the relation between "weapons and waste" that "maybe one is the mystical twin of the other ... waste is the devil twin. Because waste is the secret history, the underhistory, the way archaeologists dig out the history of early cultures ... literally from under the ground" (U 791).

From these and dozens of other references to waste in *Underworld*, one gains the sense that, for contemporary subjects in a late capitalist order,[6] waste is the random assemblage and connective tissue that binds us as identities to a highly systematized culture and history, while at the same time indicating our transience, charting the quasi-accident of our relation to abandoned objects in the world that we have made and used to fulfill our needs and desires. In this order, described by the narrator of the novel's last section, entitled after Marx's *Das Kapital* (1867), people want not "the same things, necessarily, but ... they want the same range of choices" (*U* 785); in this order, what is desired is a

> method of production that will custom-cater to cultural and personal needs, not to cold war ideologies of massive uniformity ... But even as desire tends to specialize ... the force of converging markets produces an instantaneous capital that shoots across horizons at the speed of light, making for a certain furtive sameness, a planning away of particulars that affects everything from architecture to leisure time to the way people eat and sleep and dream. (*U* 785–6)

In *Underworld* waste exists as a kind of underground empire, a realm where difference becomes sameness, linking all seemingly variegated identities into the uniform processes of production, purchase, use, and disposal that generates the illusion of difference and the seeming idiosyncrasy of individual desire. For DeLillo, the vast socio-economic system of global capitalism figures its operation in the spectacle of waste, which demarcates the complex relation between desire and fear in the lives of the novel's characters. In this relation the desire for difference, for historical particularity, is traded off against the counterdesire for system, order, and a connection to a larger, total history. Existing within the interplay of desire and counterdesire is the mortal fear that all roads lead to the same end: to be cast on the junk heap of history, to be buried with one's own trash, to be forgotten in the uniformity and rapidly convergent future of consumption's progress and remnant.

Between life and death

The collapsible antimonies of sameness and difference, system and waste are visible everywhere in *Underworld*, and their interaction constitutes what might be termed the novel's dialectic. Indeed, the novel's title bears the marks of this interaction as well as gesturing toward another pattern of significance whereby the world is rendered as total ("everything's connected," says Detweiler [*U* 289]) yet marginal, limned by the convergence of the real and the virtual, light and shadow, life and death. As previously mentioned, in the classical world "underworld" connotes the realm of the dead. And like Gabriel Conway, who in James Joyce's "The Dead" (1914) comes to view a winter landscape as the scene of all life passing into death, the multiple narrative perspectives assembled in *Underworld* overlook a contemporary landscape littered with the evidence of the mutable and transitory nature of life: the piles of waste in which formerly discrete, usable objects become inert slag; the offspring of radiation victims whose misshapen bodies are indicative of our corporeal vulnerability in the face of our technological advances; the seemingly infinite interchangeability and diffuseness of identities in crowds and objects tracked across time and history that are only seen, momentarily, like a quantum particle at a precise instant of alteration to a new physical state. This "underworld" of life-always-becoming-death is *the* world of DeLillo's novel, reflected in the image of Bruegel's *The Triumph of Death*, the apocalyptic sixteenth-century painting depicting a landscape of death, possibly an allegory of the ravages of war, that floats down (in reproduction, torn out of a magazine) along with the litter at the ball game. Yet, even given the title of Bruegel's painting, which is also the title of the novel's prologue portraying the fateful baseball game, *Underworld* does not so much dwell on the triumph or inevitability of death as on the notion that humans and objects are forever shuttling *between* life and death in a process of recycling demarcated, once more, by the underhistory of waste. Contemporary identity is, for DeLillo, precisely this shuttling; history is, precisely, the narrativization of this process.

Other resonances of "underworld" tell us more. The word is often taken to refer to underground movements and organizations of all kinds and is equally applicable to radical political entities (for example, "The Weather Underground," the group of young American revolutionaries that staged a series of guerilla actions in the 1970s protesting against the Vietnam War); supersecret government cells, such as the putative "Majestic 12," charged with hiding the presence of aliens from the American people; or the "underworld" of organized crime. In *Libra* (1988) DeLillo brought all these assemblages into sometimes accidental, sometimes planned contact with each other in his fictionalization of the assassination of John F. Kennedy and the story of Lee Harvey Oswald. *Underworld* does not deal with a singular political conspiracy as such, more with the sense that, to return to Detweiler's view, if civilization is the "organized response" to the chaotic overflow of its own detritus, the "underworld" of hidden connections between everything is vast and omnipresent. Figuratively, the underworlds of *Underworld* exist as an alternative mirror universe of shadow identities, sites, and latent, loosely coupled systems that operate in parallel to the official world of normal schooldays, managed careers, and bureaucracies of containment that are constantly subject to interruption by unexpected others and objects bursting forth from below. Each of these underworlds appears to have its own social order and system of communication.

To refer to a few among many, we find in *Underworld* "the Pocket," "a secret installation in the desert" where Matt Shay does "weapons work but of the soft-core type" (*U* 402); "the Wall," a piece of Bronx real estate located under freeway overpasses and ruled over by a master graffiti artist and his squad of acolytes; and "the Float," an arcade of junk shops and amusements catering to the paranoid and quest-obsessed, "[f]loating zones of desire. It was the what, the dismantling of desire into a thousand subspecialties, into spin-offs and narrowings, edgewise whispers of self" (*U* 319). Each of these small worlds is both total, self-contained ("The Pocket was one of those nice tight societies that replaces the world … [I]t was self-enclosed and self-referring and you did it all together in a place and a language that were inaccessible to others" [412]), and at the same time partial, traversed by selves and objects that – along with the official world above ground – make up the novel's global system in which "everything's connected." The link between manifest and hidden realms, analogous to the relation between life and death previously described, can also be viewed as the relation between reality and dream, where the novel's underworlds are symptomatic of the pathologies and anxieties that afflict the quotidian world and its citizens as they go about the daily business of managing waste, building bombs, playing baseball. In this sense, the novel's underworlds form its "unconscious," the "floating zone of desire" for life and death, system and dispersal informing the polarized dynamics of identity that play out across the lives of the novel's myriad characters.

Tracking the appearance of manifestations from this other realm is one of the main narrative tasks of the novel. The Bobby Thomson home-run baseball, for example, is viewed as it passes through various hands, from Cotter, the black teenager who scratches and claws for the ball when it bounces into the upper stands, ultimately retrieving it in the mad scramble, to Marvin Lundy, an avid collector of baseball memorabilia who scours the high and low places of America for the sacred object, to Nick Shay, into whose possession the baseball comes as an embodiment of negative capability. When Lundy visits "the Float" looking for evidence of the baseball, he walks into the shop of Tommy Chan, "maybe the country's first baseball memorabilist, if that's an actual word" (*U* 321):

> And there was Tommy in his high chair, the chair and cash register platformed, islanded higher than the surging mass of old paper that was going chemically brown, and it made Marvin think of all the game footage he'd seen during his search, fans in the Polo Grounds throwing scorecards and newspapers onto the field …. All that twilight litter. Maybe some of it eventually entering the under-ground of memory and collection, some kid's airplaned scorecard, a few leaves of toilet tissue unfurled in jubilation from the upper deck, maybe autographed delicately by a player, the scatter of a ball game come to rest all of these years later, a continent away. (*U* 321)

Metaphorically, the remnants and waste of the ball game serve in this passage as a kind of collective unconscious or mass from which emerges, by chance, a particular object to which is attached an aura of affect or memory. This process of individuation serves to generate both a particular history (one distinguishable from the unknowable mass) and a subject who is attached to the object by virtue of a word or inscription that marks an affective or mnemonic relation. As Chan remarks, "My customers come here largely for the clutter and mess. It's a history they feel a part of" (*U* 322). History, in this sense, is the resurrection of objects from the mass that confer upon selves a sense of identity, a connection to the history of the cultural collective in which they are immersed that does the double duty of distinguishing them as individuals and making them one of the crowd. Tracking the sacred object of the Bobby Thomson home-run baseball, then, becomes a process of historicizing the emergence of disparate identities across the forty years of the Cold War, connecting them together as part of a larger history that is demarcated not by its geopolitical binaries and trilateralisms but by the auratic objects that have emerged from the underworld of the collective unconscious. These objects seem to appear sporadically and at random, but like the baseball, which, similar in size and shape, is compared at several points in the novel to the core of a nuclear device, they often bear eerie resemblances and connections to their counterparts. Such connections convey the sense that, for DeLillo, history is at once a matter of accident and conspiracy, and the emergence of the individual, which can take place only as part of a process of acculturation and inscription, is at once a matter of chance and fate, ultimately spelling the integration of the self into the system of reality.

As I have suggested, in *Underworld*, what constitutes the level of the manifest in the visible appearance and relations that exist between disparate objects, identities, and events is invigorated by the latent underworld of collective fantasy and desire. To some degree, the novel might be viewed as a history of Cold War consumerist fantasies and the role that collective desire plays in the formation of both discrete and mass identities. More broadly, the underworld of desire that constitutes the novel's cultural unconscious can be described, in Susan Buck-Morss's citation and reading of Walter Benjamin's assessment of nineteenth-century consumerist culture as a "'dreaming collective' . . . composed of atomized individuals, consumers who imagined their commodity dreamworld to be uniquely personal (despite all objective evidence to the contrary) and who experienced their membership in the collectivity only in an isolated, alienating sense, as an anonymous component of the crowd."[7]

Desires of all kinds are exposed in *Underworld*, and as the Benjaminian irony that Buck-Morss notes would suggest, what appear to be the individual desires of an atomized populace are, in fact, disparate manifestations of the same, scattered eruptions of collective fantasies in specific lives. In the novel disparate episodes from the lives of individual characters over the course of forty years are connected by the running refrain of headlines announcing various crises and stages in the advance of the Cold War. Paranoia (the "organized response" to fear cited earlier but also the contradictory desire for control over historical process and utter separation from history as a discrete identity) joins in life and in death the destinies of Sister Edgar and J. Edgar Hoover, whose messianic fantasies are delivered in the form of a virulent anticommunism. The adventures of a serial killer, a subversive comedian, a performance artist, a systems engineer, and a suburban housewife are tracked and juxtaposed as they engage in seemingly unconnected acts of murder, adultery, speech, consumerism, flight, and transformation. Subtending all these acts and performative trajectories – serving, once more, as a kind of historical record of the migrations of human desire across time and space – are the unconverted piles of debris and constructed or transformed assemblages of detritus that are encountered as either the containments of fear and desire's aftermath or its transformation into art.

A remarkable instance occurs in the novel when Nick views the Watts Towers, the monumental example of found art made from junk gathered by an Italian immigrant, Simon Rodia, who spent more than thirty years in the south Los Angeles neighborhood assembling the large spires. Thomas Pynchon describes these towers as "perhaps his own dream of how things should have been: a fantasy of fountains, boats, tall openwork spires, encrusted with a dazzling mosaic of Watts debris."[8] Rodia's ironic, utopian fantasy – an apparition emerging out of the Benjaminian "phantasmagoria" of mass culture – is seen by Nick as

> an idiosyncrasy out of someone's innocent anarchist visions ... The towers and birdbaths and fountains and decorated posts and bright oddments and household colors, the green of the 7-Up bottles and blue of Milk of Magnesia, all the vivid tile embedded in cement, the whole complex of structures and gates and panels that were built, hand-built, by one man, alone, an immigrant from somewhere near Naples, probably illiterate, who left his wife and family, or maybe they left him, I wasn't sure, a man whose narrative is mostly blank spaces, date of birth uncertain, until he ends up spending thirty-three years building this thing out of steel rods and broken crockery and pebbles and seashells and soda bottles and wire mesh, all hand-mortared, three thousand sacks of sand and cement, and who spends these years with glass specks crusting his hands and arms and glass-dust in his eyes as he hangs from a window-washer's belt high on the towers, in torn overalls and dusty fedora, face burnt brown, with lights strung on the radial poles so he could work at night, maybe ninety feet up, and Caruso on the gramophone below. (*U* 276)

This eloquent evocation of a monumental "anarchist" effort to transform junk into art reminds Nick of his father, Jimmy, a bookmaker and petty criminal who disappeared from Nick's Bronx boyhood home when Jimmy, who "inferr[ed] the future out of his own lined flesh ... looked at his hand one day ... and it was blank" (*U* 276). Recalling Detweiler's theory that the containment of waste is essential to the advance of civilization and its capacity to contain its own self-destructive fears and fantasies (what Sigmund Freud in *Civilization and Its Discontents* [1930] terms civilization's "high expenditure of energy" to curtail "instinctual passions"),[9] we observe in this passage describing the Watts Towers Nick's recollection of a personal loss that undermines the certainty of his own future. Nick's insight is instigated by Rodia's sublimation into art of *his* loss of family and nation, *his* survival in an alienated, "anarchist" temporality (a "blank" future). Symbolically, the pile of junk-cum-art that is the Watts Towers is at once an "idiosyncrasy" and symptomatic of the state of identity in *Underworld*, where the leavings of commodities that satisfy the "instinctual passions" of the mass are sold via the illusion that uniquely satisfies the needs of each discrete individual. The Towers, in effect, tell the story of "our" culture: its indulgence in the fantasies of total and immediate satisfaction; its archeologies of loss founded on the disposability of objects; its "discontents," issuing from the juxtaposition of forms of alienated freedom and the fear of death, of waste.

If *Underworld* is about this, it is, of course, about many other things, including the Eliotian possibility that the wasteland can be redeemed or that the technology producing the objects that kill us is the same technology that can produce the objects that cure us.[10] In this chapter I have suggested that DeLillo's primary interest in the novel is historical and that whatever redemptive or destructive potential can be elicited from the geopolitics of the Cold War, DeLillo is fully engaged with the questions of how identity is formed by the objects we produce in a culture so given over to commodification as that of the United States during the late twentieth century, and of what those objects have to reveal about both individual and collective identity. For DeLillo, in this novel, mass culture is, in effect, the assemblage of its objects, whether these be discrete or collective, entropic or transformational, alienating or sacral. Culture is, thus, the record of collective desire – the place where it does its work, manages its defenses, and disseminates its affects. This is to attribute to collective desire a form of agency that, for DeLillo, is manifested in human history both by means of events that make headlines ("the shot heard round the world") and the quotidian, domestic activities of the consuming multitudes registered most clearly in what we leave behind in the pursuit of satisfaction.

For Nick, such recognitions about the nature of objects and our attachments to them in the pursuit of desire amid the phantasmagoria of culture brings only sadness and a sense of loss. Reconciled to his wife after the acknowledgment of her adulterous affair with Brian, growing into middle age in the Phoenix suburbs, Nick reflects:

> There is something somber about the things we've collected and owned, the household effects, there is something about the word itself, *effects*, the lacquered chest in the alcove, that breathes a kind of sadness – the wall hangings and the artifacts and valuables – and I feel a loneliness, a loss, all the greater and stranger when the object is relatively rare and it's the hour after sunset in a stillness that feels unceasing. (*U* 808)

Here, amid these musings on the comfortable middle-class life he currently enjoys, Nick is also recalling his rough childhood on the streets of the Bronx, his vanished father, and the successful institutionalization of his identity, first in reform school after the accidental killing of the waiter and then as a rising executive in the waste management industry. In *Underworld* DeLillo is interested in charting such systematizations of both individual and collective identity in a world where "the object may be said to produce the subject." Among the recognitions the novel provides, one is certainly the sense that in a world of object-produced subjects – subjects that have been induced by the matrix of object relations undergirded by collective desire – something has been lost. Standing in his suburban living room, Nick longs for some putative time before he became a self interpellated into a consumerist system, for "the days of disorder ... when I was alive on the earth, rippling in the quick of my skin, heedless and real ... the days of disarray when I walked real streets and did things slap-bang and felt angry and ready all the time, a danger to others and a distant mystery to myself" (*U* 810). But this past, too, is integral to the produced subject that DeLillo shadows in *Underworld*, a time before of the "real" and the potential return to eternal youth that, as any ad man knows, is the most seductive of consumer dreams. In desire for the freedoms of a past constructed only in the wake of an increasing attachment to the world of objects that portends a quiescent future, Nick's life embodies the history of the subject produced by objects. And if, indeed, "everything's connected" in the complex matrix of identity, desire, objects, and history that DeLillo portrays in the scattered narratives of the novel, then everything – from a (cold) war to a baseball to litter to living-room reflections on boyhood – gains historical density as revelatory of our collective fantasies and fears. These, for DeLillo, motivate our formation as subjects in an era when the survival of our world is threatened by the objects that we produce, even as our subjectivity increasingly depends on those objects. *Underworld* thus comes to rest as DeLillo's most compelling narrative exploration of what makes "us."

Notes

1. For an excellent survey of DeLillo's continuing themes and their development in *Underworld*, see John Duvall, *Don DeLillo's "Underworld": A Reader's Guide* (New York: Continuum Publishing, 2002).
2. Fredric Jameson, *A Singular Modernity: Essay on the Ontology of the Present* (New York: Verso, 2002), p. 48.
3. Two essays in *UnderWords* compellingly and differently address the concept of waste in the novel: David Cowart discusses the ways in which the novel "embraces an aesthetic of recycling" as an aspect of the novel's intertextual reach (David Cowart, "Shall These Bones Live?" in Joseph Dewey, Steven G. Kellman, and Irving Malin, eds., *UnderWords: Perspectives on Don DeLillo's "Underworld"* [Newark, NJ: University of Delaware Press, 2002], pp. 50–67) and Paul Gleason discerns DeLillo's rendition of a central modernist theme and his pondering the question of whether the contemporary wasteland of American can be redeemed (Paul Gleason, "Don DeLillo, T. S. Eliot, and the Redemption of America's Atomic Wasteland," in ibid., pp. 130–41). As I discuss waste in *Underworld*, I focus on the questions of identity that waste as both metaphor and contemporary monumental reality raises.
4. In the most comprehensive reading of the novel to date, Osteen considers the ways in which waste comments on the connections among alienation, redemption (through art), loss, and containment across the novel's multiple narrative and "underhistories." See Mark Osteen, *American Magic and Dread: Don DeLillo's Dialogue with Culture* (Philadelphia: University of Pennsylvania Press, 2000), pp. 214–60.
5. Although one of the first book-length studies of DeLillo, Tom LeClair's *In the Loop: Don DeLillo and the Systems Novel* (Urbana: University of Illinois Press, 1987) remains one of the most comprehensive assessments of DeLillo's fiction, particularly as his work engages "systems theory" and interrelated mathematical, linguistic, narrative, and philosophical systems.
6. The term "late capitalism" has been popularized in relation to postmodernism by Jameson in one of the fundamental works of postmodern theory, *Postmodernism, or The Cultural Logic of Late Capitalism* (Durham: Duke University Press, 1991), but the term finds one of its sources in Ernest Mandel's *Late Capitalism* (1972), trans. Joris De Bres (New York: Verso, 1999), where he focuses on the emergence of global markets, excessive surplus value, and the movement of capital as indicators of a historical change in the relation between labor, consumption, and produced object.
7. Susan Buck-Morss, *The Dialectics of Seeing: Walter Benjamin and the Arcades Project* (Cambridge, MA: MIT Press, 1989), p. 260. As do many of DeLillo's readers, I base my formulations here about the relationship between identity, object, and history in *Underworld* on the work of Walter Benjamin, particularly in the essays contained in *Illuminations*, ed. Hannah Arendt, trans. Harry Zohn (New York: Schocken, 1969). See "The Work of Art in the Age of Mechanical

Reproduction" (pp. 217–51) and "Theses on the Philosophy of History" (pp. 253–64). In my view, there is no doubt that DeLillo has been heavily influenced by Benjamin throughout his writing of the past twenty years, but the influence is especially evident in *Underworld* and *Mao II*. In "Theses" Benjamin writes that, in distinction from causal history, material history is a matter of "monads" and "constellations" emerging after the progression of historical events themselves and that the inconceivable totality of the past, which, for Benjamin, points toward an apocalyptic future, is "one single catastrophe which keeps piling wreckage upon wreckage" (p. 257). The notion of history as "wreckage upon wreckage" is analogous to the image of trash in *Underworld* as the repository of mass history from which emerge constellations of objects and individuals as the narrativized embodiments of particularities in relation to the totalities of "world" and "history."

8. Thomas Pynchon, "A Journey Into the Mind of Watts," *New York Times Magazine* (June 12, 1966), pp. 34 ff. Pynchon's comment occurs in an essay devoted primarily to the racial politics of the 1966 Watts riots. One of the many parallels between Pynchon and DeLillo is their common interest in junk, trash, recycling, and the transformation of inert matter into artistic forms. For more on this shared thematic, see Cowart, "Shall These Bones Live?"

9. Sigmund Freud, *Civilization and Its Discontents* (1930), trans. James Strachey (New York: Norton, 1961), p. 59.

10. Again, Paul Gleason's essay "Don DeLillo" offers strong arguments for reading *Underworld* as ironically redemptive.

PART IV

Themes and issues

9

RUTH HELYER

DeLillo and masculinity

Don DeLillo's fiction suggests that masculinity, rather than being inherent, is an insecure construction based on dominant societal norms and presented via mediated images. His writing offers a number of hypermasculine characters torn between upsetting and upholding the status quo; they display the inadequacy of stereotypes while suggesting that the concept of individuality is flawed and unsustainable. Literature can potentially aid the embedding of social conditioning; however, it can also provide a critical purchase from which to scrutinize social norms. While it is difficult to identify ideal alternatives in any cultural text, literature at least offers a forum for thinking about difference and boundary breaching. This is what DeLillo's writing does in its treatment of masculinity. Rather than replace one defunct cultural narrative with an equally invalid alternative, it displays the insecurity of masculinity without offering a facile replacement. What the reader instead becomes aware of is an emergent male self-consciousness, which is crucially and increasingly knowing about the performative nature of men's roles. For example, when Jack Gladney, the satirical protagonist of *White Noise* (1985), muses to himself about what his father-in-law might think of him, he reveals his own feelings of inadequacy, which may or may not reflect what Vernon thinks.

In a bizarre double-bluff, Jack presumes that others judge his level of masculinity according to his lack of manual skills, while at the same time acknowledging that his awareness of this ranking scenario effectively negates it. This is underpinned by a further level of awareness that Vernon may not give a second thought to Jack's skills or lack of them. Acknowledging the centrality of self-awareness to his argument reiterates the potentially ironic nature of Jack's critical comments about himself: "What could be more useless than a man who couldn't fix a dripping faucet – fundamentally useless, dead to history, to the messages in his genes?" (*WN* 245). The reader colludes with Jack in the knowledge that the manual skills he is referring to are not inherent in the male members of the race; they are acquired according to necessity and have historically become associated with being a "real" man.

Masculine identity via occupation

Jack struggles to perform an authentic masculine identity. His awareness of the ongoing battle between his conventional principles and chaotic setting prompts him to insist that "people need to be reassured by someone in a position of authority that a certain way to do something is the right way or the wrong way" (WN 171–2). The general feelings of chaos which unnerve Jack, tied to the surface nature of everyday life, are compounded by the more specific chaos climaxing around the toxic spill in his home town. His feelings of inadequacy are multiplied by his fear of death, his only recourse the strong masculine identity he has deliberately connected to ideas of academic self-aggrandizement. Within the associations of masculinity with occupation there is a distinctive hierarchy. His performance as masculine academic aims to elevate and protect: "I'm not just a college professor. I'm the head of a department. I don't see myself fleeing an airborne toxic event. That's for people who live in mobile homes out in the scrubby parts of the county" (WN 117). Jack cannot help but stereotype his fellow humans, totally caught up in the "need to structure and classify, to build a system against the terror in our souls" (N 81) and as a consequence he feels paranoid and unsafe when without his trademarks: "I wanted my academic gown and dark glasses" (WN 142). The other staff members of the School of American Environments (all men) strive to appear manly, following their leader Alfonse Stompanato, who is described as "large, sardonic, dark-staring, with scarred brows and a furious beard fringed in grey" (WN 65).

Despite masculine performance being closely tied to the dominant ideals of the work ethic acted out in the Western world, Stompanato's staff spend their time analyzing trivia – there are professors who do nothing but read cereal packaging. There is an uncomfortable fit between traditionally physical masculine activities and the diversity that can now be aligned with earning power and providing – the conventional strongholds of masculinity. Beyond the discussions around what constitutes sanctioned masculine modes of work, Nick Shay in Underworld (1997) feels that the accepted framework in which to perform them is false and restricting: "The regular hours ... the same every day. Clocking in, taking the train ... going in together, coming home together" (U 685). And likewise, "Nick didn't think it was necessary to have one job for life and start a family and live in a house with dinner on the table at six every night" (U 724). When Nick has to hone his actions to fit those of a working adult and family man, he finds it a conscious effort to adhere to schedules, and he reflects on his lack of satisfaction with so-called normal life. He is therefore glad when he finds out about his wife's affair with his work colleague Brian Glassic, feeling that such an act has the potential to free him from some of the unwelcome responsibilities that being a breadwinner has brought him: "Relieved of my phoney role as husband and father ... feel free for just a moment, myself again ... giving it all up ... the children ... the grandchild, they could keep the two houses, all the cars, he could have both wives ... None of it ever belonged to me except in the sense that I filled out the forms" (U 796).

Despite any lack of genuine concern about what his wife is doing, Nick knows that to be an acceptable male he must respond to the slight on his honor by assaulting Brian. His blows are token ones as he relies on his dialogue rather than his physicality to transmit his feelings to Brian. He attempts to fulfill what is expected of him with the minimum amount of violence, therefore acknowledging that there is a blueprint for masculine behavior, while still demonstrating his consciousness of the performed nature of this behaviour. This societal requirement to behave in a "manly" way manifests itself early in Nick's life with his hoodlum existence and his refusal (or inability) to forget about his father's desertion.

Masculine identity via family

When Nick's father disappears, he and his brother Matt have to be more reliant on each other. Nick tries to care for his brother in his tough-guy way, while Matt focuses on being a cerebral chess genius. Nick tries to use his missing father as something not to imitate, always struggling with the adage "You do what they did before you" (U 31), but it never comes naturally to him to behave reliably, predictably, or as a provider to a family. Indeed, later in life, as quoted above, he, too, welcomes any excuse to escape from his familial responsibilities. As a teenager, he gives his younger brother an example of what not to act out – a violent murder. This act does, however, offer Matt a certain amount of street credibility in their rough neighborhood, so despite Nick's wish for Matt not to emulate him his brother gains in stature from having a sibling who is a murderer.

Mothers as well as fathers in DeLillo's work are implicated in perpetuating a certain masculinity. Eric Packer in *Cosmopolis* (2003), the product of a tough neighborhood not unlike Nick's, is also subjected to the early departure of his father. Mike Packer dies young, leaving Eric, like Nick, to be raised by his mother. Eric's narrative focuses on their frequent trips to the dark womb-like world of matinée cinema. The deep attachment Eric feels for his mother climaxes in him shooting his bodyguard for daring to whisper her name as a code to make his gun fire, a choice which reflects the passionate relationship they experienced (C 183–6). In *Libra* (1988) DeLillo portrays Lee Harvey Oswald as another fatherless boy, similarly close to his mother – in fact, sleeping in the same bed until he is eleven years old. Oswald's almost claustrophobic closeness to his mother makes his confused feelings for her veer between possessive love and violent hatred. When Nick in *Underworld* has sex with Klara Sax, many years his senior, he could be said to be succumbing to this urge, to be as close as possible to a mother or motherlike figure.

Jack in *White Noise* holds onto the offspring of his various marriages, creating a hybrid family, hoping that demonstrating his ability as a socially commendable father (whether biologically theirs or not) will prevent the children from undergoing identity crises similar to his own. He takes Heinrich, his eldest son, to watch an asylum burning down, a ferocious scene that he believes cannot help but unite a father and son:

> There were other men at the scene with their adolescent boys. Evidently fathers and sons seek fellowship at such events. Fires help draw them closer, provide a conversational wedge. There is equipment to appraise, the technique of firemen to discuss and criticize. The manliness of firefighting – the virility of fires, one might say, suits the kind of laconic dialogue that fathers and sons can undertake without awkwardness or embarrassment. (*WN* 239)

In *Underworld* Nick's narrative repeatedly returns to his childhood experiences on the fringe of "The Family" – the Mafia. His own father is always a void in this dialogue, with no such uniting experiences to remember. Instead, he reiterates his theory that the Mob were at the center of his father's disappearance. Nick is excited by what he perceives as the glamor of the Mob, but afraid of the level of brutality capable of making someone totally disappear. It is the glamor and power that he tries to keep by insisting there are suspicious circumstances behind his father's disappearance, when in reality it seems unlikely that a small-time ticket-tout would be worth the Mob's time. Nick aspires to joining the high-ranking mobsters, in his mind at least, and describes their ranking system and what it is to be a "made man": "Once you're a made man, you don't need the constant living influence of sources outside yourself. You're all there. You're made. You're handmade. You're a sturdy Roman wall" (*U* 275). The phrase "made man" makes it clear how created, acted out, and performed this role is; promotion to sergeant is further enhanced by the term "handmade," with all its connotations of tradition and authenticity. Many years later, Nick acts as a mobster to entertain his staff. Threatening them in the idiom of an Italian gangster, he relies on the standardized image to pretend to be what he actually aspired to be when young. Nick's performance acts out the performance he teetered so close to as a fledgling hoodlum and his staff perpetuate this by in turn mimicking him mimicking himself. The mimicry creates some distance among his varying selves in which to analyze the confusion of fantasizing about and adopting differing personas.

Masculine identity via sport and physical exercise

Nick attempts to affect a similar distance between himself and his killing of George, a local waiter whose drug-taking and unconventional life he finds fascinating. He always describes the shooting in the third person, as a performance to be observed (*U* 781). He tries to be equally detached from his passion for sport, taking his radio to a deserted rooftop to listen to the historic baseball game of 1951 between the Giants and the Dodgers. He therefore effectively avoids the intense emotional involvement the crowd feel with the game and the need to feel, reveal, and share such emotions as hatred, love, loyalty, and despair. These feelings are contained by the sports arena but not contained sufficiently for Nick to feel comfortable. Emotions are acted out, theatricalized, and controlled within the stadium, the narrative portraying it as a place where men can conduct sanctioned relationships with other men, such homosocial bonds forming the backbone of patriarchy. The crowd illustrates a celebration of male physical prowess free from marriage, domesticity, heterosexuality, and children. Race and class are also temporarily put aside, illustrated by the illusory friendship between a white middle-class man, Bill Waterson, and a working-class, African American adolescent, Cotter Martin, which lasts only as long as the game.

Building an admirable physique is seen to be part of this celebration. In *Underworld* Nick heaves 7-Up crates, in *White Noise* Heinrich diligently performs chin-ups in his cupboard. Yet his exercise regime, aimed at honing a manly body, cannot stop his premature hair loss. Jack berates him, "Why do you want to chin? What does chinning accomplish?" Heinrich replies, "What does anything accomplish? Maybe I just want to build up my body to compensate for other things" (*WN* 181). Heinrich claims that men are merely machines consisting of bundles of stimuli; however, this does not prevent him from straining to conform to the socially approved appearance of a man. Part of his masculine maturation is "learning how to determine his worth from the reactions of others" (*WN* 131). This necessitates treating his body as separate from his mind, accepting it as something to be trained, altered, and not allowed to reveal any weakness that would compromise his masculinity.

For cultural theorist Jean Baudrillard, the demands of extreme physical exertion are linked to controlling death. If man can control, even modify, his body, then he can control his destiny and distance himself from the chaos around him by harnessing raw energy rather than allowing it to inflict itself on him:

> Decidedly, joggers are the true Latter Day Saints and the protagonists of an easy-does-it Apocalypse. Nothing evokes the end of the world more than a man running straight ahead on a beach, swathed in the sounds of his walkman, cocooned in the solitary sacrifice of his energy, indifferent even to catastrophes since he expects destruction to come only as the fruit of his own efforts, from exhausting the energy of a body that has in his own eyes become useless. Primitives, when in despair, would commit suicide by swimming out to sea until they could swim no longer. The jogger contemplates suicide by running up and down the beach. His eyes are wild, saliva drips from his mouth. Do not stop him. He will either hit you or simply carry on dancing around in front of you like a man possessed.[1]

Baudrillard's thoughts on running are epitomized by Jack: "It felt strange to be running. I hadn't run in many years and didn't recognize my body in this new format, didn't recognize the world beneath my feet, hard-surfaced and abrupt. I turned a corner and picked up speed, aware of floating bulk. Up, down, life, death. My robe flew behind me" (WN 186). While running, Jack feels the paradoxical mixing of fear and elation that Baudrillard points out, the jarring, limited earth contrasting with boundless floating air. He senses his death as intimately linked to the ground and its boundaries: "a heaviness in my legs that seemed the very pull of the earth, its most intimate and telling judgement, the law of falling bodies" (WN 227). Although Jack is no jogger and is running only to catch up with a colleague, his articulation of the way the physical exertion makes him feel is acutely pertinent. The mix of fear and elation, dread and enjoyment resonates with the physical extremity of sexual activity's propensity to push pleasure over the edge into oblivion and therefore the perceived need to control, contain, and define.

Masculine identity via sexuality

DeLillo's male characters' sexual performances fulfill George Bataille's assertion that "Men act in order to be."[2] In Underworld one of Nick's early girlfriends accepts his need to display his potency constantly with acts of random sexual performance: "She knew he'd had sex with other girls, handjobs, blowjobs, whatever else, putting it in, taking it out, putting it in, keeping it in, bareback, rubber" (U 704). In Cosmopolis Eric attempts to have sex with all his lovers on the last day of his life, resulting in encounters which are neither original nor spontaneous, but instead planned, calculated interpretations of available influences. Even his apparently accidental encounter with his new wife, with whom he supposes he ought to be having more sex, lacks spontaneity. When it finally happens, in a dark alley on a demolition site, the fact that they have both just taken part in a mass naked scene for a film emphasizes the scripted nature of the encounter, complete with cameras and directions; they are performers: "That's what this resembled, the next scene in the black-and-white film that was being screened in theatres worldwide" (C 177).

Similarly, in *White Noise*, Jack fondles his wife, Babette, in the supermarket queue, the kitchen, the car, anywhere he remembers to act out the sexual facets of his masculinity. He creates and recreates himself through his desire for a created other, primarily by fulfilling stereotypes: himself constructed as Important Scholar and Babette as Dirty Blonde complete with wild hair, legwarmers, and erotic literature. Outside stimulation is required, from props and memories, to stimulate Jack's performance as an acceptable male; there is no spontaneity – instead, a script is self-inflicted in line with society's enforced norm. Part of this is trying to conform with the images deflected back from his sexual partners and being what they want him to be: "As the male partner I think it's my responsibility to please" (WN 28). His feelings of inadequacy are fired by his pursuit of a unity and completeness that never existed. This fantasy of sexual rapport masks the lack in both the other and the self, resulting in Jack creating a romantic narrative structure to act out around his unsatisfactory life.

Jack fears that the onrush of death will precede satisfaction, and this prompts his sexual performances. The compulsion of sex is linked to a fascination with death, born of the similar feelings that both embody: extreme release and lack of control. Jack says of sex and death that he would "hate to think they were inextricably linked" (WN 217), yet his irrational behavior suggests he has already acknowledged their alliance. Bataille, whose writings center on the life-shaping power of the fear of death, would see Jack's behavior as demonstrating a certain typicality, as a man "constantly in fear of himself,"[3] attempting masculine definition by being "the mirror of death."[4]

Sex and death are further linked through their shared predisposition for being unknowable. The impossibility of knowing the full intimacy of death, or indeed sex, requires that men (like George in *Underworld*) must put themselves at stake to obtain satisfaction, fulfillment, even knowledge. DeLillo describes the shooting of George as "all about risk, of course, the spirit of the dare ..." (U 781). Such risk-taking compromises scripted performance, the safety of any such performance instantly undermined by the vastness of what seems unknowable when pleasure is aligned with uncertainty and chance. As Heinrich wisely states, "knowledge changes every day"

(WN 280). Part of the mediation of accepted masculine images is that men need to keep permanently tuned in for the next installment. Rather than this safe drip-feed of the evolving outline for perfect manliness, Bataille insists that men must take risks if they want to find out more than they already know or experience more than they are already experiencing. Acting out safe identities must be forfeited: "'Communication' cannot take place from one full and intact being to another: it requires beings who have put the being within themselves *at stake*, have placed it at the limit of death, of nothingness."[5] In *Libra* Oswald demonstrates Heinrich's respect for knowledge, spending "serious time at the library" (WN 33); however, he realizes that risks must be taken if you are to make your mark and rise above the stereotype, even facing a death attempt to prove his seriousness about eschewing his constructed identity in order to adopt what one of his Russian interrogators calls "A second and safer identity" (166). Although described as "safe," this identity requires him to face death.

Masculine identity via death

The fear of death and the subsequent fear of sex's potential also to overwhelm are irrevocably tied to a fear of letting go of the comfort of planned and scripted constructions. These constructions are control mechanisms designed to subdue fear. Jack is attracted to the comfort of ignorance: "Does knowledge of impending death make life precious? What good is a preciousness based on fear and anxiety? It's an anxious quivering thing" (WN 284). He questions whether fear is another word for self-awareness and, consequently, risk-taking a pastime designed to make risk-takers feel more alive, more tangible and clearly aware of themselves. This perhaps explains his son's friend Orest Mercator choosing to sit in a cage full of deadly snakes in order to make his emotions comply with his own construction of life. Jack demonstrates recklessness himself by stealing a car and running red lights, to "escape the pull of the earth, the gravitational leaf-flutter that brings us hourly closer to dying. Simply stop obeying" (WN 303). Nick's statement in *Underworld* reiterates the tendency for stereotypical masculine responsibilities to tie down and stultify: "I long for the days of disarray, when I didn't give a damn or a fuck or a farthing ... the days of disorder. I want them back, the days when I was alive on the earth, rippling in the quick of my skin, heedless and real ... angry and ready all the time, a danger to others and a mystery to myself" (U 806–10).

Identity is a performance, intrinsically fake and with the potential to therefore be safe. In *Libra* Oswald struggles to fit in, a loner who is bullied by his peers, the system, even family members. It is undoubtedly safer to try to blend in with the accepted clothes, hair, and accent. Win Everett in *Underworld* tellingly calls this fitting in "Spying on ourselves" (*U* 18), reiterating the self-awareness and self-policing behind constructing identities with a view to being accepted. Recklessness is associated with reality, if such an elusive notion is attainable. Jack is aware of the build-up of anger within him and, while he does not question its authenticity, he does sense an impending implosion. His way of projecting the free play of this surplus energy, of what Bataille terms "an unbroken animal that cannot be trained,"[6] into an outward explosion is by shooting Willie Mink in a radical release of energy that confronts destructive potential, while at the same time adhering to what is expected of a man whose wife is an adulteress. In *The Accursed Share* (1988), Bataille discusses such energy as being "always in excess."[7] This excess circulates, waiting to be squandered or recycled:

> Life suffocates within limits that are too close; it aspires in manifold ways to an impossible growth; it releases a steady flow of excess resources, possibly involving large squanderings of energy. The limit of growth being reached, life, without being in a closed container, at least enters into ebullition: Without exploding, its extreme exuberance pours out in a movement always bordering on explosion.[8]

Recycling is an option that DeLillo's male characters frequently turn to. Benno, in *Cosmopolis*, builds his surroundings from recycled objects; Nick, in *Underworld*, creates his professional persona from recycling waste products. Jack, in *White Noise*, claims material goods to be intolerable burdens yet is powerless to resist buying goods to replace what he throws away. The recycling is not limited to material goods, but extends to styles, events, and beliefs in the form of parody, pastiche, and déjà vu, even a recycling of desire. Jacques Lacan connects this recycling to the manner in which humans learn how to read images as part of a developing sense of the various constructed versions of "Me" and "I." These images of self become thoroughly assimilated into life as empty reflections that can be appropriated. This means that they are used in the formation and reduplication of relationships between humans, both with others and with the objects around them, part of the creation of varying forms of reality.[9] The inherent falseness and reconstituted nature of images ensure that they negate any aspirations of authenticity. This lack of authenticity cancels any claim for feeling genuine desire, simultaneously ensuring that men are uncomfortably aware of the restricted dimensions of that which deserves to be the *object* of this contrived desire. That which is worthy of desire is as much a mediated image as is the ideal male. It is difficult to cast DeLillo's men in this role given their leanings toward inadequacy, sexual promiscuity, acquisitiveness, selfishness, incest, coldness in relationships, violence, vandalism, and even murder.

Masculine identity via violence

DeLillo's fiction abounds with violent acts, the priority being "which body crushes the other" (*U* 797). This swaggering masculinity results in seventeen-year-old Nick taking machismo to its limits by fatally shooting an acquaintance. Many of the violent acts are performed by men against themselves. For example, Eric in *Cosmopolis* demands that one of his bodyguards shoots him with a stun gun, he shoots another of the bodyguards himself, and then shoots himself in the hand, before being shot and killed; also in the narrative a man burns himself to death; Jack, in *White Noise*, shoots Mink and facilitates his own wounding by giving Mink the gun, going directly against the advice his colleague Murray Siskind has proffered that killing Mink will preserve his own life; in *Underworld* George provides the gun for Nick to shoot him with; Oswald in *Libra* almost willfully allows himself to be set-up and sacrificed as a fall guy, instantaneously shooter and shot at and Rey Hartke, in *The Body Artist* (2001), shoots himself. These acts echo Bataille's proclamation, "I imagine myself covered with blood, broken but transfigured and in agreement with the world, both as prey and as jaw of TIME, which ceaselessly kills as it is ceaselessly killed."[10] There is an acceptance of the circularity of violence, pain and self-conscious identity formation. The violent act becomes part of the performance, planned and rehearsed in the mind's eye, but the pain inflicted pushes the experience of that performance into the realms of the unrehearsed (hence the need, illustrated in *White Noise* by SIMUVAC, to use the actual in order to rehearse for the imagined). The ability of pain to hurt and shock gives it a destabilizing power and the potential to cause something like genuine spontaneity:

> The world collapsed inward, all those vivid textures and connections buried in mounds of ordinary stuff. I was disappointed. Hurt, stunned and disappointed. What had happened to the higher plane of energy in which I'd carried out my scheme? The pain was searing. Blood covered my forearm, wrist and hand. I staggered back, moaning, watching blood drip from the tips of my fingers. I was troubled and confused. (*WN* 313)

Jack feels let down. He has carried out society's expectation by avenging his wife's infidelity, so why is he left feeling nothing but pain, fear, and confusion? Obeying social pressures to conform to stereotypical identities is never satisfactory; no performance can ever be good enough as the image of what is normal and what is perfect changes and evolves. DeLillo's men gravitate toward the force and violence traditionally expected of them, but it is an unpleasant surprise to find that this violence does not solve anything or give the real world any more clarity. Violence against the self has to escalate into death and self-annihilation before anything new and unmediated is revealed. Jack's search for an intense connection with physicality, "the visceral jolt" (WN 308), becomes too real when Mink returns his fire, agonizingly shattering his wrist. The intensity of the pain and luminous red blood forces the would-be murderer to divert from his carefully scripted and contained actions. Indeed, Jack saves Mink by taking him to hospital, the exact opposite of his plan.

In Cosmopolis the fatal attack on Nikolai Kaganovich and the stabbing of Arthur Rapp, live on the television money channel, are events that are televised and watched repeatedly. However, they take the viewer no closer to experiencing death. Only those providing the spectacle go beyond the violent end. Masculinity is mediated and copied, with television serving as the most prolific purveyor of images: "The flow is constant ... For most people there are only two places in the world. Where they live and their TV set" (WN 66). But there has to be a fall guy. It is not merely about acting, and those who are viewed as behaving in a validly brave and physical manner, even to the point of death, have to actually die. There is nothing fake or inauthentic about this: even when the death is part of a filmed and mediated performance, it is still death.

Ironically, while technology has the potential to save humans and enhance life, what it seems more commonly to do is frighten and alienate us from our own (frail) bodies. The television is used to uphold desirable masculinity, making actual men feel inadequate. Jack illustrates this in White Noise, his technological health check distancing him from his own dying (WN 141). Similarly, in Cosmopolis the spycams in Eric's car reveal events to him before they happen: "Eric watched himself on the oval screen below the spycam, running his thumb along his chinline ... he realized queerly that he'd just placed his thumb on his chinline, a second or two after he'd seen it on-screen" (C 22). This alteration of accepted chronology serves to distance Eric from his image, his identity, and his life. Mediated images are never straightforward. Furthermore, they are filtered through preconceived notions, as Victor Seidler terms it: "We can be so used to constructing our experience according to how we think that things ought to be, that it can be difficult to acknowledge any emotions and feelings that go against these images."[11] Cosmopolis suggests a world turned full-circle where the sophisticated technology of voice-activated guns, mobile offices, and constant surveillance, rather than enhancing life, mitigates against its full and satisfying development. Masculine identity is part of this struggle; DeLillo's men perfectly encapsulate the conflicting pressures of society and soul. The "messages in his genes" that Jack refers to in White Noise are as dead and contested as the "history" he credits them with, yet men still strive to behave in the way they feel they ought to in order to fulfill their traditional roles, tellingly illustrated by Jack's wistful fantasizing about manual skills and less humorously by Oswald's willingness to kill and be killed.

Notes

1. Jean Baudrillard, *America* (London: Verso, 1999), p. 38.
2. Georges Bataille, *Eroticism*, trans. Mary Dalwood (London: Boyars, 1987), p. 171.
3. Ibid., p. 7.
4. Georges Bataille, *Visions of Excess: Selected Writings 1927–1939*, ed. Allan Stoekl, trans. Allan Stoekl, C. R. Lovitt and D. M. Leslie, Jr. (Minneapolis: University of Minnesota Press, 1985), p. 239.
5. Georges Bataille writing about Nietzsche, quoted by Jacques Derrida in *Writing and Difference* (London: Routledge, 1978), p. 263.
6. Georges Bataille, *The Accursed Share*, trans. Robert Hurley (London: Zone Books, 1988), p. 24.
7. Ibid., p. 23.
8. Ibid., p. 30.
9. Jacques Lacan, *Ecrits: A Selection*, trans. Alan Sheridan (New York: Norton, 1977), pp. 1–8.
10. Bataille, *Visions*, p. 239.
11. Victor J. Seidler, *Unreasonable Men: Masculinity and Social Theory* (London: Routledge, 1994), p. 138.

136

10

MARK OSTEEN

DeLillo's Dedalian artists

When Don DeLillo was asked in a 1979 interview – the first he ever gave – why he shunned publicity and rarely spoke about his work, he replied, "Silence, exile, cunning, and so on."[1] He was quoting James Joyce's *A Portrait of the Artist as a Young Man* (1916), wherein protagonist Stephen Dedalus famously vows to use those three "arms" to defend his art from the intrusions of nationalism, religion, and domesticity.[2] DeLillo's novels about artists – *Great Jones Street* (1973), *Mao II* (1991), and *The Body Artist* (2001) – sustain a dialogue with these modernist, "Dedalian" aesthetic principles. Each novel depicts the lure of silence and exile, as each artist figure coils inward in order to spring outward, often with a new work that redefines his or her artistic practice.

This pattern indeed forms a link in an intertextual chain that leads back to the Greek myth from which Stephen takes his name. Daedalus was, of course, the artificer who built a nearly inescapable labyrinth for King Minos of Crete, where he kept the half-bull, half-human Minotaur and fed him human sacrifices. Taking one victim's place, the Athenian prince Theseus killed the Minotaur and escaped afterward using a thread given to him by Minos's daughter, Ariadne. Later, Daedalus himself was imprisoned in the labyrinth but, by fashioning wings from feathers and wax, escaped with his son, Icarus. Failing to heed his father's warnings, Icarus flew too close to the sun; his wax wings melted and he fell into the sea. Daedalus subsequently put aside his wings, but after enviously murdering his clever nephew Perdix, he was transformed by Athena into a bird.

DeLillo's artists repeatedly reenact this pattern of seclusion and emergence, entrapment and escape, and their metamorphoses render them temporarily monstrous, malformed, or moribund before they die or emerge in a new guise. DeLillo's artists embody both the Minotaur and Daedalus, who leaves the labyrinth but loses something priceless in his flight to freedom. Thus in *Great Jones Street*, rock star Bucky Wunderlick quits his band midtour, exiling himself in a tiny room far from the "tropics of fame" (*GJS* 4);

hoping to embrace silence, he finds that his withdrawal only permits others to exploit him. His planned return leaves Bucky a half-myth, half-mute. Bill Gray, the missing novelist of *Mao II*, likewise discovers that his self-imposed exile has become a trap he can escape only through self-immolation. However, this novel – in which crowd photographs are interspersed at certain chapter and section breaks – alters the circular trajectory of *Great Jones Street* by presenting another, more viable model for artistic engagement in the photographer who takes Bill's portrait. *The Body Artist* consummates this pattern, dramatizing how protagonist Lauren Hartke reuses her past to fly from the labyrinth of grief and engender living art from the very stuff of death. In these novels DeLillo demonstrates the limits of silence, exile, and cunning, and, by adopting the same forms he anatomizes – rock music, photography, journalism – reveals that artists must both engage their society and maintain a critical detachment from its blinding glare and deafening buzz.

Wordless things: *Great Jones Street*

During his final, abortive tour, Bucky Wunderlick's fans only mimed their screams, prompting him to envision a future of "huge stadium[s] filled with wildly rippling bodies, all totally silent" (*GJS* 2). Taking a cue from them, he withdraws, planning to "return with a new language for them to speak" or perhaps to encourage them to "seek a divine silence attendant to my own" (*GJS* 3). In the first eleven chapters of the novel, Bucky, ensconced in his barren room on Great Jones Street, tests what Susan Sontag terms an "aesthetics of silence," in which "disavowal of the work becom[es] a new source of validity, a certificate of unchallengeable seriousness." Through silence, she writes, an artist attempts to free himself "from servile bondage to the world, which appears as patron, client, consumer, antagonist, arbiter, and distorter of his work."[3] Figures playing exactly these roles swirl and swarm about Bucky, attempting to steal his music, exploit his name, or sacrifice him for their ends. Bucky's silence thus becomes what Sontag calls "a form of speech ... an element in a dialogue" with his fans, his agent, his girlfriend, and finally with himself.[4]

Bucky has long been plunging toward silence or meaninglessness: as reproduced in the novel's "Superslick Mind Contracting Media Kit," his lyrics have devolved from politically charged laments for Viet Cong women to scalding confessions (*GJS* 111–12) to those of his latest album, *Pee-Pee-Maw-Maw*, which contains lines such as "Blank mumble blat / Babble song, babble song ... / The beast is loose / Least is best" (*GJS* 118). Most recently, he recorded the already legendary Mountain Tapes, which germinated as he sat "wedged in a block of silence" in an anechoic chamber far from the city (*GJS* 121). His ascetic discipline ultimately yielded "strange little autistic ramblings," "genuinely infantile" lyrics offering "[t]ributes to [his] own mute following" (*GJS* 148). These, he believes, are "[m]aiden words" that will restore his authentic voice (*GJS* 203). But he soon learns what a character in an earlier DeLillo novel, *Americana* (1971), calls a "lesson in the effect of echoes" (*A* 58): that "the less you say, the more you are" (*GJS* 128) – that is, silence and exile are also commodities. As the novel proceeds, the Mountain Tapes – brought to Bucky by his girlfriend, Opel – and an experimental word-blocking drug become interchangeable symbols of his quest to muffle the deafening echoes of fame and quell the marketplace's insatiable appetite.

Two objects, a phonograph record and a telephone, represent Bucky's current state. As I have argued elsewhere, the lyrics of his song "Diamond Stylus" figure him as a spinning phonograph record "Circling into word-time" (*GJS* 112).[5] As the central hole in the disk, Bucky no longer speaks but only enables the speech of others by permitting himself to be picked up and reused time and again. Caught in this futile, labyrinthine spinning, Bucky sees suicide as his sole exit. Like the vinyl record, his room telephone is a technology created to transmit sound. The silent telephone represents his alienation from the world at large: disconnected, unable to speak, though "made for no other reason," it becomes "an object rather than an instrument," its descent into "total dumbness" rendering it beautiful, mysterious (*GJS* 31). Bucky aspires to the condition of the telephone, whose dial-tone seems to him a mode of "silence endowed with acoustical properties" (*GJS* 166). Eventually, however, it draws him back into the market's web, becoming a string that his manager, Globke, can use to manipulate him into going back on tour and delivering new "product."

Two human figures represent the perils Bucky faces and the new identity he hopes to forge. His upstairs neighbor, hack writer Eddie Fenig, exemplifies the artist enslaved by the market. Unlike the taciturn Wunderlick, Fenig cannot stop talking; in his writing, he is not a man of letters but a "man of numbers" (*GJS* 51), defining his work by sheer quantity, compulsively producing whatever he believes will feed the market's unslakable maw, from pornography for children to financial writing for millionaires. For Fenig, the market is a Minotaur, a "living organism" that "sucks things in and then spews them up" (*GJS* 27), not a labyrinth but a demonic merry-go-round that "spins and gyrates ... going faster and faster and throwing off anybody who can't hold on" (*GJS* 141). Fenig is DeLillo's mordant early portrait of the artist as a facsimile, a two-dimensional figure resembling the picture-bearing bubblegum cards that the cynical drug dealer Watney carries with him. Bucky speculates that in Fenig's closet are "four more Fenigs, laced, hooded, neatly creased" (*GJS* 223).

Bucky's other alter-ego is his downstairs neighbor, Mrs. Micklewhite's severely disabled son. This character cannot write, or even form a word, yet his muteness evokes Bucky's most human responses. In an epiphanic moment, Bucky encounters this boy, whose haunting cries have obtruded occasionally from below to remind him of the "beauty and horror of wordless things" (*GJS* 52). Drawn by his "embryonic beauty" and fascinated by his "radical divestment," Bucky touches the boy, hoping to find a clue to his own unborn self and the maiden words he seeks. Although the encounter ends sardonically, with Mrs. Micklewhite's warning, "Careful, he bites" (*GJS* 162), this scene, occurring at the center of the novel, initiates Bucky's movement out of the labyrinth. The Micklewhite boy is the only character who does not respond at all to Bucky's notoriety, and the only one who entirely eludes commodification (his father once tried to sell him to a carnival, but "who'd buy him?" his mother asks rhetorically [*GJS* 134]). Similar personages appear in many of DeLillo's novels – from the numerous bizarre, childlike characters in *Ratner's Star* (1976) and nine-year-old novelist Tap Axton in *The Names* (1982), to Jack Gladney's ululating toddler Wilder in *White Noise* (1985) and the aphasic Mr. Tuttle of *The Body Artist*. Uttering what DeLillo describes as "the word beyond speech,"[6] these characters serve as models for DeLillo's artists, who try to emulate their quasi-autistic conditions in order to rediscover their voices or acquire new ones.

Although he eventually imitates the Micklewhite boy's muteness, Bucky's quest to elude commodification fails when a violent cultlike group called the Happy Valley Farm Commune injects him with the silence-inducing drug that has spurred many of the novel's plot machinations. "[A]colytes of [his] silence" (*GJS* 194), Happy Valley has erected Bucky as a symbol of "the idea of privacy" (*GJS* 193); but because "there's no silence with the tapes on the market," they must blow up the factory where the tapes are held (*GJS* 246). Bucky, of course, half-desires this treatment and has voiced his sacrificial yearnings on the Mountain Tapes. Perhaps, he feels, this drug-induced muteness will finally release him from the echo chamber of fame. Enjoying his newly infantile state, Bucky envisions himself as a kind of "living chant" (*GJS* 264). But the market is more cunning than he, turning wordlessness itself into his "act" and perpetuating rumors about a saintly Wunderlick wandering the urban desert performing good deeds. Worse: the drug's effects eventually wear off.

Great Jones Street is DeLillo's first analysis of the problems with Stephen Dedalus's modernist aesthetic principles. Instead of permitting Wunderlick to find his voice, silence and exile merely allow others to put words into his mouth, drowning out his words with echoes. This lesson in the effect of echoes is one that DeLillo's artists are repeatedly taught, but learn only when, as in *The Body Artist*, they are cunning enough to incorporate those echoes – of their audience, of their own suffering, of other artists' voices – and thereby foster a dialogue with their community. By doing so, they locate themselves neither in the tropics of fame nor in the chilly regions of exile, but in a temperate zone between the two.

Portraits of the artist: *Mao II*

The garishly colored Andy Warhol silkscreens of Mao Zedong that decorate the dustjacket cover of *Mao II* recall Watney's bubblegum cards and alert us to this later novel's major themes: the nature of authority and the power of image-makers to deface or remodel that authority. *Mao II* revisits the themes of *Great Jones Street*, but whereas in the earlier novel DeLillo borrows from the procedures and promotional tactics of pop music, in the later one he incorporates photographs – of a vast gathering in Tiananmen Square, a mass wedding, the Hillsborough Stadium soccer disaster, the Ayatollah Khomeini's funeral, and three Middle Eastern boys in a Beirut bunker – to examine the social obligations of art and the pitfalls of exile. The photos also illustrate one side of what DeLillo has described as this novel's "argument about the future," which pits individual consciousness against "the mass mind" in a battle for the imagination of the world.[7] These crowd images represent one vision of postmodern authorship, in which authors do not write books but employ visual and electronic media to form their followers' minds, glorify themselves, and incite and publicize violence. Among these "spectacular authors," as I have termed them,[8] are the Rev. Sun Myung Moon, who presides over the mass wedding depicted in the opening scene; Warhol, whose cunning manipulations of his and other famous images provide a counterpoint to novelist Bill Gray's fumbling attempts to elude, then exploit his fame; Khomeini, whose scowling face inspires mourners to outlandish acts of violence or grief; and a terrorist leader named Abu Rashid.

The other side of the argument is embodied by Gray, who published two slim novels thirty years earlier and has since gone into hiding. In claiming that the "writer who won't show his face is … playing God's own trick" (*M* 37), Gray is alluding to Stephen Dedalus's notorious description of the godlike author who exists "within or behind or beyond or above his handi-work, invisible, refined out of existence."[9] But Gray (sometimes mistakenly viewed as a DeLillo stand-in) represents the death throes of this modernist model of authorship. For one thing, the self-exiled Gray no longer feels the pulse that would propel his art. Nor does he need a Micklewhite boy to expose his failure, for his laboriously composed but inert, unpublished novel reminds him of it daily. A "humpbacked, hydrocephalic" thing (*M* 55), a "cretin, a distort" (*M* 92), the mound of typescript embodies the monstrous "second self" that his exile has spawned (*M* 37). Moreover, as with Wunderlick (and the real-life J. D. Salinger), his disappearance has only fed public curiosity: as *Mao II* opens, "Bill is at the height of his fame" (*M* 52). Perhaps worst of all, his withdrawal has made him subject to the machinations of Scott Martineau – his fan, factotum, and finally captor.

First seen scanning bookstore shelves "for Bill" (*M* 20) – that is, for the commodified Bill represented on his dust jackets – Scott is Bill's personal Happy Valley Farm Commune, a manservant-cum-kidnapper who uses Bill to absorb his own fear. Scott embodies Bill's doubt and self-hatred, constantly denigrating his unpublished novel and maintaining that "the withheld work of art is the only eloquence left" (*M* 67). The other denizen of Bill's hideaway is Karen Janney, one of the brides at the Moonie wedding, whom Scott found wandering, freshly deprogrammed, in White Cloud, Kansas, a village commemorated in a famous Eve Arnold photograph.[10] Whereas Arnold's book, in which the photograph appeared, documented the vanishing ethnic and folk cultures of America's heartland, Karen, according to Bill, comes from "the future" (*M* 85): first matched with her Korean husband via a photograph, she is the perfect consumer of the novel's spectacular images and serves as our eyes when the book's photos appear in the narrative.

Scott first spies photographer Brita Nilsson in New York, standing "slightly apart" from a bustling crowd (*M* 22). This physical position adumbrates DeLillo's metaphorical position regarding the artist's relation to society: although among the crowd, she remains somewhat detached from it, buffeted by its currents but not immersed in them. Gray is the latest subject in her project to photograph "the unknown, the untranslated, the inaccessible, the politically suspect, the hunted, the silenced" writers of the world (*M* 66) – a species count, as it were, of a soon-to-be extinct breed, an elegiac enterprise rather like Arnold's. At once flattered and threatened by her camera, Gray tells Brita that the photographic session is "like a wake," with himself as the actor "made up for the laying-out" (*M* 42) and remains suspicious throughout, apparently agreeing with Sontag that "to photograph people is to violate them" and that "all photographs are *memento mori*."[11]

Yet the novel's opening setpiece, the mass wedding in Yankee Stadium, depicts a grander motive and outcome. Here the chanting mass seems "lifted by the picture-taking, the forming of aura," attaining an afterlife through the camera's ministry (*M* 15). Similarly, but less ironically, Brita's aim is less that of a mortician, as Bill believes, than that of a physician hoping to revive her subjects' human shambles "by the energy of her seeing" (*M* 37). Although the novel acknowledges the degree to which photographs package their subjects and turn persons into objects of consumption, Brita's photos nonetheless reveal a serious artist at work. Late in the novel, for example, after Bill has escaped from his handlers in a painfully misguided attempt to help free another captive writer, Scott examines the contact sheets of the photo session and sees in them glimpses of "Brita thinking, a little anatomy of mind and eye": a photographer attempting to "deliver her subject" by making pictures that "erased his seclusion ... and made him over" (M 221). Brita's photographs, then, are self-portraits of an artist residing "within or behind or beyond or above" the handiwork that bestows what Laura Barrett describes as a "kind of immortality."[12]

In contrast, Bill loses control over both his writing and his body. Moving eastward in his quixotic attempt to participate in a reading honoring Jean-Claude Julien, a Swiss poet taken hostage by a terrorist group, Bill realizes that writing has not only failed to protect him but is "bad for the soul" and "narrow[s] everything to failure and its devastations. Gave your cunning an edge of treachery and your jellyfish heart a reason to fall deeper into silence" (M 198). His devotion to Dedalian principles has devolved into cowardice and even betrayed his muse. Writing for himself alone has "caused his life to disappear"; far from offering rejuvenation, it has become a brand of murder or vampirism (M 215). Caught in this self-fashioned labyrinth, Bill is less Daedalus than self-cannibalizing Minotaur.

Yet even in the midst of his disintegration, Bill mounts a spirited defense of modernist authority in a series of conversations with a man named George Haddad. Earlier, Bill had remarked on a "curious knot that binds novelists and terrorists. In the West we become famous effigies as our books lose the power to shape and influence ... Now bomb-makers and gunmen have taken that territory. They make raids on human consciousness. What writers used to do before we were all incorporated" (M 41). With Haddad, he continues, "The danger they represent equals our own failure to be dangerous" and points to Samuel Beckett as the last writer to "shape the way we think and see. After him, the major work involves midair explosions and crumbled buildings" (M 157). Putting aside the eerie prescience of these words in the wake of September 11, 2001, it is hard to credit Gray's assertions. Were novelists ever so powerful? Was the notoriously reticent and difficult Beckett really a major influence on mass consciousness? Haddad (a terrorist sympathizer, if not worse) picks up Gray's thread to declare that terrorists are "heroes for our time"; shrewdly appropriating Bill's modernist ideal, he even claims that novelists like Bill admire "their discipline and cunning." Only such "lethal believer[s]," Haddad argues, resist incorporation by the media and capitalism (M 157).

Although Bill's rather desperate defense of the novel's "democratic shout" against Haddad's chilling celebration of "total authority" is poignant (*M* 158–9), it seems unconvincing, given his own refusal to engage with other voices. Yet Haddad's portrayal of the terrorist as a principled solitary outlaw is even more specious. For postmodern terrorists are creatures of the global communications network, spectacular authors who, without television and the internet, could not disseminate images of their work, publicize their political messages, or recruit followers. Moreover, as Haddad himself betrays when he discusses trading Bill for Julien, terrorists treat hostages as bargaining chips, fungible commodities in the same global marketplace they claim to oppose. The novelist/terrorist polarity, then, is false on many levels, not only because it perpetuates false notions of both but also because it ignores how terrorism relies upon the very instruments of the capitalism it excoriates.

Bill's ignominious death after being hit by a car in Athens (he expires anonymously on a boat en route to Beirut) does nothing to bolster his case and leaves Scott in possession of his manuscripts, photos, and legacy. Scott decides to allow Bill's "aura" to deepen and gather force by withholding the documents from the public. Bill's death has, ironically, refreshed Scott: is it not wonderful, he concludes, that life is so "filled with second chances" (*M* 224). Does Bill's ignoble demise signify that novelists are irrelevant, having been supplanted by image-makers and merchants? In interviews conducted around the time of *Mao II*'s publication, DeLillo gives seemingly contradictory responses, as if engaging in what Frank Lentricchia and Jody McAuliffe call "self-argument."[13] Thus in one interview he echoes Gray, insisting that writers must refuse to be "incorporated into the ambient noise. This is why we need the writer in opposition, the novelist who writes against power ... against the corporation or the state or the whole apparatus of assimilation."[14] But in a 1993 interview, he maintains that a writer cannot "separate himself from the crowd ... It is indispensable to be fully involved in contemporary life, to be part of the ... clash of voices."[15] To remain immersed, yet removed; involved, yet distant. How does one perform this difficult balancing act? DeLillo shapes a possible answer through Brita, who embodies the potential for an art that appropriates the tools of spectacular authors to contest their attempts to control history and subjectivity.

Although a weathervane for cultural shifts – "everything that came into her mind ... seemed at once to enter the culture, to become a painting or photograph or hairstyle or slogan" (*M* 165) – Brita is more than a trendsetter or follower, like Karen. She uses her craft to create a counternarrative to the dominant ones. Hence, in the novel's final section (the only portion narrated in the present tense), she travels to war-ravaged Beirut, a "millennial image mill" where militias fire at the photos of other militia leaders (*M* 229), to photograph terrorist leader Abu Rashid. As in the photo that frames the section – three boys in a bunker, one pointing either a gunsight or a camera viewfinder toward the viewer – image-makers and warriors seem indistinguishable. Rashid, surrounded by young boys with their heads under hoods, each wearing Rashid's photo on his shirt, boasts that they are "all children of Abu Rashid" and proclaims his ability to change history (*M* 233). But he seems not to realize that he is just as fungible as the hostages he trades: as with the Maos on the novel's jacket, photographs can transform him into a facsimile easily replaced by some other photo, some other Abu. Unlike the session with Bill, where Brita's aim was commemoration and resurrection, here she shoots Rashid to disarm him, to steal his force. Likewise, at the session's end, she removes one boy's hood and snaps his picture (*M* 236), as if to acquire the boy, to supplant Rashid's image with one she has authored, and thereby demonstrate the limits of Rashid's control. Departing, she shakes Rashid's hand, "pronouncing her name slowly" (*M* 237) as if to say, "You are nothing without me."

Brita's gesture suggests her cunning awareness of her social and political power: photographs may glorify or diminish, even figuratively murder or revivify, as the situation affords. Although they represent her mind at work, her photos also present portraits of the culture in which she does that work. Unlike Bill, whose escape from his self-created labyrinth merely leads him into another kind of prison, Brita's travels from Bill's house to New York to Beirut place her at the center of global culture, yet permit her to remain "somewhat apart," as if floating slightly above the action, shooting down. In one interview DeLillo sketched similar goals, stating, "I try to record what I see and hear and sense around me – what I feel in the currents, the electric stuff of the culture."[16] A novelist, it seems, must also be a photographer who simultaneously documents and criticizes the culture in which he resides. *Mao II* thus shows DeLillo remodeling his vision of authorship, from an ambivalent endorsement of Dedalian principles toward a negotiated compromise with the society of spectacle, in which the artist refashions the society's own tools to attain a position "within or behind or beyond or above" it. Politically and aesthetically potent works thus issue not from a solitary island but cunningly from within the culture itself.

Second chances: *The Body Artist*

In an essay published at the same time as his masterpiece *Underworld* (1997), DeLillo concludes that "Fiction is all about reliving things. It is our second chance."[17] *Underworld* bears out this contention, as DeLillo not only plumbs his early life in the Italian-American section of the Bronx but revisits and rewrites postwar American history. The novel's historical and fictional artists – provocateur Lenny Bruce, sculptor Klara Sax, graffiti writer Ismael Muñoz, film-maker Sergei Eisenstein, visionary builder/sculptor Simon Rodia – also embody second chances. Klara, for example, repaints World War II-era bombers, turning weapons of war into instruments of peace; Rodia built Watts Towers, a glorious sculpture garden-cum-monument, from cast-off bottles and crockery. Revealing the "redemptive qualities of the things we use and discard," these works also symbolize DeLillo's method of assembling *Underworld* from a montage of scenes, characters, and events (*U* 809). Watts Towers, in particular, testifies to the ideal of the second chance, to art's cunning capacity to salvage from loss something lasting.

DeLillo's compressed, poetic novel *The Body Artist* traces this process on a more personal scale, limning again DeLillo's now-familiar artistic trajectory of inward coil and outward spring, but with a variation, as protagonist Lauren Hartke flies from a labyrinth of grief by transmuting mourning into an unsettling work of performance art. She engenders her transformation through an undertaking – that is, ritual relinquishment of her husband – in which she revisits mundane conversations and minor characters from her recent life and learns to speak in a voice that is hers, paradoxically, because it issues from someone else. Her work, *Body Time*, proves how artistic cunning need not be a defensive reaction but instead may nurture a new self from the stun of intrusion. The catalyst for Lauren's rebirth is an aphasic, echolalic man whom she names Mr. Tuttle after her high school science teacher. The latest in DeLillo's gallery of disabled muses, Mr. Tuttle teaches Lauren the "[m]aiden words" she needs to germinate a new identity and inspire her audience (*GJS* 203). Through the thread left by Mr. Tuttle, Lauren discovers the Ariadne – and the Dedalus – within herself. In this novel an artist learns that lesson in the effect of echoes that DeLillo's earlier artists strained for, but failed to hear. Indeed, by echoing other works in the novel's themes and plot, DeLillo further enacts the theme of second chances and represents artistic gestation as a kind of ghostly possession.

An actor and film director who reinvented his past and lived as though identity were nothing but masquerade, Lauren's husband, Rey, was in some respects a ghost even before he died. Lauren, too, seems to lack a fixed identity, as indicated in the opening scenes of the novel, which shift from first to third to second person as Lauren and Rey prepare breakfast and depict Lauren's groping for words and shifting subjectivity. DeLillo mirrors the couple's jockeying for control over the breakfast implements using a similar battle among the birds at their window feeder. Indeed, the novel's omnipresent birds – blue jays, crows, ravens, gulls, "the color-changing birds, the name-saying birds" (*BA* 71) – come to represent Lauren's shape-shifting subjectivity and quest to shed her old skin. When she first returns to her rented house after Rey's death, everything about her seems "plunged into metamorphosis" (*BA* 36), but in fact she has barely begun her own transformation. Her friend, journalist Mariella Chapman, admonishes Lauren not to "fold up into" herself (*BA* 39), but actually Lauren needs to fold inward so that she may eventually emerge like a butterfly bursting from its pod or a bird taking wing.

What enables Lauren's artistic explosion is her relationship with Mr. Tuttle. At once ghost, projection, "heteroclite muse,"[18] symbol of Lauren's inchoate new self, and live tape recorder of her marital conversations, Mr. Tuttle is Lauren's artistic inseminator and this novel's version of the Micklewhite boy. Lauren is jolted when, soon after she finds Mr. Tuttle, she hears from his lips "the clipped delivery, the slight buzz deep in the throat, her pitch, her sound" (*BA* 50) as if he is "assuming her part in a conversation with someone" else (*BA* 51). The birds at her feeder, uneasily alert for the "jay that mimics a hawk," dramatize her unsettled condition (*BA* 53). Then, as Lauren reads Mr. Tuttle a book about childbirth, she realizes that he is speaking to her in Rey's voice and recalls that Rey once told her that "she was helping him recover his soul" (*BA* 61). Rey once said, "I regain possession of myself through you. I think like myself now, not like the man I became. I eat and sleep like myself ... when I was myself and not the other man" (*BA* 62). Mr. Tuttle, we realize, is doing the same for her, not by becoming himself but by becoming both her and Rey. She and Mr. Tuttle thus represent the two forces behind her art: she the body and he the inspiration – literally, in that he knows "how to make her husband live in the air that rushed from his lungs" (*BA* 62). Mr. Tuttle embodies inspiration as a form of ghostly possession, as a lesson in the effect of echoes.

Mr. Tuttle's ventriloquistic parroting of past conversations enables Lauren first to inhabit her grief then to stand apart from it and rehearse her new self. But he does more than echo. As the novel proceeds, Mr. Tuttle sometimes chants a haunting Heideggerian poetry: "Being here has come to me. I am with the moment, I will leave the moment ... Coming and going I am leaving ... Leaving has come to me" (*BA* 74). In these Zen-like utterances Lauren hears the "stir of true amazement ... [t]he wedge into ecstasy" (*BA* 75): that "purer" or "alternate speech" that DeLillo's artists so habitually seek.[19] Now inspired by Mr. Tuttle, Lauren begins to listen to other voices, including the stilted electronic message on Mariella's answering machine (*BA* 67), which she replays over and over, probing the relationship between electronic devices and her own entrapped condition. As with Bucky Wunderlick, these devices both symbolize her numbness and teach her to restore her voice, paradoxically, by teaching her to listen to others.

Mr. Tuttle's mixed verb tenses – as when he substitutes "it rained very much" for "it is going to rain" (*BA* 44) – and time-lapsed condition eventually begin to affect Lauren's state of mind. As if miming his temporal fluidity, she repeatedly practices "checking the time," perhaps in order to demolish the linear time that doomed her husband (*BA* 73). Yet she remains deeply ambivalent about temporality. On the one hand she seeks to scour away the past through monastic exercises that will permit her to "disappear from all her former venues of aspect and bearing and to become a blankness, a body slate erased of every past resemblance" (*BA* 84). Yet she also desires to recapture the past through Mr. Tuttle, to repossess her husband and regain her previous life. Her impulse to revive Rey climaxes when Mr. Tuttle rehearses in precise detail a conversation that Lauren and Rey held the day he died. Although she recognizes Rey's words in Mr. Tuttle's mouth, "she didn't think the man was remembering. It is happening now ... in his fracted time, and he is only reporting, helplessly, what they say." Through Mr. Tuttle's ventriloquism "Rey is alive" (*BA* 87), yet "fracted" – both broken and newly reconstituted. And just as the narrative discourse in these sentences slides from Lauren's idiom to the narrator's past tense, so the shifting verb tenses capture Lauren's perception of time's shuttling flight. But once Lauren draws inspiration from Mr. Tuttle, he begins to fade, and lose his voice; he eventually vanishes, leaving "not a single clinging breath of presence" (*BA* 96). Initially forlorn, she gradually recognizes that leaving must "come to him" in order for her new voice – which is also his – to come to her. Lauren has, indeed, incorporated Mr. Tuttle: answering the telephone, she uses "his voice, a dry piping sound, hollow-bodied, like a bird humming on her tongue" (*BA* 101). Lauren can resuscitate both Rey and Mr. Tuttle while also exorcizing her grief and guilt by undertaking – that is, at once raising and burying – both of them in *Body Time*.

In an inserted magazine profile, Mariella describes Lauren's appearance as "colorless, bloodless and ageless ... rawboned and slightly bug-eyed" (*BA* 103): in short, she resembles a newborn or a plucked bird, prepared to acquire new shape and color. According to Mariella, Lauren's work shows her "always in the process of becoming another or exploring some root identity" (*BA* 105). Among the identities that *Body Time* depicts are figures and voices from the novel's earlier pages: Mariella's answering machine, an Asian neighbor, an executive compulsively checking her watch, and, at the end, a naked man lip-syncing to a voice (probably Mr. Tuttle's) on tape. Mariella concludes that *Body Time* is "about who we are when we are not rehearsing who we are" (*BA* 110), but its metacommentary on performance is even more complex than that. Indeed, Lauren's appropriation of Mr. Tuttle's voice is not exactly a performance but a blend of acting and being: since his voice echoed hers, she can now become herself by using him as her phone or recording device. Further, the novel's many shifts in narrative angle – DeLillo's own shape-shifting, birdlike motion – suggest that there is no "who" who is not performing: that, like certain birds, humans become themselves only by imitating and appropriating others. We are, in short, an effect of echoes.

DeLillo's text is also an effect of echoes, for its intertextual threads include the *Alcestis* of Euripides, Sophocles's *Ajax*, and Beckett's *Krapp's Last Tape* (1958), among many others.[20] More importantly, it is crucial for understanding DeLillo's presentation of the artist's relation to society that Lauren's art is not the solitary work of a novelist, nor even a two-person dialogue such as those that Brita Nilsson's photo shoots engender, but avant-garde theater. Intentionally "obscure, slow, difficult and sometimes agonizing" (*BA* 109), *Body Time*'s lingering, stuttering, then epileptic movements are designed to disrupt narrative time and explode theatrical conventions. Emerging from Lauren's grief in order to transmute it, *Body Time* embodies second chances not only for Lauren, who revives and undertakes Mr. Tuttle and Rey, but also for audience members, who cannot watch passively but must engage in a spirited give-and-take with Lauren's impersonations and subversions. Lauren's echoes thus reverberate against the audience's experiences to enable the formation – even if briefly – of a genuine community. As Mariella writes, the piece is "about you and me. What begins in solitary otherness becomes familiar and even personal" (*BA* 109–10). It is a wake for dying selves.

DeLillo's embrace of theater (also shown by his plays *The Day Room* [1986], *Valparaiso* [1999], and *Love-Lies-Bleeding* [2006]) therefore marks a decided movement away from Dedalian defensiveness toward an embrace of social engagement. Bucky Wunderlick remains mostly a passive recipient of his fans' fetishes and fears; Brita Nilsson's photographs, although they fashion a form of afterlife, cannot renew themselves with each viewing. Lauren's art, in contrast, exists solely in the interaction between her metamorphoses and her audience's expectations and responses, so that each performance is different. The artist's primary engagement with society, DeLillo suggests here, takes place through a process of renewal that is itself constantly renewed, an act of salvage that, even when motivated by grief or despair, transcends death. Hence, as Lauren emerges from her labyrinth, she does not fly solo but carries passengers with her, thereby achieving an art that lies "outside the strict limits of the written word" and beyond Dedalus's self-protective formulation.[21] The Dedalian artist is liberated not by exile and silence but by a cunning collaboration with his or her audience.

Notes

1. Thomas LeClair, "An Interview with Don DeLillo," in Thomas DePietro, ed., *Conversations with Don DeLillo* (Jackson: University Press of Mississippi, 2005), p. 4.
2. James Joyce, *A Portrait of the Artist as a Young Man: Text, Criticism, and Notes*, ed. Chester G. Anderson (New York: Viking, 1968), p. 247.
3. Susan Sontag, "The Aesthetics of Silence," in *A Susan Sontag Reader* (New York: Vintage, 1982), p. 183.
4. Ibid., p. 187.
5. Mark Osteen, *American Magic and Dread: Don DeLillo's Dialogue with Culture* (Philadelphia: University of Pennsylvania Press, 2000), p. 52.
6. LeClair, "An Interview," p. 10.
7. Vince Passaro, "Dangerous Don DeLillo," in DePietro, ed., *Conversations*, p. 81.
8. Osteen, *American Magic*, p. 193.
9. Joyce, *A Portrait*, p. 215.
10. Eve Arnold, *In America* (New York: Alfred A. Knopf, 1983), p. 118.
11. Susan Sontag, *On Photography* (New York: Farrar, Straus and Giroux, 1977), pp. 14–15.
12. Laura Barrett, "'Here But Also There': Subjectivity and Postmodern Space in *Mao II*," *Modern Fiction Studies* 45 (1999), p. 796.
13. Frank Lentricchia and Jody McAuliffe, *Crimes of Art and Terror* (Chicago: University of Chicago Press, 2003), p. 36.
14. Adam Begley, "The Art of Fiction CXXXV: Don DeLillo," in DePietro, ed., *Conversations*, p. 97.
15. Maria Nadotti, "An Interview with Don DeLillo," in DePietro, ed., *Conversations*, p. 110.
16. Begley, "The Art of Fiction," p. 107.
17. Don DeLillo, "The Power of History," *New York Times Magazine* (September 7, 1997), p. 63.
18. David Cowart, *Don DeLillo: The Physics of Language* (Athens: University of Georgia Press, 2002), p. 204. For a comprehensive list of critical views of Tuttle, see Laura Di Prete, "Don DeLillo's *The Body Artist*: Performing the Body, Narrating Trauma," *Contemporary Literature* 46.3 (2005), p. 484.
19. LeClair, "An Interview with Don DeLillo," p. 8.
20. Mark Osteen, "Echo Chamber: Undertaking *The Body Artist*," *Studies in the Novel* 37 (2005), pp. 65, 68–9, 77.
21. Don DeLillo, "The Artist Naked in a Cage," *New Yorker* (May 26, 1997), p. 6.

11

DAVID COWART

DeLillo and the power of language

In Don DeLillo's first novel, *Americana* (1971), the narrator remembers juvenile inebriation as a slipping into "the river which is language without thought" (*A* 189). The figure recurs in *The Names* (1982), in which, commenting on the displacement of Aramaic, "the language of Jesus," by Arabic, the language of Mohammed, a character declares, "The river of language is God" (*N* 150,152). Neither of these pronouncements quite makes sense – unless, as DeLillo intends, one pauses to reconsider familiar or received ideas about language, what it means, and how it works. Whoever does this enters a labyrinth long thought to harbor a poststructuralist minotaur; in fact, it harbors only a cunning artificer.

Although he did not, like Dedalus, build the labyrinth, DeLillo is very much its master. Certainly his writings feature, as given or constant, a thematics of language. In a number of interviews, the author has affirmed the centrality, in his thinking and in his writing, of ideas about the great ocean of words in which, dolphin-backed, he swims. As early as the writing of *End Zone* (1972), his second novel, he comments, "I began to suspect that language was a subject as well as an instrument in my work."[1] "[B]efore everything," he remarks in a 1993 *Paris Review* interview, "there's language. Before history and politics, there's language."[2] In another interview, in 1997, he restates this credo: "For me the crux of the whole matter is language."[3] But DeLillo's meditations on language tend to take place in a kind of parallel universe – a vantage from which the author can reframe, reconfigure, or subvert certain of the tendentious and reductionist elements in linguistics, psychology, and literary theory. Poetic and startling without ever lapsing into the merely fanciful, DeLillo's language games remind readers that there are more things in heaven and earth than are dreamed of in the poststructuralist episteme.

One cannot, in any event, overemphasize the centrality of the language theme in any and all of DeLillo's novels, stories, plays, and essays. As my chief examples of DeLillo's engagement with this subject, I shall focus on one novel in which it figures prominently, *The Names*, and another, *The Body Artist* (2001), in which it seems relatively peripheral. An especially important mid-career fiction, the first looms as, for this critic at least, DeLillo's definitive work. The second, like Herman Melville's *Billy Budd* (1924), Henry James's *The Turn of the Screw* (1898), Thomas Mann's *Tonio Kröger* (1903), or Ernest Hemingway's *The Old Man and the Sea* (1952), demonstrates a master's ability to do on a small canvas what he normally does on a much larger scale. In *The Body Artist*, moreover, one sees how ideas about language, even when not thematically foregrounded, offer themselves as keys to the DeLillo text.

Language and its discontents

Literary artists share a reverence for their medium, and from time to time they feel obliged to defend it against practices that erode its precision. William Wordsworth, the most familiar example, undertook to reform the increasingly artificial diction of poetry at the end of the eighteenth century. He argued that poetry would lose nothing – would in fact gain – if written "in a selection of language really used by men."[4] Better to write "fish," in other words, than "finny tribe." Although Wordsworth had DeLillo-like doubts about crowds ("the encreasing [sic] accumulation of men in cities") and media ("the rapid communication of intelligence"),[5] he lived in an age in which literary art was still powerful and language itself not so easily corrupted by the "tidal mendacity" (as George Steiner once called it) of politics and journalism.[6] Thus he did not associate the preciosity of poets with political influences or consequences. He deplored the progressive coarsening of culture but stopped short of blaming those who, in his view, had allowed poetic expression to degenerate. In calling for a less mannered literary discourse, then, Wordsworth expected only an indirect societal or political import – insofar as the plain-spoken poet, "carrying sensation into the midst of the objects of ... science,"[7] would the more effectively annex or take possession of subject matter seemingly remote from versified sentiment.

No doubt poets must wage some such campaign in every generation, but certain conflicts can seem more fraught than others. In the twentieth century literary artists had again to rescue their medium – language – from a host of debasing influences. Revering the Stéphane Mallarmé who sought "to give the words of the tribe a more pure sense," T. S. Eliot struggles, in *Four Quartets* (1944), with words that "[d]ecay with imprecision."[8] Ezra Pound invokes the Confucian principle of Ching Ming ("precise verbal definitions").[9] Robert Frost undertakes to rake the leaves away where water wells up, a place coded for centuries as the very source of inspiration, the muses' dwelling place. Thus "I'm going out to clean the pasture spring"[10] translates: "I'll rid discourse itself of choking clutter."

Seeing that corruption of – or merely inattention to – language takes a political as well as an artistic toll, the moderns sought greater precision, clarity, and concreteness in their own management of words. Not that they always got it right. Pound believed passionately that the health of a civilization depends on the health of language and respect for the arts, yet somehow he became an apologist for the century's most hideous politics. His Italian contemporary Giuseppe Ungaretti (whom DeLillo quotes in his 2005 play *Love-Lies-Bleeding*) was less deceived. A veteran of World War I, Ungaretti insisted on concrete diction, especially in any record of military experience, and so anticipated Hemingway's famous rejection of such abstract, once-valorizing terms as "sacred," "glorious," "sacrifice," and "in vain."

George Orwell, at the century's mid-point, deplored the ubiquity of Latinate fog in political utterance. Closing on the millennium, his successors continued the struggle. Like the moderns, the postmoderns saw the corruption of language as an issue at once political and artistic, and they devoted much literary energy to resisting the Cold War's warping influence on public discourse. In the language of nuclear deterrence, as anatomized in DeLillo's *End Zone*, the disparity between "words and phrases like thermal hurricane, overkill, circular error probability, post-attack environment, stark deterrence, dose-rate contours, kill ratio, spasm war" and the actualities they cloak in bureaucratic plausibility – "[h]orrible diseases, fires raging in the inner cities, crop failures, genetic chaos, temperatures soaring and dropping, panic, looting, suicides, scorched bodies, arms torn off, millions of dead" – becomes especially appalling (*EZ* 21, 240). Cold War rhetoric almost made one nostalgic for the simple mendacities of "sacred," "glorious," "sacrifice," and "in vain."

A kind of black hole of political discrimination, the Cold War spawned warmer versions of itself in Korea, Malaysia, and Vietnam. Yet even as the casualties grew in Southeast Asia, American academics began to wrestle with fresh questions about the referential limitations of language. The Tet Offensive in early 1968 was bracketed by the public presentation (1966) and the translation into English (1970) of Jacques Derrida's frequently anthologized essay "Structure, Sign, and Play in the Discourse of the Human Sciences," which became one of poststructuralism's seminal texts. According to Derrida and his followers, language remains radically self-referential, meaning always short-circuits, and signifier and signified can never be fully congruent. Commonplace or transcendental, the signified perpetually absconds, perpetually reveals itself as, after all, only another signifier, marker for the elusive idea of a semiotic foundation. Discourse, narrative, speech, writing – all found themselves immured, as it were, in reflexivity.

Battered by public corruption of language in one quarter and such academic assertions about its radical superficiality in another, the literary artists of the late twentieth century proved almost lapidary in their devotion to the medium. Even as, occasionally, the writers themselves thematized the representational inadequacy of language, they amazed readers with demonstrations of its endless performativity. Whatever its rhizomatic features, language in the work of the great postmodernists keeps affirming the value of its own infinitely varied complexity.

Like Wordsworth, who witnessed the French Revolution, or the moderns, who perpended the deaths of ten million between 1914 and 1918, DeLillo came of age as a writer under war's looming shadow – notably that of the conflict fought in Vietnam. Publishing his first novel during the final phase of that war, he found himself part of the 1930s-born literary cohort (they included E. L. Doctorow, John Barth, Philip Roth, Thomas Pynchon, and Toni Morrison) that joined a slightly older generation of writers (Ralph Ellison, Kurt Vonnegut, Joseph Heller, Norman Mailer, Grace Paley) in resisting various official discourses that threatened plain English with Orwellian metastasis. Indeed, the jargon with which officialdom sought to obfuscate the progressive disaster in Vietnam – "pacification," "strategic hamlet," "protective-reaction strikes" – seemed eerily to recapitulate the examples in Orwell's "Politics and the English Language": "rectification of frontiers," "transfer of population," "elimination of unreliable elements."[11] Apologists for this war, as DeLillo remarks in his 1978 novel *Running Dog*, depended heavily on such "hybrid gibberish" (*RD* 208).

Yet DeLillo never became a political novelist, never wrote an *Armies of the Night* (1968) or *Middle of the Journey* (1947) or *The Plot Against America* (2004). Even when he writes about the John F. Kennedy assassination (in *Libra* [1988]) or the Cold War (in *Underworld* [1997]), he seems little invested in politics *per se*. Rather, he focuses on the fine grain of American consciousness under the various stresses to which it has been subject over the course of several dramatic decades. He also keeps his eye – or rather his excellent ear – on language and its redemptive vitality, whatever enormities the politicians, journalists, and social scientists subject it to. In his inexhaustible fascination with language, DeLillo becomes an unusual kind of historian, and in a trenchant 1997 article, he asserts the profound affinity of history and the word. Although cheered by "the tendency of the language to work in opposition to the enormous technology of war that dominated the [Cold War] era," DeLillo sees that the struggle can never be declared a success. As century and millennium come to an end, he draws attention to the need for literary artists, keeping their medium answerable to social, political, and historical contingency, to resist the "single uninflected voice, the monotone of the state, the corporate entity, the product, the assembly line." DeLillo hails a dynamic idea of language as the chief resource of writers who seek to stand "against the vast and uniform Death that history tends to fashion as its most enduring work." Subverting that monolith, language becomes "a form of counterhistory." When kept in good working order, it "lives in everything it touches and can be an agent of redemption, the thing that delivers us, paradoxically, from history's flat, thin, tight, and relentless designs, its arrangement of stark pages."[12]

The Body Artist: language, trauma, time

In his thirteen major fictions to appear by 2003, DeLillo demonstrates a seemingly inexhaustible ability to conjure fresh questions about language. Thus *End Zone* features characters who "engage in wars of jargon with each other,"[13] and from time to time in subsequent work DeLillo recurs brilliantly (and with unerring ear) to the parsing and parodying of the argots, specialized vocabularies, and nitlike clichés of the late twentieth century. But like Vladimir Nabokov's novelist hero Sebastian Knight, who makes of parody "a kind of springboard into the highest region of serious emotion,"[14] DeLillo aims at more than the mere exposure of vulgarity in language, the *poshlost* that manifests itself in jargon and stale catchphrases. Thus he constantly ranges beyond parody to engage language as the currency, the medium of exchange, in the vast and complex marketplace of human existence. In *Mao II* (1991) he dissects a wide range of expression: the painfully limited lexicon of cult members; the stylistic grammar, in a *faux*-Warhol painting, of derivative art; the "throttled squawk" with which deranged homeless people try to communicate ("a different language completely, unwritable and interior, the rag-speak of shopping carts and plastic bags, the language of soot" [*M* 180]). In *Cosmopolis* (2003) he inventories the vocabulary that complements and historicizes technology. In *Great Jones Street* (1973) he imagines that a powerful drug might divorce one from language completely (only a DeLillo would attempt to imagine and represent such a condition). In *White Noise* (1985) he vets the idea that the side effects of another powerful drug might make one unable to differentiate a phrase such as "hail of bullets" from actual shooting. In *Ratner's Star* (1976) he imagines a think-tank team striving to develop a metalanguage by which to circumvent the propositional indeterminacy theorized by Ludwig Wittgenstein and Kurt Gödel (who reframe, in terms of symbolic logic, the uncertainty postulated by Werner Heisenberg). This conceit also figures in DeLillo's 1979 play *The Engineer of*

Moonlight, which concerns the frustrations of an empiricist (the engineer of the title) who seeks a language – scientific, mathematical, or other – that will pierce though the world's veil of appearance and put him in touch with reality. The name of his wife, Maya, comments ironically on his doomed enterprise – as does the pun in the surname of her predecessor, Diana Vail.

In *The Body Artist* DeLillo introduces another moon-addled language gamer, the nameless autistic savant who declares: "[t]he word for moonlight is moonlight" (*BA* 82). Hearing this pronouncement, the novel's heroine does not dismiss it as mere tautology, for she understands the poetic nuance: the *word* for moonlight is dreamy and ethereal and otherworldly. Not intrinsically, of course, but because one's more or less uncanny experience of moonlight confers a certain flavor upon its verbal marker. Thus she thinks the statement "logically complex and oddly moving and circularly beautiful and true." The polysyndeton (the repetition of "and") signals a breathless discovery: that in the guileless statement of a retarded man semiotic alps on alps arise. The recognition here, highly characteristic of this author, concerns those qualities of language often neglected in reductive analysis. One pauses over this remark (and the rhapsodic response to it) because it intimates, again, something of DeLillo's rigorous and subtle thinking about language. Another writer – or theorist – would pounce on the phrase's tautological aspect as the whole point, the moonlight-to-moonlight loop one more link in the signifying chain that is not attached, after all, to the thing language supposedly represents.

How, then, as Shakespeare's Peter Quince asks, to get moonlight into a chamber? In one form or another, the question exercises all who traffic in the benign illusion of artistic representation. One answer comes from a character in Richard Powers's *The Gold Bug Variations* (1991) who speaks of "putting Shakespearean moonlight into a twenty-six-letter chamber."[15] Language, codified as alphabet, proves able to contain every kind of sublime magic, Shakespearean or otherwise. Or, to put it another way, language is the gossamer substance, the pale fire, the *moonlight*, in that alphabetical chamber.

A miracle of thematic economy, *The Body Artist* incorporates, without strain, rather a lot of conceptual and thematic material. It concerns a performance artist, Lauren Hartke, whose husband commits suicide, after which she grieves – alone, she thinks – in the house they had rented by the sea. But in the midst of her anguished solitude, she discovers another person in the house. Apparently the victim of some unspecified mental disability, he cannot give his name. He speaks in riddling echoes that modulate toward the uncanny. Lauren mentally refers to him as "Mr. Tuttle" because he resembles a person of that name, a shabby high school science teacher she once had. As

Laura di Prete has shown, the story lends itself to analysis as a brilliantly original meditation on mental trauma and its after effects. "Not unlike Morrison's *Beloved* (1987)," di Prete observes, "DeLillo's narrative imagines trauma as necessarily bound to the emergence of a 'foreign body,' a phantom-like figure in full flesh that makes the workings of traumatic memory access-ible."[16] Di Prete sees Mr. Tuttle, then, as the reification of the heroine's mental distress. In dealing with him, Lauren works through the trauma of her husband's death. The novel's ecphrastic inclusion of *Body Time*, a new performance piece by Lauren, signals the recovery of her mental equilibrium. After its presentation, Lauren finds herself free of Mr. Tuttle.

DeLillo suggests that this secret sharer, who disappears as mysteriously as he had previously materialized, can never be fully recuperated to the world that Lauren, her psychological balance restored, must occupy. Yet he lingers as the trace of something beyond the phantasmatic embodiment of trauma. He embodies a primitive idea of language, the medium in which Lauren must come to terms with – and articulate – painful experience. Although "meant," like any other human being, "to locate his existence" amid "verbs" and "parts of speech" (*BA* 100), this smallish man of indeterminate age speaks largely in echoes, like one arrested (as in fact he may well be) at the earliest phase of language acquisition.

A walking linguistic conundrum, Mr. Tuttle is the vehicle for a number of enigmatic revelations about language as environment. "If you don't know *where* you are," observes Ralph Ellison's Invisible Man, "you probably don't know *who* you are."[17] Lauren Hartke comes to a better understanding, in the story's last three words, of "who she was" as a result of her unsought immersion (*BA* 124), through interaction with the strange Mr. Tuttle, in language (the locus or "where" of all self-knowledge). DeLillo obliges his character to locate herself temporally as well: she must come to terms with the "when" that also dwells in language. Lauren resists seeing "[p]ast, present and future" as "amenities of language" (*BA* 99), but she finds the temporal everywhere in the linguistic. To her horror, she discovers that Mr. Tuttle can reproduce conversations she had with her late husband. Even more disturb-ing – and truly mysterious – is his ability to "echo" words not yet uttered. "He said, 'Don't touch it' in a voice that wasn't quite his. 'I'll clean it up'" (*BA* 81). Here he ventriloquizes the voice of Lauren, who will – days later (*BA* 93) – provide the verbal template. "This," she thinks, "is a man who remembers the future," who "violates the limits of the human" (*BA* 100). Mr. Tuttle seems to exist in some strange exemption from temporality: "There has to be an imaginary point, a nonplace where language intersects with our perceptions of time and space, and he is a stranger at this crossing, without words or bearings" (*BA* 99). Unmoored in time, Mr. Tuttle's words never coalesce as part of any real language with a lexicon and grammar that make possible the creation of an infinite series of fresh sentences. Mr. Tuttle's discourse parodies the famous pronouncement of Martin Heidegger: we do not speak language, language speaks us. Intimating that nowhere is this more true than in the language that is time itself, DeLillo imagines the extent to which language at once survives within a damaged human being and becomes, even in its attenuation, an index to or measure of his humanity.

The attenuation notwithstanding, Mr. Tuttle's echoic speech models language in its more advanced manifestations. In parroting the phrases of Lauren Hartke and her husband, Mr. Tuttle rehearses the perennial tease of referentiality, every link in the signifying chain itself an echo with no traceable origin, no final referent or signified. Strangest of all: both Lauren and DeLillo do what Mr. Tuttle does. Throughout, there is an elaborate counterpoint of repeated phrases and actions and images: the hair in the mouth (*BA* 11, 69), the lamp that gets bumped when one disrobes (*BA* 35, 112, 122), the "bottle with a pistol-grip attachment" (*BA* 32, 114), the wax paper (*BA* 34, 113), the Japanese woman (*BA* 35–6, 105, 115), and so on. None of these iterative elements is intrinsically meaningful – each functions as arbitrary morpheme or lexical unit that may or may not lend itself to sense. One experiences this book, this echo chamber, as Lauren experiences Mr. Tuttle. He allows Lauren and the reader to see that language, for all its marvels, is not sentient, not self-knowing. Even so, it frees its speakers from time and circumstance and allows them, among other things, to transmute grief into art. But art, too, is a language in which the emergence of fresh semes depends on small variations. Lauren's *Body Time*, in which certain gestures recur over and over with, as aural "accompaniment, the anonymous robotic voice of a telephone answering machine delivering a standard announcement" and "played relentlessly" (*BA* 106), unfolds like one of the minimalist compositions of Philip Glass, John Adams, or Steve Reich, in which larger forms emerge from basic elements repeated and repeated and repeated. DeLillo's *The Body Artist*, itself "logically complex and oddly moving and circularly beautiful and true," works in much the same way.

How many languages do you speak? *The Names*

Namelessness such as Mr. Tuttle's is an attribute of the all and the nothing, as one learns in *Underworld*. Cold War humanity lived under the shadow of "the thing with no name, the bomb that would redefine the limits of human perception and dread."[18] Hearing that one of its disillusioned designers called it *merde*, the artist Klara Sax has a small epiphany: "Something that eludes naming is automatically relegated ... to the status of shit" (*U* 77).

Another character suggests, however, that in fact little actually manages to go nameless. In a much discussed scene, Father Paulus catechizes a wayward boy in "the physics of language." Exhibiting a shoe, the Jesuit challenges young Nick Shay to "[n]ame the parts." When the youth falters, the teacher suggests that knowledge must begin with nomenclature: "You didn't see the thing because you don't know how to look. And you don't know how to look because you don't know the names" (*U* 540). By implication, one grows by taking the trouble to learn just how much of the world has yielded itself to the onomastic imperative.

Yet a name has only a provisional referent, and it can and does float free of what it identifies. According to the familiar biblical story, however, it was not always so. In a text embedded in Paul Auster's *City of Glass* (1985), one reads that

> Adam's one task in the Garden had been to invent language, to give each creature and thing its name. In that state of innocence, his tongue had gone straight to the quick of the world. His words had not been merely appended to the things he saw, they had revealed their essences, had literally brought them to life. A thing and its name were interchangeable.[19]

A similar gloss on Genesis figures in the Richard Powers novel previously cited: "In the first nomenclature, what Adam called a creature was what it *was* – an exact lookup table for the living library. But that perfect equivalence between name and thing was scattered in ten thousand languages, punishment for an overly ambitious engineering project."[20] (From Shakespeare's Childe Roland to Robert Browning's, from Dante's vision of Ugolino's prison to Gérard de Nerval's *tour abolie* and the towers that Eliot catalogues in *The Waste Land*, how often that project – the heaven-scraping edifice at Babel or something very like it – reasserts itself in the Western imagination.)

But as Auster and Powers engage the myth of Edenic language and the myth of its corruption after Babel, so do writers such as Pynchon and DeLillo invoke the New Testament countermyth of Pentecost, in which the renewal of spiritual purpose takes a specifically linguistic form: the Gift of Tongues. Pentecost means "fiftieth" (that is, the fiftieth day after Easter), and some critics discern a reference to Pentecostal expectation in the title of Pynchon's second novel, *The Crying of Lot 49* (1966), whose central character grapples with spiritual dead ends, with "the absence of surprise to life," with "the exitlessness ... that harrows the head of everybody American you know."[21] Early in her story, Oedipa Maas contemplates a Remedios Varo painting of "frail girls" immured in "the top room of a circular tower" that one recognizes as a postmodern version of the great erection that got humanity into trouble in Genesis. For Pynchon as for many of his fellow postmodernists, the curse of Babel lies not in the proliferation of languages but in the universal recursivity at the heart of a Symbolic Order always already at a remove from the Real. In DeLillo this spiritual desperation fosters less oblique expressions of Pentecostal desire. Fascinated with the survival of glossolalia or "speaking in tongues" among Pentecostal congregations, DeLillo recurs to the idea in interviews and makes it central to his great work, *The Names*. DeLillo critiques the twinned myths of Adamic language and its Pentecostal restoration in this, the novel he has characterized as a turning point in his career, "the book that marks the beginning of a new dedication."[22] Its very title announces an engagement with the Ur-conceptualization of language, a grappling with ideas going back to Plato and St. Augustine, if not to Adam. Like Socrates in Plato's *Cratylus*, DeLillo scrutinizes the notion that all language begins in names and naming. But beyond ancient thinking about nominality, the author provides an unusual guided tour of the major and minor arcana of sign systems, referentiality, and, in every sense of the word, "writing."

The story: while in Athens for a year, James Axton visits his estranged wife Kathryn and their son on the Greek island where she helps with an archeological excavation. There he meets the dig's organizer and principal investigator, Owen Brademas, and hears about a mysterious itinerant cult whose members greet strangers by asking, "How many languages do you speak?" The question suggests an inchoate or perverse Pentecostalism; those who ask it seem to imagine that in learning one language after another they can emulate the disciples who gained the ability to speak in the tongues of all nations, thereby transcending the curse of Babel. Strangely susceptible to the cult, Owen has direct, personal knowledge of the yearning to "speak in tongues." As a child, he attended a Pentecostal church but found himself unable to "get wet," unable to immerse himself in glossolalia's "babbling brook" (N 306), that tributary of the divine "river of language" (N 152) evoked elsewhere in DeLillo's story. He tells the Axtons about these experiences, which become the subject of a "nonfiction novel" written by the precocious Tap, James and Kathryn's son.

The cult embraces more than heteroclite Pentecostalism. As presently becomes known, its adherents observe a bizarre and murderous ritual. They identify and stalk a deranged or disabled person, waiting for the prospective victim's initials to coincide with those of a place. When the initials converge, the cultists convene – and slay, for example, the "apparently feeble-minded" Michaelis Kalliambetsos, who has wandered into the village of Mikro Kamini (N 73). Dedicated to visionary or mystical (or merely twisted) ideas about language and the alphabet, the cult seems fixated, so far as Owen or James can tell, on the venerable idea that words originate in names. Thus focused on referentiality, the cultists may seek experience of some literalized Logos, a still point in the turning world of signifiers, some strangled echo of the single, divine Word that, according to the Gospel of St. John, contains creation itself at the instant of its biblical Big Bang. But if, as James surmises, the cultists actually call themselves "The Names," they demonstrate, in the act of naming, the very problem they seek to resolve. "The word for moonlight is moonlight" may be sheer poetry, but no such wit redeems the tautology that DeLillo invites the reader to formulate: the name of The Names is The Names.

Interpretations of the cult's defining ritual tend to be framed in the poststructuralist terms current in the late twentieth century and thus, perhaps, subject to certain epistemic limitations. In *The Names* DeLillo engages, with particular energy, what a theorist would call the problematics of representation. One doubts, however, that the author would find such a phrase congenial. In 1990, when an interviewer asked if he took an interest in the "theoretical work being done in philosophy and literary criticism these days," DeLillo responded, "No, I don't" and added, "I don't think of language in a theoretical way."[23] This disclaimer bears scrutiny. The author may simply wish to avoid the kind of pronouncement that will, as James says, "surrender my text to analysis and reflection" of a particular kind (*N* 20). One has only to think of certain writers who *do* proclaim their theoretical sophistication to see the kind of sterility risked. Rather than saying that he knows nothing of theory, then, DeLillo affirms only that he does not think within its box. If he knows about the alleged crisis of representation, he declines to let it ruin his authorial day. Nor does he pay obeisance to Ferdinand de Saussure, Michel Foucault, Roland Barthes, Derrida, Jacques Lacan, and the others responsible, in the final decades of the twentieth century, for floating signifiers, free play, *différance*, negative doctrines of referentiality, and the Death of the Author. Indeed, it might not be going too far to suggest that the thinking of the poststructuralists may have a point or two in common with that of Ta Onómata, the cultists. Like the terrorists in *Mao II*, they embrace ideas inimical to the idea of the artist's creative autonomy. "Years ago," remarks that novel's Bill Gray, "I used to think it was possible for a novelist to alter the inner life of a culture. Now bombmakers and gunmen have taken that territory. They make raids on human consciousness." A writer himself, Gray adds that "what terrorists gain, novelists lose. The degree to which they influence mass consciousness is the extent of our decline as shapers of sensibility and thought. The danger they represent equals our own failure to be dangerous" (*M* 156–7).

Whatever his awareness of literary theory, DeLillo seems never to have been particularly daunted by twentieth-century ideas about language that, interrogating the Adamic premise, emphasize the problematic link between signifier and signified. Yet interpreters of *The Names* have with some legitimacy viewed the cult's matching of the initials of the sacrificial victim and those of the place in which he or she perishes as an attempt, through a violent and irretrievable act, to arrest the fluidity in language, the "free play" of signifiers. The ritual death effects a murderous marriage. "[T]hrough a terminal act of connection," one critic observes, the cultists "attempt the binding of symbol and object into one-to-one correspondence."[24]

What goes unnoticed here is the possibility that the imagined, violent simplification parodies the reductive logic of theory. Like any other attempt to cut the Gordian knot of signification, the ritual remains obscure, little more than a gesture toward the Adamic, foundational dream. If anything, the cult's program exists to reveal any final hierogamy of signifier and signified as a congruence of the arbitrary, the reflection in any and every word of the radical meaninglessness at the heart of things. In fact, James and Owen deny transcendental implications in the cult's observances. "No sense," James reflects, "no content, no historic bond, no ritual significance. Owen and I ... knew in the end we'd be left with nothing. Nothing signified, nothing meant" (*N* 216). Owen goes further: "These killings mock us. They mock our need to structure and classify ... They intended nothing, they meant nothing. They only matched the letters" (*N* 308).

Yet Owen seems to accept their logic. When James meets him, Owen is already turning his back on archeology to indulge a passion for epigraphy, the study of ancient inscriptions. This fascination scarcely extends to the "content" of the inscriptions – even though, to read them, he teaches himself ancient languages and writing systems. Etymologically writing (*graphein*) on the outside or surface (*epi*), epigraphy becomes yet another figure that problematizes language as something radically superficial, a gossamer gloss on the world of physical reality. It is significant that Owen cannot sustain a professional commitment to archeology, the business of recording and penetrating strata, moving into depths at once spatial and temporal. Never able, as a child, to join his parents and the rest of the congregation in the experience of glossolalia, he remains as an adult largely oblivious to spiritual possibility. Nor can he deliver himself from perceptions that a reader recognizes as relentlessly poststructuralist.

Owen will succumb to an anomie that makes him unable to deny moral membership in the cult, but James, shaken by his failure to "name the parts" of his own political identity, seems to move toward a degree of moral clarity. He discovers himself to be a CIA stooge at the same time that he discovers his place, as American, in the political grammar of Third World resentment and international terrorism that has long promoted a single question among nervous travelers: "Are they killing Americans?" (*N* 45, 95). Toward the end of his year in Athens, the question becomes less academic. A pair of gunmen – terrorists? ordinary thugs? – shoot an American, whom they may have mistaken for James.

The story ends with visits to language-filled temples – one on the prairie that framed Owen's childhood, the other high above the city of Athens, where James has tried, among other things, to come to terms with the dissolution of his marriage. Perversely, James has so far made a point of not visiting the Acropolis, even though he lives in its shadow. When at last, chastened, he climbs up to the Parthenon for the long-postponed encounter with antiquity, he marvels at "hearing one language after another, rich, harsh, mysterious, strong." His last words as narrator present a final epiphany: "This is what we bring to the temple, not prayer or chant or slaughtered rams. Our offering is language" (*N* 331). He discovers, in other words, a kind of residual holiness that turns tourists into pilgrims who bring their varied languages to one of the oldest altars in the Western world. Insofar as the ruined Parthenon looms above an ancient center of civilization (on the *acro polis* or high city) and insofar as it is thronged with languages, it becomes a sacralized Tower of Babel, a monument to piety rather than presumption – the locus, DeLillo hints, of a kind of postmodern Pentecost. In a brilliant and daring maneuver, DeLillo adds a powerful epilogue in the form of an excerpt from the "nonfiction novel" in which James's son Tap tells the story of Owen Brademas, whom he renames "Orville Benton" (like a more innocent cultist, Tap matches the initials, which happen also to spell "Ob," the "name" of a familial pseudo-language resembling pig Latin). Young Orville, in Tap's book, struggles with his inability to achieve religious ecstasy, to speak in tongues. Although naïve, Tap's rendering of this struggle has a redemptive energy: even as he depicts the main character's failure to possess a language of spiritual transformation, the young author devises a language of enormous vitality. Recalling DeLillo's characterization of *The Names* as "the book that marks the beginning of a new dedication," one discerns in Tap the author's own self-projection as born-again writer.

The French psychoanalyst Lacan has said that the infant, learning the *Nom du Père*, enters the Symbolic Order and so becomes estranged from the Real. But Frankfurt School critic Walter Benjamin, reading Genesis closely, notes that "God did not create man from the word, and he did not name him. He did not wish to subject him to language, but in man God set language, which had served *him* as medium of creation, free. God rested when he had left his creative power to itself in man."[25] *Pace* Lacan, then, human beings once knew "the name of the Father" without impairment of the immediacy with which they knew – and named – the world. To affirm as much need not make either a Benjamin or a DeLillo an old-fashioned believer. One doubts, indeed, that the author of *The Names* and *The Body Artist* would gainsay the "rockbound doubt" of his own James Axton (*N* 92) – or for that matter dispute Lia Macklin's vision (in *Love-Lies-Bleeding*) of the "nowhere" that swallows the dead. Yet DeLillo always treats religious hunger with respect, and with regard to language, his is invariably a spiritualizing discourse.

Notes

1. Tom LeClair, "An Interview with Don DeLillo," in Thomas DePietro, ed., *Conversations with Don DeLillo* (Jackson: University Press of Mississippi, 2005), p. 5.
2. Adam Begley, "Don DeLillo: The Art of Fiction CXXXV," in DePietro, ed., *Conversations*, p. 107.
3. David Remnick, "Exile on Main Street: Don DeLillo's Undisclosed Underworld," *New Yorker* (September 15, 1997), p. 47.
4. I quote here from the 1850 version of Wordsworth's famous "Preface" to *Lyrical Ballads*. See *The Prose Works of William Wordsworth*, 3 vols., vol. 1, ed. W. J. B. Owen and Jane Worthington Smyser (Oxford, 1974), p. 123.
5. Ibid., p. 128.
6. George Steiner, *Language and Silence: Essays on Language, Literature, and the Inhuman* (New York: Atheneum, 1967), p. 14.
7. Ibid., p. 141.
8. T. S. Eliot, "Burnt Norton," *Four Quartets*, in Eliot, *The Complete Poems and Plays* (New York: Harcourt, Brace & World, 1971), p. 121.
9. Ezra Pound often recurs to this principle in the *Cantos*. The gloss is from his translation of and commentary on Confucius's *Ta Hsio*. See Confucius, *The Great Digest, The Unwobbling Pivot, The Analects*, trans. Ezra Pound (New York: New Directions, 1951), p. 31.
10. Robert Frost, "The Pasture," in *The Poetry of Robert Frost*, ed. Edward Connery Lathem (New York: Holt, Rinehart, and Winston, 1969), p. 1.
11. George Orwell, "Politics and the English Language," in Orwell, *Shooting an Elephant, and Other Essays* (New York: Harcourt, 1950), p. 88.
12. Don DeLillo, "The Power of History," *New York Times Magazine* (September 7, 1997), p. 63.
13. LeClair, "An Interview with Don DeLillo," p. 5.
14. Vladimir Nabokov, *The Real Life of Sebastian Knight* (1941) (Norfolk, CT: New Directions, 1959), p. 91.
15. Richard Powers, *The Gold Bug Variations* (New York: William Morrow, 1991), p. 167.
16. Laura di Prete, *Foreign Bodies: Trauma, Corporeality and Textuality in Contemporary American Culture* (New York: Routledge, 2006), p. 87.
17. Ralph Ellison, *Invisible Man* (New York: Random House, 1952), p. 500.
18. Don DeLillo, *Underworld* (New York: Scribner, 1997), p. 422.
19. Paul Auster, *City of Glass*, in *The New York Trilogy* (Los Angeles: Sun & Moon Press, 1994), p. 69.

20. Powers, *The Gold Bug Variations*, p. 317.
21. Thomas Pynchon, *The Crying of Lot 49* (Philadelphia: Lippincott, 1966), p. 170.
22. Begley, "The Art of Fiction," p. 284.
23. Anthony DeCurtis, "'An Outsider in This Society': An Interview with Don DeLillo," in Frank Lentricchia, ed., *Introducing Don DeLillo* (Durham: Duke University Press, 1991), p. 61.
24. Paula Bryant, "Discussing the Untellable: Don DeLillo's *The Names*," *Critique* 29 (Fall 1987), p. 19.
25. Walter Benjamin, "On Language as Such and on the Language of Man," in Benjamin, *Selected Writings*, 4 vols., vol. 1, *1913–1926* ed. Marcus Bullock and Michael W. Jennings, trans. Edmund Jephcott (Cambridge, MA: Harvard University Press, 1996), p. 68.

12

JOHN A. McCLURE

DeLillo and mystery

A discrimination of mysteries

Like many postmodern novelists, Don DeLillo plays seriously with the forms of popular fiction. He draws regularly on the forensic plotlines of detective mysteries and espionage fiction. Who is plotting to blow up the New York Stock Exchange (*Players*) (1977)? Who has the film of Adolf Hitler's last days (*Running Dog*) (1978)? For whom is James Axton really working (*The Names*) (1982)? Who has Dylar, the drug that supposedly represses the fear of death (*White Noise*) (1985)? Who killed JFK (*Libra*) (1988)? The plots of esoteric fiction, filled with quests for secret knowledge and cosmic conspiracies, also fascinate him. *The Names* features a search for a secret cult obsessed with obscure languages and ritual murder, and *Libra* muses, as its title indicates, over the secrets encoded in the esoteric systems of astrology. In these popular narrative traditions, all mysteries are for solving, all disruptive forces can be managed, and human dignity is closely linked to the acquisition of exact knowledge.

But DeLillo is preoccupied as well with a third and very different discourse of mystery. Many of his novels – including *Players*, *The Names*, *White Noise*, *Mao II* (1991), and *Underworld* (1997) – climax in dramatic episodes of worshipful communion that recall the religious "mysteries" of DeLillo's Catholic heritage.[1] In these episodes characters unfulfilled by quests for knowledge and control or by practices of privileged superficiality find comfort in experiences of sacramental communion that recall the "mysteries" of the Catholic sacraments, sacred practices that channel grace to those who perform them from sources that cannot be fully understood. (The English word "sacrament" is derived from the Greek word for mystery.) And these characters have experiences of profound unknowing that resemble those described by apophatic mystics such as St. John of the Cross and the anonymous medieval author of *The Cloud of Unknowing*. These Catholic mystics argue that conventional (*kataphatic*) efforts to know God conceptually are futile. The Ultimate is and must remain, even as it is approached, utterly unnamable and profoundly mysterious: those who seek it must surrender to mystery.

Unlike the mysteries of popular crime, espionage, and occult fiction, then, these religious mysteries are not for solving. They point toward powers that are, in the words of the contemporary Catholic theologian Nicholas Lash, permanently beyond human "comprehension and control." These powers can be mentioned "but never fixed within the categories of our understanding" or placed "upon the map of things," or made "manageable."[2] Yet they are benign: by practicing the sacramental mysteries or the arts of unknowing, one experiences the inexplicable mystery of divine presence, and one is rendered less anxious and more responsible by these acts of honoring and abiding in the unknown.

It could be argued, of course, that DeLillo is simply an aficionado of mystery in all its forms and that the deployment of different sorts of mystery in his work is one more sign of the playful eclecticism of a certain postmodern aesthetic. But I will argue instead that DeLillo's work urges the reader to perform a discrimination of mysteries – to check his or her fascination with forensic and esoteric mysteries and explore the possibility of apophatic and sacramental modes of being. Forensic and esoteric mysteries alike, DeLillo's novels suggest, condition us to seek existential comfort in fragile or unattainable forms of knowledge and power: absolute rational knowledge and control in the case of forensic narratives, magical knowledge and control in the case of esoteric thrillers. Religion in its more dogmatic and militant forms, DeLillo's novels argue, also feeds on and reinforces such dreams of mastery. It invites us, as Richard Rorty and Gianni Vattimo put it, to "escape [our] finitude by aligning [ourselves] with infinite power."[3] But such promises, DeLillo's plots insist, are ultimately unfulfillable. There can be no final escape through rational, magical, or religious practices from nagging intuitions of ignorance, vulnerability, and insubstantiality because such intuitions reflect fundamental aspects of the human condition. The belief that these aspects of existence can be fully overcome tends, in fact, to make things worse by sponsoring projects of mastery ("management" and "control" in Lash's lexicon, and DeLillo's) that damage individuals and communities alike. Nor can one find relief from existential anxieties by pursuing a second popular strategy, the deliberate cultivation of superficiality. In DeLillo's work it is only by coming to terms with permanent mystery, by accepting finitude and fragility, and by reasoning from this position that humans are able to live less anxiously, act more responsibly, and make contact with the mysterious benignities that circulate in the world.

DeLillo's turn toward the Catholic mysteries is not a return to the religion itself. On the contrary, he seems committed to deepening the Catholic discourse of mystery to the point where Catholic dogma, the Catholic cosmos, and theism itself disappear or survive only as inspired products of the speculative imagination. In this his thinking resembles that of the contemporary American philosopher William Connolly. The "postsecular" position that Connolly lays out in *Identity/Difference* (1991) rejects both the religious discourse of a "sovereign God" and "the modern project of mastery," calling instead for the cultivation of a "nontheistic reverence for life and the earth."[4] What remains of the religious in the wake of Connolly's turn from transcendence and mastery is the sacramental sense of a world infused with mysterious presence and a chastened humanity called into communion with (and responsibility for) life and the earth.

Moments of mystery in DeLillo's fiction

If the forensic narratives of the popular mystery genres celebrate their protagonists' escape from unknowing, then the religious narratives to which DeLillo is drawn celebrate a certain coming into mystery. In the pages that follow, I will trace characters' movements toward this state of being in four novels (*Players*, *The Names*, *White Noise*, and *Underworld*), focusing on the climactic episodes in which the acceptance of mystery is sealed. These episodes share certain features. In each of them the experience of mystery delivers the protagonist from a life dedicated without satisfaction to self-distraction or the solution of conventional mysteries. In each it takes place during a collective rite and creates, for the protagonist, a powerful sense of communion with other humans and with something more, a spiritual presence that remains unnamed. In each case, this rite unfolds in an unbounded public space rather than a church or even indoors: people come and go freely, no one is excluded, and those who gather do not share any institutional identity. Nor is what happens during these ceremonies scripted or controlled in any formal way: there are no prescribed movements, no priests or elders directing the unfolding of events. In each case, finally, what happens remains discursively unsecured by any theological vocabulary. But as indicated above, the eventfulness of these rites is not entirely unmappable. As we move from text to text, we find DeLillo emphasizing a set of features that link his institutionally unhoused and discursively unmapped encounters with mystery to Catholic sacramental and apophatic traditions. And we find him embracing, in his more recent works, a third religious mystery, that of spirit-filled ecstasy, which is sharply challenged in his earlier fiction.

In *Players* the mysteries affirmed are emphatically immanent ones: the path of redemption leads downward out of a sterile secular condition of egotistical "transcendence" into mysteries of carnal communion and responsibility. Lyle and Pammy Wynant, the novel's protagonists, are both "players," privileged young Americans who make an art of superficiality and imagine that they have the know-how to manage any mysterious forces they might encounter. Lyle, a stockbroker, gets entangled in a terrorist plot to blow up the New York Stock Exchange and is gradually dismantled, mentally and physically, by his amateurish attempt to live out the role of the mystery-solving espionage agent. Pammy plays carelessly with the powers of love and sex and is also unmade by the consequences, but in a more enabling way.

Pammy's presenting problem, as the novel opens, has to do with her practice of familiar forms of abstraction. An employee of a Manhattan firm named the Grief Management Council, she has perfected the arts of denial. Pausing to unlock her apartment door one evening, she is assaulted by an unwanted feeling: "She remembered what had been bothering her, the vague presence. Her life. She hated her life. It was a minor thing, though, a small bother. She tended to forget about it. When she recalled what it was that had been on her mind, she felt satisfied at having remembered and relieved that it was nothing worse" (*P* 32). Pammy recoils as well from any reminders of her mortality. She is drawn to "the earthly merit" of some peaches she buys (*P* 32) but finds that she cannot "deal with the consequences of fruit, its perishability, the duty involved in eating it" (*P* 35).

Pammy's efforts to distance herself from such troubling feelings and insights lead to a life of artful play, irresponsibility, and perpetual anxiety. But a careless decision and its consequences teach her to honor "the processes of the physical world" (*P* 201) and to take "responsibility," a key word in the novel's moral vocabulary, for her actions. On vacation with her colleague Ethan Segal and his bisexual lover Jack Laws, Pammy has sex with Jack in a grassy field. The event triggers a kind of letting go, as Pammy, deeply aroused, is "able to break through . . . nearly free from panic and the tampering management of her own sense of fitness," first to "study her own involvement" and then to experience, unreflectively, "a transporting" and "exalted" experience of mysterious "replenishments," "the mysteries of muscles and blood" (*P* 168). Pammy escapes here from her obsession with mental "management" into experience of replenishing "mystery." But she quickly recoils both from the visceral intensity of this experience ("The earth had hurt. The goddamn ground" [*P* 169]) and from the kind of empathetic grounding it threatens to produce. Wondering why she was "so concerned about" Jack (*P* 169), she assures him, when he, too, begins to worry about the consequences of their act, that it's "No big deal." "Not for you," Jack responds, insisting that it is a big deal for him and for his lover Ethan, who, unlike Pammy, "is responsible . . . is willing to be that . . . is willing to be responsible" (P 170).

Jack's suicide a few days later finally elicits a grief that Pammy cannot manage. But her breakdown is also a breakthrough. Struggling with her own emotions and watching Ethan mourn, Pammy realizes that "people unconsciously honored the processes of the physical world, danced fatalistically with nature whenever death took someone close to them" (P 201). And she improvises a version of that sacramental dance for herself. Deciding not to fly back to New York, she submits, as if to acknowledge the stubborn truth of distance and to expose herself to her own feelings, to the ordeal of an "eleven-hour bus ride" (P 203). Her conscious goal is "to be back in the apartment, closed away again, spared the need to react tenderly to things" (P 204). Once home, however, she continues to work "unconsciously" (P 201) toward an emotional opening and an honoring of the most basic human processes: Jack's life and death, her grief, the very rhythms and risks of mortal life which she has trained herself to deny. Unable to sleep, she descends from her cloistered apartment to the teeming street, which DeLillo depicts as a site of secular carnal mystery and communion. Having descended in order to get herself a roast-beef sandwich, Pammy discovers, to her surprise, that "Everyone was eating. Wherever she looked there were mouths moving, people handling food, passing it around." This is not the communion of the Church, nor is New York the heavenly city; indeed, it is more like a carnival feast and like that other city of the Bible, Babel or Babylon, a "babble king of cities" (P 206). But what Pammy experiences is a sort of communion, a benign being-with-others that suggests the possibility of deeper openings.

The experience seems to give her the strength to pass a final test when she finds herself literally "under the sign" of mortality: "She walked beneath a flophouse marquee. It read: TRANSIENTS." Her first response is an old one – abstraction. The word takes on "an abstract tone, as words had done before in her experience," and threatens to evade "the responsibilities of content" (P 207). But Pammy has learned to "deal with the consequences" of embodied being, to pay attention to troubling messages. Her final act is a literal conversion, or turning: "Pammy stopped walking, turned her body completely and looked once more at the sign. Seconds passed before she grasped its meaning" (P 207). The mysteries affirmed here, like those affirmed by Connolly in his description of postsecular thinking, are worldly ones; Pammy's progress has entailed a kind of transcendence downward, out of the sterile world of privileged isolation, superficiality, and grief management into the teeming carnality of the street, with its rituals of communion, reflection, and surrender.

Like Pammy's partner Lyle, James Axton, the protagonist of *The Names* (1982), is torn between a life of calculated, superficial pleasures and the intensities of forensic and esoteric mysteries. He is a self-declared tourist, an international risk analyst, an unwitting agent of the CIA, and an amateur investigator of a sect of assassins. But at the novel's end, after all these modes of being have been ethically unmasked, he is granted a rendezvous with redemptive mystery similar to Pammy's. Based in Athens, he finally makes a long-delayed "pilgrimage" to the Acropolis (N 5), where in company with other tourists he is mysteriously transformed. The "scarred, broken, rough" stones of the Acropolis bespeak a larger condition of brokenness and suffering that recalls, but does not repeat, the Christian thematics of the Crucifixion (N 330).

James's refusal to visit the Acropolis at the novel's outset is based in part on a misconception of what he will find there. He assumes that the temples celebrate classical Hellenistic ideals – "Beauty, dignity, order, proportion" (N 3), the "aloof, rational, timeless, pure" (N 330) – that will mock his superficiality and the messy, many-sided, and time-haunted world he occupies but seeks to avoid. But when, cured of his half-feigned complacency, he does make his pilgrimage, he discovers a site and a celebration he can affirm. His first impression is of "space and openness, lost walls, pediments, roof." "I'd seen the temple a hundred times from the street," Axton recalls,

> never suspecting it was this big, this scarred, broken, rough ... It wasn't aloof, rational, timeless, pure ... It wasn't a relic species of dead Greece but part of the living city below it. This was a surprise. I'd thought it was a separate thing, the sacred height, intact in its Doric order. I hadn't expected a human feeling to emerge from the stones but this is what I found ... I found a cry for pity ... this open cry, this voice we know as our own. (N 329–30)

The temple James finally reaches engenders a form of sacred experience closer to kenotic traditions of Christology, with their emphasis on the suffering communion of the divine with the human, than to Hellenistic philosophy. The "mauled" stones cry out like Christianity's crucified divinity (N 330), in a "voice we know as our own." But it seems to be humanity or nature or the cosmos itself that cries here, the earth-life to which we belong, which we fashion, and which fashions us.

The tone of the passage cited above is solemn and somber. But the gathering at the Acropolis is ultimately a celebration. As in Pammy's Manhattan street, so here there is companionship and the pleasure of talk:

> People came through the gateway, people in streams and clusters, in mass assemblies. No one seems to be alone. This is a place to enter in crowds, seek company and talk. Everyone is talking. I move past the scaffolding and walk

down the steps, hearing one language after another, rich, harsh, mysterious, strong. This is what we bring to the temple, not prayer or chant or slaughtered rams. Our offering is language. (N 331)

The play of mostly indecipherable languages here and elsewhere in DeLillo's work recalls, as Amy Hungerford suggests, the mysterious language of the Latin mass.[5] And the "Our" of the last sentence in the passage invites us to contrast this ceremony to others depicted in the novel. For *The Names* criticizes not only the triumphalistic rationalism of a certain Hellenistic ideal but also what it sees as the violent irrationalism of ecstatic religiosity. The congregants at the Acropolis retain a composure scorned at the novel's other center of worship, the "vortex in the courtyard of the Grand Mosque" in Mecca, where the congregants "burn away [the] self" in "a whirlwind of human awe and submission" (N 296). And the open liturgy of the international tourists' distinct but recognizably human voices represents an emphatically unfused and earthly alternative both to the single hieratic language of the old Latin mass and to "the worldwind" [sic] of "the spirit's voice" that possesses the novel's American Pentecostals (N 337). If the fusional mysteries of vortex and "worldwind" promise an alignment with infinite power (the will or spirit of God) through acts of violent self-unmaking, the ceremony that DeLillo improvises here enables its participants to acknowledge and honor the co-presence of anguish and joy, community and difference, in the "rich, harsh, mysterious" world they inhabit. Such acknowledgment, DeLillo insists, does not provide some total release from the anguish of human finitude. But it can release people like James from their headlong and hopeless flight from this anguish and from the preoccupation with violent power that it sponsors.

Like Pammy and James, Jack Gladney, the protagonist of *White Noise*, models a number of fashionable modes of self-empowerment. Some of his schemes constitute radically secularized rites of worship and replenishment; he seeks refuge from anxiety, as Mark Osteen observes, in the novel's many "postmodern temples – the supermarket, the mall, the TV, the motel."[6] Others are sponsored by academia, where the possession of commanding knowledge is said to provide the professor with a secure identity and power. And still others are part of the popular culture of systematic distraction: the white noise of television and the situation comedy of family banter. Several critics have argued that these strategies of self-consolidation have a certain effectiveness;[7] they keep the characters going from day to day and give them some respite from the terror in their souls. But far from securing Jack emotionally, they leave him and his wife, Babette, exposed to intolerable forms of mental anguish and lead them to increasingly desperate acts of betrayal and violence.

In the end, however, Jack finds a certain respite from this life in yet another episode of spontaneous congregation:

> We go to the overpass all the time ... We find little to say to each other ... People walk up the incline and onto the overpass, carrying fruit and nuts, cool drinks, mainly the middle-aged, the elderly, some with webbed beach chairs which they set out on the sidewalk, but younger couples also, arm in arm at the rail, looking west. The sky takes on content, feeling ... It is hard to know how we should feel about this. Some people are scared by the sunsets, some determined to be elated, but most of us don't know how to feel. (WN 324)

The people who gather on the overpass to watch the sunsets are delivered by the experience, Jack suggests, out of all sorts of false "knowledge" into an inexplicably consoling form of radical unknowing: "it is hard to know ... most of us don't know ... we don't know whether we are watching in wonder or dread, we don't know what we are watching or what it means" (WN 324). They are delivered from the "white noise" of their culture's endless distracting chatter into near silence: "No one plays a radio or speaks in a voice that is much above a whisper" (WN 325). And they are delivered out of frantic activity into something like contemplation.

DeLillo, who earlier in the novel introduces both a great toxic cloud and the phrase "a cloud of unknowing" (WN 290) alludes in this scene to religious practices described in the medieval text. "When you first begin," the anonymous author of *The Cloud of Unknowing* writes,

> you find only darkness, and as it were a cloud of unknowing ... Do what you will, this darkness and this cloud remain between you and God, and stop you ... from seeing him in the clear light of rational understanding ... Reconcile yourself to wait in this darkness [for] if you are to feel him or to see him in this life, it must always be in this cloud, in this darkness.[8]

DeLillo's congregants are rewarded for their readiness to wait in unknowing with mysterious gifts: "Something golden falls, a softness delivered to the air ... It is not until some time after dark has fallen ... that we slowly begin to disperse, shyly, politely, car after car, restored to our separate and defensible selves" (WN 325). The gift of "something golden," some mysterious sort of "deliverance," coincides with an experience of communion that – like the experience of divinity – is only indirectly registered here at the moment of its passing and the restoration of the ordinary state of things. But by depicting such a gifting, at the climax of this novel about the fruitless quest for security through the cultivation of superficiality and the accumulation of knowledge, DeLillo may be seen to pass an ancient religious judgment on secular dreams of self-deliverance.

In the works discussed so far, DeLillo seems intent on purging spiritual mystery not only of its identification with theistic power and grandeur but also of any practices of ecstatic self-surrender. He assigns such practices to traditions he distrusts: Islam, Pentecostalism, and the Unification church. And he links them, paradoxically but plausibly, to a will to fuse oneself with absolute power. But in *Underworld*, and again in *Cosmopolis* (2003), DeLillo includes the ecstatic within his episodes of redemptive congregation. Bringing his imagination to bear on the Bronx world of his youth, he comes back as well to his Catholic roots, celebrating, albeit cautiously, the popular Catholicism of saints, ecstatic devotions, and the work of the Spirit.

Underworld tracks the spiritual development of Sister Alma Edgar, a "cold war nun" of the old school, authoritarian and world-despising (*U* 245). Sister Edgar devotes her life to the poverty-stricken residents of the Bronx, but her fear of contamination from the wasted human subjects of her dutiful care is such that she seems condemned to a self-isolation and emotional aridity as withering as that which afflicts the privileged protagonists of *Players*.

But like Pammy, Sister Edgar is delivered from this fate. When Esmeralda, a twelve-year-old runaway, is raped and killed in the wastelands of the South Bronx and people begin to see visions of her face on a billboard, Sister Edgar, who has kept a fastidious, even phobic distance from the polyglot, multiracial, and multifaithed community she serves, decides to make a pilgrimage to the site. Her decision appalls Sister Grace, her more religiously progressive colleague. For Gracie (who is named, ironically, for the very spiritual power she seems to have forgotten), the billboard "is something for poor people to confront" inasmuch as "the poor need visions." Sister Edgar's response is quietly devastating: "I believe you are patronizing the people you love," she says, and then, "You say the poor. But who else would saints and angels appear to? Do saints and angels appear to bank presidents?" (*U* 819). DeLillo suggests here that the progressive Church has capitulated too fully to secular modes of thinking and has lost its faith in the traditional Catholic mysteries of the more-than-human. But DeLillo, too, in his earlier work, has avoided the popular devotional spirituality of "saints and angels." Sister Edgar's pilgrimage tends to lend credence to this spirituality. She and Gracie make the journey to the street corner site where Esmeralda has appeared superimposed on a billboard advertisement for Minute Maid orange juice. Standing amid the crowd of "working people, shopkeepers . . . drifters and . . . charismatics" (*U* 820), Sister Edgar sees "Esmeralda's face take shape under the rainbow of bounteous juice and above the little suburban lake and there is a sense of someone living in the image, an animating spirit – less than a tender second of life, less than half a second and the spot is dark again" (*U* 822). The astonishing vision releases Sister Edgar not only from the corrosive despair triggered by Esmeralda's death but also from the long isolation of her life. She feels

> something break upon her. An angelus of clearest joy. She embraces Sister Grace. She yanks off her gloves and shakes hands, pumps hands with the great-bodied women who roll their eyes to heaven. The women do great two-handed pump shakes, fabricated words jumping out of their mouths, trance utterance – they're singing of things outside the known deliriums.   (*U* 822)

This scene, like the others I have discussed, brings a mixed crowd of congregants together and into face-to-face relation with a powerful symbol of suffering, finitude, and mystery: the face of a murdered girl, glowing briefly on a billboard in the squalor of the Bronx. But it also brings them into contact with something more, a powerful force that breaks over the gathering and fundamentally transforms it. The novel calls this something a "spirit," a "godsbreath" (*U* 821), an "animating spirit" (*U* 822). As Sister Edgar experiences this double solicitation to her carefully sequestered feelings, the distancing mechanisms of a lifetime dissolve. She feels everything "near at hand, breaking upon her, sadness and loss and glory and . . . pity and a force at some deep level of lament that makes her feel inseparable from the shakers and mourners . . . she is nameless for a moment, lost to the details of personal history, a disembodied fact in liquid form, pouring into the crowd" (*U* 823). Identified earlier in the scene as "a figure from a universal church with sacraments" (*U* 822), Sister Edgar here both receives and dispenses the mysterious power identified, in charismatic theology, with the work of the Spirit. She is released from a lifetime of emotional self-discipline and phobic isolation by the power of "something break[ing] upon her" from the "living . . . image" of Esmeralda on the sign (*U* 822). And she herself becomes in turn a vessel of redemption for others, "pouring" the spirit that fills her into the crowd.

This is the most Catholic of DeLillo's many scenes of congregation, the one that comes closest to recreating the Catholic cosmos and affirming the Catholic mysteries. But even here the supernatural appears in the fleeting image of a murdered girl, framed by a billboard advertisement identifying canned orange juice with the fecundity of the natural world, among a religiously polyglot crowd at an unauthorized and soon-to-be-dismantled site of worship. DeLillo affirms, that is to say, the most antipatriarchal, earth-positive, popular, and inclusive aspects of his tradition.

Cosmopolis, one of DeLillo's most recent novels, shares that openness to ecstatic traditions (including Islam and Pentecostalism) that sets *Underworld* apart from the earlier works. The funeral of the rapper Brutha Fez – an astonishing pageant of "plainsong rap," "ancient Sufi music," "mystical" break-dancing, and "charismatic speech" – is perhaps the most moving and hopeful moment in the novel. It brings people of different races and religions – Muslims and Catholics, African Americans, Arabs, and Anglos – together in a moment of "communal grace" that "appease[s] their grief" (C 134–8).

Conclusions

In each of the scenes of redemptive gathering that we have discussed, then, DeLillo dramatizes religiously inflected rites that produce a complex experience of partial redemption, an experience compounded of a mysterious sense of communion and a profoundly painful acknowledgment of fragility, finitude, and brokenness. But even as DeLillo fashions these powerful representations of postsecular mystery, he questions their validity, suggesting that they may represent, in the end, nothing more than one more mode of self-mystification. Each scene contains within it possibilities for irony. How seriously can we take the festival of nonstop consumption that Pammy discovers on the streets of New York? What is the relation between the "cloud of unknowing" and the toxic clouds that produce the theatrical sunsets in *White Noise*? And is the juice that "pour[s] forth" on the billboard in *Underworld* the product of the spirit or of advertising (U 816)? The strategic positioning of these scenes draws us deeper into uncertainty. In *White Noise*, for instance, DeLillo sets the overpass episode at the end of a narrative chain that conducts us from one absurd and self-generated "moment of transcendence" to another: from the collective rapture produced by the sight of the most photographed barn in America to the "supernatural" consolations of the supermarket. I have read the overpass scene as breaking that chain, but it is possible to see it as a final episode of self-mystification. Or as the penultimate episode, for in *White Noise* as in his other works DeLillo positions his scenes of apparently successful communion with mystery just before final episodes that return us to blank confusion and pain. So in *The Names*, for instance, the ceremony at the Acropolis is followed by a fragment from Tap Axton's novel-in-progress that depicts its protagonist's terrified flight from a fierce Pentecostal service into a landscape of meaningless chaos, "the nightmare of real things" (N 339). And in *Underworld* Sister Edgar's moment of communion is followed by a scene in which she appears to have died and been transported into another dimension, not heaven but the trackless wastes of cyberspace. *White Noise* itself brings us back from the overpass to the supermarket, where we are informed by Jack, in the final words of the novel, that "[e]verything we need that is not food or love is here in the tabloid racks. The tales of the supernatural and the extraterrestrial. The miracle vitamins, the cures for cancer, the remedies for obesity. The cults of the famous and the dead" (WN 326).

What are we to make of these ultimate scenes? Are they designed to erase completely the sense of possibility, of authentic mystery, generated by the scenes of redemptive gathering? Or to drive home the fragility and impermanence of such experiences? Or are they to be read according to a different logic, branching rather than sequential, as ways of understanding how things can turn out, in the absence of any adequate opening to mystery?

DeLillo seems determined to leave any resolution of this question to his readers. "And what do you remember," the anonymous narrator of *Underworld* asks an unspecified second person, in the wake of the moment of ecstatic communion at the billboard,

> when everyone has gone home and the streets are empty of devotion and hope, swept by the river wind? Is the memory thin and bitter and does it shame you with its fundamental untruth – all nuance and wishful silhouette? Or does the power of transcendence linger, the sense of an event that violates natural forces, something holy that throbs on the hot horizon, the vision you crave because you need a sign to stand against your doubt? (*U* 824)

DeLillo has been telling us, all along, that spiritual experiences such as those we have been examining are mysteriously sponsored, mysteriously formed, and unverifiable. He cannot tell us, then, with the confidence of a detective who has cracked a case, or a magus who has attained the key to all knowledge, or the priest of an ancient faith, exactly why such experiences occur and what they mean. The Church would say that there are in fact divine mysteries, but DeLillo can say only that certain events, which may be related to some form of more-than-human benignity, occur, and that they seem to be healing.

Notes

1. For DeLillo's comments on his relation to his Catholic heritage, see interviews with Anthony DeCurtis, "'An Outsider in This Society': An Interview with Don DeLillo," in Frank Lentricchia, ed., *Introducing Don DeLillo* (Durham: Duke University Press, 1991); Vince Passaro, "Dangerous Don DeLillo," *New York Times* (May 19, 1991), pp. 34 ff; Tom LeClair, "An Interview with Don DeLillo," in Thomas DePietro, ed., *Conversations with Don DeLillo* (Jackson: University Press of Mississippi, 2005), pp. 3–15; David Remnick, "Exile on Main Street," *New Yorker* (September 15, 1997), pp. 42–8; and Maria Moss, "Writing as a Deeper Form of Concentration: An Interview with Don DeLillo," *Sources* (Spring 1999), pp. 82–97.
2. Nicholas Lash, *The Beginning and the End of "Religion"* (Cambridge: Cambridge University Press, 1996), pp. 61, 53, 59.
3. Richard Rorty and Gianni Vattimo, *The Future of Religion* (New York: Columbia University Press, 2005), p. 56.

4. William Connolly, *Identity/Difference* (Ithaca: Cornell University Press, 1991), p. 155.

5. See Amy Hungerford, "Don DeLillo's Latin Mass," *Contemporary Literature* 47.3 (Fall 2006), pp. 343–80.

6. Mark Osteen, *American Magic and Dread: Don DeLillo's Dialogue with Culture* (Philadelphia: University of Pennsylvania Press, 2000), p. 166.

7. See, for example, Frank Lentricchia, *New Essays on "White Noise"* (Cambridge: Cambridge University Press, 1991), p. 113, and for a counterperspective, Thomas Ferraro, "Whole Families Shopping at Night," in ibid., p. 20.

8. Anon., *The Cloud of Unknowing and Other Works* (New York: Penguin, 1981), pp. 61–2.

JOSEPH M. CONTE

Conclusion: Writing amid the ruins: 9/11 and *Cosmopolis*

The fall of the Towers

Many lives came to an abrupt end on the morning of September 11, 2001, among them those of a financial analyst with Cantor Fitzgerald in the World Trade Center who did not return to meet his wife at a suburban New Jersey commuter train station; a busboy in the Windows on the World restaurant with a second job lined up that evening in the Bronx; and a firefighter from Queens who had expected a day of camaraderie at the fire station. The 1990s had been marked by the technological acceleration and financial excesses of the information economy; but the freeze-frame shot of American Airlines Flight 11 penetrating the glass and steel carapace of the North Tower at 8:46 am brought this symbol of the United States's preeminent place in multi-national capitalism to ruins. Don DeLillo, who had nearly finished drafting his thirteenth novel, *Cosmopolis* (2003) at the time, shared in the collective seizure of the American mind. "Terror," he observes, "is now the world narrative, unquestionably. When those two buildings were struck, and when they collapsed, it was, in effect, an extraordinary blow to conscious-ness, and it changed everything."[1] After the terrorist attacks, DeLillo claims, "I took a long pause. I just didn't want to work for a while, although I wrote an essay on the attacks themselves. The attacks didn't affect the novel directly, but they certainly affected me."[2]

The action of *Cosmopolis* is confined to a single day in April 2000, as Eric Packer, a 28-year-old billionaire currency trader and fund manager, attempts to make his way in a luxurious and technologically sophisticated stretch limousine through the gridlock of mid-town Manhattan to get a haircut. As Packer expends his vast personal fortune in order to leverage a dip in the Japanese yen, an unpredictable gyration of the market presages the "dotcom bubble" collapse. While some reviews of this post-9/11 novel have suggested that the novelist's imagination may have been overtaken by events, attention to the essay that DeLillo wrote during his pause in the completion of his novel, "In the Ruins of the Future: Reflections on Terror and Loss in the Shadow of September," published in December 2001, reveals that he has more presciently understood the character of this major phase-change in American culture than most of the "first responders" in newspapers, journals, and broadcast media.[3]

Although he declines to regard his fiction as prophetic, DeLillo's novels are deeply seamed with moments of senseless violence and deliberate acts of terrorism – either emanating from the American psyche or calculated to disturb it with maximum effect. His many observant readers have commented on the premonitory quality of the catastrophes that occur in his works. The airborne toxic event that descends upon a small college town in *White Noise* (1985) seems prelude to the release of methyl isocyanate gas from the Union Carbide plant in Bhopal, India, that same year.[4] His magnum opus, *Underworld* (1997), is punctuated by the Texas highway killer whose random drive-away shootings prefigure the Washington, D.C. sniper attacks of 2002. *Mao II* (1991) notably features the "curious knot that binds novelists and terrorists" (*M* 41), the latter in the guise of the anti-Western militia chief Abu Rashid in civil war-torn Beirut. Appearing two years before the initial attack on the World Trade Center by the Islamist terrorist group al-Qa'eda in 1993, the novel regards the Towers through the reflex lens of photographer Brita Nilsson: "my big complaint is only partly size. The size is deadly. But having two of them is like a comment, it's like a dialogue, only I don't know what they're saying" (*M* 40). Summarizing this theme of frightening prognostication, the critic Vince Passaro, in "Don DeLillo and the Towers," calls our attention to the cover photograph of *Underworld*: "there it was, the two towers, dark and enshrouded (by fog, much as they had been by smoke early last Tuesday morning); before them the stark silhouette of the belfry of a nearby Church ... and off to the side, a large bird, a gull or a large pigeon, making its way toward Tower One. It's eerie and religious."[5] DeLillo would regard these episodes – the prevalence of terrorist acts in his fictions, the shadow cast by the Towers – not as premonitions of events as they have come to pass but as the gift of the novelist for expressing the latent crises in the culture before others have fully recognized them. Thus, confronted with the otherwise unspeakable loss of 9/11 – that is, not expressible in its enormity in any literary, artistic, or journalistic representation after the fact – the observant reader nevertheless experiences a kind of cognitive consonance when a writer such as DeLillo has already suggested that such an event might happen.

Eric Packer's crosstown route on 47th Street in Manhattan takes him from his residence in the international district near the United Nations headquarters and the Japan Society on First Avenue, threading past Times Square and the Nasdaq Center to the south, and reaching the industrial lofts, tenements, and an underground garage past Eleventh Avenue; from dawn to nightfall; and from the bastions of wealth and global power to the squalid indigence of an abandoned warehouse. Of course, the World Trade Center on the lower West Side – still standing in April 2000 – is not to be seen on this route. But Packer's conspicuously appointed 48-room penthouse triplex apartment, furnished with a lap pool, gymnasium, shark tank, and dog pen for his borzois, is situated in an 89-story building, at "nine hundred feet high, the tallest residential tower in the world, a commonplace oblong whose only statement was its size. It had the kind of banality that reveals itself over time as being truly brutal. He liked it for this reason" (*C* 8–9). Packer's building is thus the residential complement of the Twin Towers, at 110 stories and 1,368 feet the tallest buildings in the world at the time of their completion in 1973. Although approving, Packer's assessment of the gigantism of his building echoes Brita Nilsson's view of the Towers. Packer's building is symbolic of his brutal avariciousness, which is finally more disdainfully egotistical than it is mercantile; the collapse and destruction, however, is that of Packer's fortune and his life, not the building's. Alphonse Stompanato, chair of the department of American environments at the College-on-the-Hill in *White Noise*, advances a version of catastrophe theory that is mordantly humorous but instructive: "we're suffering from brain fade. We need an occasional catastrophe to break up the incessant bombardment of information" (*WN* 66). In millennial American culture, the catastrophe of the Towers seizes on consciousness, its terror breaking through the anomie of multinational capitalism and media saturation.

From the Cold War to the Age of Terror

One lesson of the 9/11 attacks is that we should no longer expect that changes in world culture will present themselves swathed in gradualism; rather, we should expect them to have the instantaneity of a paradigm shift in which suddenly none of the rules and explanations of the earlier regime applies. It may be that the dynamics of such a phase-change have been at work covertly before a new order is revealed, but the change, when it arrives, is not incremental but totalizing. DeLillo's *Cosmopolis* merits some comparison with James Joyce's *Ulysses* (1922), whose action follows the wandering of Leopold Bloom on June 16, 1904, as the modern epitome of what may be encapsulated in a single day. It is not a narrative gimmick that Eric Packer's crosstown odyssey in *Cosmopolis* takes place on the day in April 2000, when the financial market suddenly lost its momentum and wobbled toward a collapse. DeLillo states that "I realized that the day on which this book takes place is the last day of an era."[6] Its narrative compression, the "sense of acceleration of time and of reality itself,"[7] correlates with the assessment of his essay "In the Ruins of the Future," which measures the acts of terror that in one day rewrote some three thousand life stories and changed the narrative of the American future.

DeLillo begins his essay by describing the world much as it was on that day in April 2000:

> In the past decade the surge of capital markets has dominated discourse and shaped global consciousness. Multinational corporations have come to seem more vital and influential than governments. The dramatic climb of the Dow and the speed of the Internet summoned us all to live permanently in the future, in the utopian glow of cyber-capital, because there is no memory there and this is where markets are uncontrolled and investment potential has no limit.[8]

Eric Packer is the lord of this domain, the very avatar of cyber-capital. As he brings his multibillion dollar investment fund to bear on the value of the Japanese yen, he asserts the preeminence of global capital over the power of even the Group of Eight national economies. By comparison, the President of the United States in his motorcade, which impedes Packer's progress to the West Side, appears as a soft, "gynecoid" figure on the flat-panel monitors of Packer's white, anonymous stretch limousine. The leader of the Free World appears as "the undead. He lived in a state of occult repose, waiting to be reanimated," a corollary of the embalmed Lenin in his Red Square mausoleum (C 77). Packer no longer trades in or forecasts stocks that would have been associated with some sector of industrial or commercial production; now he concerns himself solely with charting and predicting the movement of money itself, seeking the "hidden rhythms in the fluctuation of a given currency" (C 76). The question of profit and loss is, in a sense, immaterial as he hedges the relative price of currencies in an electronically connected global market. It is a virtual economy, as Packer's "chief of theory," Vija Kinski – more a postmodernist than an economist – waxes: "I love the screens. The glow of cyber-capital. So radiant and seductive" (C 78). Echoing DeLillo's assessment of the turn-of-the-millennium utopianism, she opines, "It's cyber-capital that creates the future. What is the measurement called a nanosecond?" (C 79). The international currency markets the Nikkei and the Nasdaq never close. This is liquid-crystal globalism, virtual, instantaneous, and networked.

But all is changed utterly in a day. DeLillo apprehends that on September 11, "the world narrative belongs to terrorists" who target America's technological modernity, its secularism, its imperialism, and the "power of American culture to penetrate every wall, home, life, and mind."[9] It is a counternarrative that repudiates US hegemony as the world's only future. Discussing *Cosmopolis* with interviewers, he states that the novel is poised liminally "between the end of the Cold War and the beginning of the Age of Terror."[10] Readers of *Underworld* will appreciate DeLillo's treatment of the Cold War, from the US discovery of Soviet nuclear testing in 1951 in the novel's prologue, "The Triumph of Death," to the post-Soviet entrepreneurialism in disposing of contaminated waste in Kazakhstan in the epilogue, "Das Kapital." The bilateral animus and the geographic spheres of influence of the NATO and Soviet blocs have dissipated. Yet, with a Cabinet staffed with Cold War warriors and a National Security Advisor in Condoleezza Rice who was a Soviet Union specialist, the Bush administration retained a dangerous "feeling of nostalgia for the Cold War"[11] through the very moment of shocked inaction by the President on the morning of September 11, 2001. DeLillo suggests in his essay that a counternarrative to the binary opposition of the United States and Russia needs to be articulated, one that describes the transnational politics of a new global order. In contrast to the thinking in the Oval Office, Packer deploys some of his cyber-capital to pick up a piece of Cold War kitsch, a decommissioned Soviet strategic bomber, "an old Tu-160. NATO calls it a Blackjack A," nuclear weapons and cruise missiles not included. Not purchased from the Russians, of course, but on the "black market and dirt cheap from a Belgian arms dealer in Kazakhstan" (C 103). It seems no more than a provocative anecdote meant to illustrate the transcendence of global capital over nation-states until one learns that after conceiving the episode, DeLillo read about a wealthy American in California who "owns a decommissioned MiG, a Soviet fighter plane."[12]

Just as the Cold War had its analysts, the Age of Terror must have its theorists. Jean Baudrillard's essay "The Spirit of Terrorism" offers a counternarrative by describing the singularity of globalization that has displaced the antithetical ideologies of the Cold War. He asks, "When the world has been so thoroughly monopolized, when power has been so formidably consolidated by the technocratic machine and the dogma of globalization, what means of turning the table remains besides terrorism?"[13] As global capital has established a permeating hegemony over world culture, terrorism is a retrovirus that emerges as the dark agent, the counterforce, in this struggle for dominion. "Terrorism is the act that restores an irreducible singularity to the heart of a generalized system of exchange."[14] In place of the ideological antithesis between capitalism and communism in the Cold War, globalization and terrorism each contend within a singular dynamic for a deterritorialized, transnational power. Fronted by multinational corporations and networked consumerism, globalization suffuses and appropriates world cultures. As DeLillo's minister of theory, Vija Kinski, states, there is nowhere one can "exist outside the market" (C 90). As we know, the terrorists occupy no strategic territory; they are not outside but inside the dominant system. Baudrillard concurs that

> there is no longer a boundary that can hem terrorism in; it is at the heart of the very culture it's fighting with, and the visible fracture (and the hatred) that pits the exploited and underdeveloped nations of the world against the West masks the dominant system's internal fractures. It is as if every means of domination secreted its own antidote.[15]

He regards the ordeal of 9/11 as the first salvo in a fourth World War, after the end of European imperialism, Nazism, and Communism; but it is a war of "fractal complexity, waged worldwide against rebellious singularities that, in the manner of antibodies, mount a resistance in every cell."[16]

DeLillo's assessment of the Age of Terror, expressed in "In the Ruins of the Future," is comparable in some respects to Baudrillard's: "With the end of Communism, the ideas and principles of modern democracy were seen clearly to prevail, whatever the inequalities of the system itself. This is still the case. But now there is a global theocratic state, unboundaried and floating and so obsolete it must depend on suicidal fervor to gain its aims."[17] It is disconcerting to regard how representative democracy, or "freedom on the march," has subsequently been employed as a shill for globalization in the war in Iraq. In turn, the improvised explosive device deployed in automobiles, backpacks, and roadside caches has become the weapon *du jour* in Baghdad, Bali, London, and Madrid by clandestine, border-crossing terrorists in support of a transnational Islamist theocracy. Yet Baudrillard cautions that the "phantom of America" should not be taken as the incarnation of globalization, any more than the "phantom of Islam" should be equated with terrorism. Global capitalism and the Islamist theocracy are narrative and counternarrative, the technological future and the fundamentalist past, in the fashioning of a new global order.

The episode that concludes Part One of *Cosmopolis*, as Packer's limousine passes Times Square and crosses Broadway from the East Side to the West Side of Manhattan, involves a violent demonstration by red-and-black-clad anarchists at the Nasdaq Exchange, trading floor for technology stocks in the new economy. In their attack on the fortress of cyber-capital, the protesters are the new Luddites, setting off a bomb outside an investment bank and changing the electronic stock ticker to declare, "a specter is haunting the world – the specter of capitalism," a variation of the first sentence of *The Communist Manifesto*, written as a response to the ills of industrial capitalism in 1848 (C 96).[18] Although not advocates of a transnational Islamist theocracy, the anarchists who rock Packer's limousine behave as vectors of the counternarrative. Kinski, riding with Packer, sounds much like Baudrillard in her understanding that because "market culture is total," it "breeds these men and women. They are necessary to the system they despise" (C 90). Cyber-capital and terrorism contend within the singularity of global power. As presented through Packer's sensibility, the episode is a "market fantasy" that illustrates the interdependence of the system of domination and its antidote, the host and its vector: "The protest was a form of systemic hygiene, purging and lubricating. It attested again, for the ten thousandth time, to the market culture's innovative brilliance, its ability to shape itself to its own flexible ends, absorbing everything around it" (C 99). Packer's confidence that such antiglobalization protests serve only to confirm the totality of the system is shaken by the self-immolation of one of the protesters in the street. This act of ritual suicide, evoking the Buddhist monks in South Vietnam and the four Americans who in the mid-1960s immolated themselves protesting against the war in Vietnam, may be a "thing outside" the reach of globalization. Although Kinski declares the gesture unoriginal, self-immolation represents a pure form of protest against totalizing political systems and other forms of oppression; the extreme act works as a statement that counters the totality of the market's absorption with a body consumed by fire. Unlike the suicidal attacks of 9/11, however, ritual self-immolation involves no other victims and is intended as an appeal to nonviolence.

Technology and the lethal believer

The 9/11 attacks staged a morality play in which the proponents of a twenty-first century figured in virtual space, technological complexity, and globally networked information systems are confronted by the fanatical adherents of an anti-enlightenment religion, moral absolutism, and medieval retribution. Americans are inclined to believe that they have "invented the future."[19] Technology becomes our belief system, "our fate," a miracle that "we ourselves produce." Unmatched technological superiority is "what we mean when we call ourselves the only superpower on the planet."[20] In *Cosmopolis* Packer possesses an almost preternatural ability to recognize the patterns in currency values that shift in nanoseconds and cyber-capital that is traded instantaneously on the Nikkei and Nasdaq markets. He assumes the hieratic role of the prophet. His fortune depends on his recognition that

> speed is the point. Never mind the urgent and endless replenishment, the way data dissolves at one end of the series just at it takes shape at the other. This is

the point, the thrust, the future. We are not witnessing the flow of information so much as pure spectacle, or information made sacred, ritually unreadable. The small monitors of the office, home and car become a kind of idolatry here, where crowds might gather in astonishment. (C 80)

So attuned is Packer to the future that he repeatedly literalizes the rhetorical trope known as "hysteron proteron"; that is, as he scans the several digital monitors mounted in his limousine, he experiences an effect before its cause. Among Packer's premonitions is observing himself onscreen recoiling in shock from the Nasdaq bombing before the actual blast occurs. Kinski declares it a sign of his genius – how else could Packer anticipate fluctuations in world currency? – evidence of the "polymath, the true futurist" (C 95). Yet she warns that while technology "helps us make our fate ... it is also crouched and undecidable. It can go either way" – indeed, the Japanese yen defies Packer's hedged bet and rises (C 95).

Packer bears witness to the imminent coming of the technological sublime. In historical terms, he apprehends the shift from the postwar order of the military-industrial complex that directed both strategic arms and anticommunist incursions to a world order based on the "interaction between technology and capital. The inseparability" (C 23). Prophets are adept at reading the signs in nature of the advent of messianic power, and while Packer traverses the city in his limousine he tracks the flow of information on digital monitors. Although he has sex with his new wife and several mistresses during the course of his day, Packer disdains the body (what he calls "meat space" [C 64]), preferring instead to scan the spectacle of financial data with the deep acuity of an autistic savant for the "organic patterns" of "birdwing and chambered shell" (C 24) that might be found there. Reading the eloquence of the alphanumeric graphs of finance, he apprehends "in the zerooneness of the world, the digital imperative that defined every breath of the planet's living billions" (C 24). Seeking to reveal latent patterns in the otherwise irregular and unpredictable behavior of the market, Packer intuitively grasps the fractal complexity of financial data and believes he has "found beauty and precision here, hidden rhythms in the fluctuations of a given currency" as surely as there are repeating figures in nature (C 76).

In Packer's last experience of hysteron proteron – as he realizes that he is already dead, shot by his stalker, Benno Levin – he is granted a vision of the ultimate union of cognition and information technology. As the Abrahamic faiths promise the afterlife of the soul, so the technological sublime holds forth the transcendence of the disembodied mind

as data, in whirl, in radiant spin, a consciousness saved from void. The technology was imminent or not. It was semi-mythical. It was the natural next step.

It would never happen. It is happening now; an evolutionary advance that needed only the practical mapping of the nervous system onto digital memory. It would be the master thrust of cyber-capital, to extend the human experience toward infinity as a medium for corporate growth and investment, for the accumulation of profits and vigorous reinvestment. (*C* 206–7)

As his mind dissipates into the void, Packer espouses the doctrine and the financial prospectus of the world religion of cyber-capital.

This millennial tale of the mind's rapturous relationship with technology has its believers and its apostates. Among the "credible threats" (*C* 19) to the wellbeing of Eric Packer is a disgruntled former employee of the investment fund, Richard Sheets, a computer analyst whose perceived slights include being demoted to "lesser currencies" (*C* 151) such as the Thai baht. Under the alias Benno Levin, he writes his Confessions (*C* 58, 149) – to premeditated murder and to a darkly Augustinian conversion narrative in which he rejects faith in cyber-capital – presented as interludes to Packer's odyssey. Now offline and squatting in an abandoned tenement near Eleventh Avenue, Levin resembles those "men in small rooms" (*L* 181), whose ranks include for DeLillo all makers of plots, including novelists and terrorists, writing "ten thousand pages that will stop the world" (*C* 152). Although Levin is not to be regarded as a martyr in the cause of a global theocratic state, his murderous design puts him in loose alliance with those who refuse to be absorbed in the dominion of an information economy and a virtual future. Levin shares, however, the fanatical intent of the terrorist as described by George Haddad in *Mao II*:

> Who do we take seriously? Only the lethal believer, the person who kills and dies for faith. Everything else is absorbed. The artist is absorbed, the madman in the street is absorbed and processed and incorporated . . . Only the terrorist stands outside. The culture hasn't figured out how to assimilate him. It's confusing when they kill the innocent. But this is precisely the language of being noticed, the only language the West understands. (*M* 157)

After 9/11, one regards this passage as an accurate profiling of radical Islamists, the "lethal believers" such as Mohamed Atta al-Sayed who infiltrated Western modernity while harboring a fundamentalist determination to see it destroyed. The technological sublime – the conviction that science and technology can emancipate and uplift humanity with their promise of a brightly burnished future that eradicates the past – is deemed a godless and indulgent infidel belief. Benno Levin the disaffected apostate can be more closely aligned with such assassins of influential men as Lee Harvey Oswald or Mehmet Ali Ağca (the Turkish radical who shot Pope John Paul II in St. Peter's Square in 1981), but the antipathy toward globalism and Western technocracy is a common trait.

Blood sport

Cosmopolis is hardly the first American novel to critique the vain obsessions of an elite class of businessmen. The *nouveau riche* title character of William Dean Howells's cautionary tale *The Rise of Silas Lapham* (1885) is ruined financially – but spiritually redeemed – when his business speculations fail. Sinclair Lewis's *Babbitt* (1922) enters the lexicon as synonymous with narrow-minded commercial success that remains dismayingly ignorant of the complexities of modern life. In this lineage Eric Packer has no pretense to philanthropy or social largesse. His cruel diet is his competition. It is a blood sport, and he regards the assassination of his rival Arthur Rapp, managing director of the International Monetary Fund, "killed live on the Money Channel" (C 33), as "refreshing. The prospective dip in the yen was invigorating" (C 35). Making the point explicit with his female bodyguard, who is assigned to protect him from such assaults, Packer states, "The logical extension of business is murder" (C 113). One imagines that Packer regards assassination as the ultimate form of hostile takeover. He also finds "contentment" in the report of the death of Nikolai Kaganovich (C 81), the head of a Russian media conglomerate that is establishing a post-Soviet monopoly in telecommunications and online pornography. Packer recognizes a fraternal bond with Kaganovich, found "facedown in the mud in front of his dacha outside Moscow, shot numerous times just after returning from a trip to Albania Online" (C 82), in that this transnational entrepreneur exhibits the essential qualities of shrewdness and cruelty; he is a wolfhound, a borzoi in pants. There is a League of Rogues who compete for dominion in cyber-capital. Although vestiges of Cold War mutual deterrence remain, Packer and Kaganovich are rivals in a global market that is unfettered by the trade regulations of nation-states. Assassination – whether it be by antiglobalist protesters, organized crime, or local militias – is presented as the reciprocal tactic of international business practice.

It seems that it is a day "for influential men to come to sudden messy ends" (C 132). The concatenation of attacks in *Cosmopolis* is the natural extension of the business cycle, so they harbinger the stunning collapse of the dotcom bubble of which Packer Capital is a chief proponent. It is a system on the edge of chaos. The egregious assault on the Nasdaq Exchange that is meant to recall the bombing on Wall Street by anarchists on September 16, 1920 – which was then heralded as an act of war – includes a parachutist whose exposed member is logotyped in red and black. The asymmetry between the bastions of global capital and the protesters requires that their largely symbolic assaults must be spectacular. These are not strategic assaults in which the armored vehicles or ballistic missiles of opposing forces are arrayed in a contest over geographic territory; rather, the intent of terrorism is to deliver the most lurid impact possible on the public consciousness. Baudrillard regards the attacks on 9/11 in this vein: "the radical nature of the spectacle, its brutality, is the only thing about it that is original and irreducible. The spectacle of terrorism forces upon us the terrorism of the spectacle." Invoking Antonin Artaud's theory of drama as a shock to the audience's complacency, he claims, "It is our very own theater of cruelty, the only one we have left – extraordinary because it represents both the high point of the spectacular and the high point of defiance."[21] One nonlethal assailant in *Cosmopolis* in the asymmetrical warfare against globalization is André Petrescu – presumably Romanian, though his nationality is not given – who bills himself as the "pastry assassin." His "mission worldwide," he claims after having "crèmed" Packer, is to "sabotage power and wealth" (C 142–3). The very spectacularity of these assaults is required by the cruel disparity of the global political system.

How, then, to explain Packer's increasingly self-destructive behavior as he traverses Manhattan? Surely a baron of hypercapitalism can summon a legion of hairdressers to his apartment or limousine, yet he persists in this stubbornly counterproductive venture into geographic space and gridlock. Despite his chief of security's remonstrance, he insists, "[W]e still want what we want," which is the spirit of capitalism (C 101). He visits an old-fashioned Italian barber in the tenement-crowded neighborhood who, under his father's supervision, first cut his hair. Such a destination appears dangerously nostalgic and against type. But perhaps like DeLillo's Nick Shay in *Underworld*, Packer longs for "the days of disarray when I walked real streets and did things slap-bang and felt angry and ready all the time, a danger to others and a distant mystery to myself" (U 810). The desire to revisit this locale in real space that has emotional attachment – the only expression of attachment that Packer permits himself – acts as a parasite that infects his judgment in the simulated space of global finance. His leveraging of the yen has caused "storms of disorder" in the currency market (C 116), and as chaoticians will attest, perturbations in nonlinear dynamical systems can have disproportionate and unpredictable effects. Packer has brought his entire portfolio of tens of billions, and the lagniappe of his wife's inheritance of a few hundred million, to bear on the yen in a test of his genius for discerning the latent patterns in nature; if incorrect, he becomes the vector of the system's destabilization and he fatally compromises his intellectual esteem. The symptoms of a seemingly automated self-punishment include stunning himself with his bodyguard's taser, killing Torval, his chief of security, with his own voice-activated gun, and shooting himself in the hand during his confrontation with his assassin, Levin, when he might have shot Levin instead.

In "The Spirit of Terrorism," Baudrillard again provides insight into how in a chaotic and asymmetrical warfare the dominant system can be induced to self-destruct. As an avatar of hypercapitalism, Packer has committed suicide rather than fallen victim to an assassination plot. Unlike conventional warfare fought on the battlefield of reality, Baudrillard explains, terrorism assumes the terrain of symbolism:

> The tactic of the model terrorist is to provoke an excess of reality and to make the system collapse under its own weight; the terrorist hypothesis is that the system itself will commit suicide in response to multiple fatal suicide attacks, because neither the system nor power is free from symbolic obligations. In this vertiginous cycle of exchanging death, the death of a terrorist is an infinitesimal point, but one that provokes an enormous aspiration.[22]

Just as the roadside bombings in Baghdad have greater symbolic force than the actual casualties they incur, and as these suicidal attacks precipitate self-inflicted wounds upon the domestic and international symbolic imaginary – at the Guantanamo Bay detainment camp, in Abu Ghraib prison, and in the village of Haditha – so for Packer and the system of hypercapitalism the various asymmetrical, suicidal assaults take their toll. "All around this minute point," according to Baudrillard, "the entire system, the system of reality and power, fortifies itself, vaccinates itself, gathers itself together, and crumbles into ruin out of its own overefficiency."[23] Packer is a financial Icarus in meltdown, too prideful to admit miscalculation. Levin instructs him in the principles of chaos theory – and the spirit of terrorism – when he points out that Packer's search for symmetrical shapes in market cycles and natural rhythms is "horribly and sadistically precise," in effect, an overefficiency. Instead of examining for harmonic balance, Packer should have recognized that patterns in currency values would be "lopsided," misshapen, irregular, or – as in the contest between globalism and terrorism – asymmetrical (C 200).[24]

DeLillo's fiction has been closely attuned to moments of cultural transformation in American history – the public announcement of a nuclear-ized Cold War in the *New York Times* on October 4, 1951, in *Underworld*; the "seven seconds that broke the back of the American century" on November 22, 1963, in *Libra* (1988); and the beginning of the Age of Terror September 11, 2001. In his first novel published after that day on which the hellacious fury of fundamentalism impacted the gigantism of global capital, DeLillo's *Cosmopolis* depicts the collapse of an American future determined by the pure synergy of finance and technology. In the ruins of the future he finds a new syndrome of global ideological conflict. He issues a warning for democracy – in kind with Bill Gray's advocacy in *Mao II* of the novel as a "democratic shout" (*M* 159) that in its contradictions contains multitudes, against absolutist beliefs – to reclaim the essence of individual freedom in the twenty-first century. This democratic shout must be heard above the imprecations of theocracy abroad or the impingement of personal liberties and speech at home.

Notes

1. David L. Ulin, "Finding Reason in an Age of Terror," *Los Angeles Times* (April 15, 2003), p. E1.
2. John Barron, "DeLillo Bashful? Not This Time," *Chicago Sun-Times* (March 23, 2003), p. 1.
3. "In the Ruins of the Future" not only offers a penetrating reading of the relationship of globalization and terrorism but also provides a personal reflection on the tragedy. DeLillo's nephew's family had nearly been killed in their financial-district apartment house as the Towers fell. As a lifelong New Yorker, DeLillo recounts that within days he went to the site, "looking directly into the strands of openwork façade. It is almost too close. It is almost Roman, I-beams for stonework, but not nearly so salvageable. Many here describe the scene to others on cell phones. 'Oh my god I'm standing here,' says the man next to me." See Don DeLillo, "In the Ruins of the Future: Reflections on Terror and Loss in the Shadow of September," *Harper's* (December 2001), p. 38.

   In his latest novel, *Falling Man* (2007), DeLillo examines the traumatic experience and personal restitution of one man, Keith Neudecker, a corporate lawyer working in the North Tower. Stunned and injured, Neudecker accepts a ride from a stranger, giving the address of his estranged wife and son in uptown Manhattan, initiating, unconsciously, a healing process that reunites the family. Yet when he returns to the site and to his nearby bachelor apartment, he can only remark, "I'm standing here" (*FM* 25), recapitulating the expression of awe before the disaster site recorded in DeLillo's essay. It is the recognition of survivors that there is nothing virtuous – or evil – that distinguishes them from those who perished. It is the same recognition that comes to the survivors of every holocaust in history.
4. Mark Osteen, "Introduction," in Osteen, ed., *"White Noise": Text and Criticism* (New York: Viking, 1998), p. vii.
5. Vince Passaro, "Don DeLillo and the Towers," *Mr Bellers Neighborhood*, October 10, 2001, http://www.mrbellersneighborhood.com/story.php?storyid=403. Passaro states that DeLillo independently selected the image for the cover of *Underworld*.
6. Barron, "DeLillo Bashful?" p. 1.
7. Ibid.
8. DeLillo, "In the Ruins," p. 33.
9. Ibid.
10. Ulin, "Finding Reason," p. E1. See also Barron, "DeLillo Bashful?"
11. DeLillo, "In the Ruins," p. 34.
12. Barron, "DeLillo Bashful?" p. 1.

13. Jean Baudrillard, "The Spirit of Terrorism," trans. Donovan Hohn, *Harper's* (February 2002), p. 14.
14. Ibid.
15. Ibid.
16. Ibid.
17. DeLillo, "In the Ruins," p. 40.
18. The original text by Marx and Engels reads, "A spectre is haunting Europe – the spectre of communism."
19. DeLillo, "In the Ruins," p. 39.
20. Ibid., p. 37.
21. Baudrillard, "Spirit of Terrorism," p. 18.
22. Ibid., p. 16.
23. Ibid.
24. In *Falling Man* DeLillo discusses the strategy of asymmetrical warfare practiced by terrorists through the character of Ernst Hechinger, aka Martin Ridnour, an international art dealer with a shady past that might lead to the Baader-Meinhof Gang of left-wing West German radicals of the 1970s. Ridnour's commentary on anti-American terrorism is comparable to Jean Baudrillard's theory: "They strike a blow to this country's dominance. They achieve this, to show how a great power can be vulnerable. A power that interferes, that occupies ... One side has the capital, the labor, the technology, the armies, the agencies, the cities, the laws, the police and the prisons. The other side has a few men willing to die" (*FM* 46–7).

SELECT BIBLIOGRAPHY

This bibliography is meant only to introduce readers to the wealth of material written by and about Don DeLillo. Those seeking the latest and fullest bibliographic information should consult the two websites listed below under "Secondary sources."

Works by Don Delillo

Novels

Americana. Boston: Houghton Mifflin, 1971.
End Zone. Boston: Houghton Mifflin, 1972.
Great Jones Street. Boston: Houghton Mifflin, 1973.
Ratner's Star. New York: Knopf, 1976.
Players. New York: Knopf, 1977.
Running Dog. New York: Knopf, 1978.
The Names. New York: Knopf, 1982.
White Noise. New York: Viking, 1985.
Libra. New York: Viking, 1988.
Mao II. New York: Viking, 1991.
Underworld. New York: Scribner, 1997.
The Body Artist. New York: Scribner, 2001.
Cosmopolis. New York: Scribner, 2003.
Falling Man. New York: Scribner, 2007.

Major plays

Valparaiso. New York: Scribner, 1999.
Love-Lies-Bleeding. New York: Scribner, 2005.

Screenplay

Game 6. Directed by Michael Hoffman. Santa Monica, CA: Serenade Films, 2005.

Interviews

DePietro, Thomas, ed. *Conversations with Don DeLillo*. Jackson: University Press of Mississippi, 2005. This volume reprints the major interviews with DeLillo from 1982 to 2001.

Secondary sources

Websites

Don DeLillo's America. Ed. Curt Gardner. www.perival.com.

The Don DeLillo Society. Ed. Philip Nel. www.k-state.edu/english/nelp/delillo/.

Books about DeLillo

Boxall, Peter. *Don DeLillo: The Possibility of Fiction*. London: Routledge, 2006.

Cowart, David. *Don DeLillo: The Physics of Language*. Athens: University of Georgia Press, 2002. 2nd revd. edn 2003.

Dewey, Joseph. *Beyond Grief and Nothing: A Reading of Don DeLillo*. Columbia: University of South Carolina Press, 2006.

—, Steven G. Kellman, and Irving Malin, eds. *UnderWords: Perspectives on Don DeLillo's "Underworld."* Newark, DE: University of Delaware Press, 2002.

Duvall, John. *Don DeLillo's "Underworld": A Reader's Guide*. New York: Continuum Publishing, 2002.

Engles, Tim, and John N. Duvall, eds. *Approaches to Teaching DeLillo's "White Noise."* New York: Modern Language Association of America Press, 2006.

Kavadlo, Jesse. *Don DeLillo: Balance at the Edge of Belief*. Frankfurt: Peter Lang, 2004.

Keesey, Douglas. *Don DeLillo*. Twayne's United States Authors Series. New York: Twayne, 1993.

LeClair, Tom. *In the Loop: Don DeLillo and the Systems Novel*. Urbana: University of Illinois Press, 1987.

Lentricchia, Frank, ed. *Introducing Don DeLillo*. Durham: Duke University Press, 1991. Reprint of a special issue of *South Atlantic Quarterly* 89.2 (Spring 1990) on DeLillo.

—, ed. *New Essays on "White Noise."* Cambridge: Cambridge University Press, 1991.

Orr, Leonard. *Don DeLillo's "White Noise": A Reader's Guide*. New York: Continuum Publishing, 2003.

Osteen, Mark. *American Magic and Dread: Don DeLillo's Dialogue with Culture*. Philadelphia: University of Pennsylvania Press, 2000.

Ruppersburg, Hugh, and Tim Engles, ed. *Critical Essays on Don DeLillo*. New York: G. K. Hall, 2000.

GUIDE TO FURTHER READING

1 DeLillo and modernism

Gleason, Paul. "Don DeLillo, T. S. Eliot, and the Redemption of America's Atomic Waste Land." In Joseph Dewey, Steven G. Kellman, and Irving Malin, eds., *UnderWords: Perspectives on Don DeLillo's "Underworld."* Newark: Associated University Presses, 2002, pp. 130–43.

Nel, Philip. "Don DeLillo's Return to Form: The Modernist Poetics of *The Body Artist.*" *Contemporary Literature* 43.4 (Winter 2002), pp. 739–41.

Osteen, Mark. "Echo Chamber: Undertaking *The Body Artist.*" *Studies in the Novel* 37.1 (2005), pp. 64–81.

Saltzman, Arthur. "The Figure in the Static: Don DeLillo's *White Noise.*" In Saltzman, *This Mad "Instead": Governing Metaphors in Contemporary American Fiction.* Columbia: University of South Carolina Press, 2000, pp. 33–48.

2 DeLillo, postmodernism, postmodernity

Allen, Glen Scott. "The End of Pynchon's Rainbow: Postmodern Terror and Paranoia in DeLillo's *Ratner's Star.*" *Postmodern Culture* 4.2 (1994), pp. 115–34.

King, Noel. "Reading *White Noise*: Floating Remarks." *Critical Quarterly* 33.3 (1991), pp. 66–83.

O'Donnell, Patrick. *Latent Destinies: Cultural Paranoia in Contemporary U.S. Narrative.* Durham: Duke University Press, 2000.

Tabbi, Joseph. *Postmodern Sublime: Technology and American Writing from Mailer to Cyberpunk.* Ithaca: Cornell University Press, 1995, pp. 169–207.

3 DeLillo and media culture

Critchley, Simon. *Very Little ... Almost Nothing: Death, Philosophy, Literature.* London: Routledge, 1997.

Hassan, Ihab. *The Literature of Silence: Henry Miller and Samuel Beckett.* New York: Knopf, 1967.

Hutchinson, Stuart. "What Happened to Normal? Where is Normal? DeLillo's *Americana* and *Running Dog.*" *Cambridge Quarterly* 29.2 (2000), pp. 117–32.

4 DeLillo and apocalyptic satire

Keesey, Douglas. "*End Zone.*" In *Don DeLillo.* Twayne's United States Authors Series. New York: Twayne, 1993, pp. 34–47.

LeClair, Tom. "A New Map of the World: *Ratner's Star.*" In LeClair, *In the Loop: Don DeLillo and the Systems Novel.* Urbana: University of Illinois Press, 1987, pp. 110–43.

5 DeLillo and the political thriller

Carpi, Daniela. "The Thriller and Its Dissolution: The Postmodern Revision of a Literary Trend." *Textus* 14 (2001), pp. 53–68.

DeLillo, Don. "That Day in Rome: Movies and Memory." *New Yorker.* October 20, 2003, pp. 76–8.

Johnston, John. "Generic Difficulties in the Novels of Don DeLillo." *Critique* 30 (1989), pp. 261–75.

Mullen, Bill. "No There There: Cultural Criticism as Lost Object in Don DeLillo's *Players* and *Running Dog.*" In Ricard Miguel Alfonso, ed., *Powerless Fictions? Ethics, Cultural Critique, and American Fiction in the Age of Postmodernism.* Amsterdam: Rodopi, 1996, pp. 113–39.

6 White Noise

Engles, Tim. "'Who are You Literally?': Fantasies of the White Self in *White Noise.*" *Modern Fiction Studies* 45 (1999), pp. 755–87.

Lentricchia, Frank. "Tales of the Electronic Tribe." In Lentricchia, ed., *New Essays on "White Noise.*" Cambridge: Cambridge University Press, 1991, pp. 87–113.

Peyser, Thomas. "Globalization in America: The Case of Don DeLillo's *White Noise.*" *Clio* 25 (1996), pp. 255–71.

Wilcox, Leonard. "Baudrillard, DeLillo's *White Noise*, and the End of Heroic Narrative." *Contemporary Literature* 32 (1991), pp. 346–65.

7 Libra

Olster, Stacey. "A Mother (and a Son, and a Brother, and Wife, et al.) in History: Stories Galore in *Libra* and the Warren Commission Report." In John N. Duvall, ed., *Productive Postmodernism: Consuming Histories and Cultural Studies.* Albany: State University of New York Press, 2002, pp. 43–59.

Thomas, Glen. "History, Biography, and Narrative in Don DeLillo's *Libra.*" *Twentieth-Century Literature* 43 (1997), pp. 107–24.

Willman, Skip. "Art after Dealey Plaza: DeLillo's *Libra.*" *Modern Fiction Studies* 45 (1999), pp. 621–40.

8 Underworld

Apter, Emily. "On Oneworldedness; Or Paranoia as a World System." *American Literary History* 18 (2006), pp. 365–89.

Evans, David H. "Taking Out the Trash: Don DeLillo's *Underworld*, Liquid Modernity, and the End of Garbage." *Cambridge Quarterly* 35.2 (2006), pp. 103–32.
Spencer, Nicholas. "Beyond the Mutations of Media and Military Technologies in Don DeLillo's *Underworld*." *Arizona Quarterly* 58.2 (2002), pp. 89–112.
Wilcox, Leonard. "Don DeLillo's *Underworld* and the Return of the Real." *Contemporary Literature* 43 (2002), pp. 120–37.

9 DeLillo and masculinity

Connell, R. W. *Masculinities*. Cambridge: Polity, 2005.
Edwards, Tim. *Cultures of Masculinity*. London: Routledge, 2006.
Kimmel, Michael. S., *et al.*, eds. *Handbook of Studies on Men & Masculinities*. London: Sage, 2004.
Nel, Philip. "Homicidal Men and Full-Figured Women." In Tim Engles and John N. Duvall, eds., *Approaches to Teaching DeLillo's "White Noise."* New York: Modern Language Association of America Press, 2006, pp. 180–91.
Wesley, Marilyn. *Violent Adventures: Contemporary Fictions by American Men*. Charlottesville: University of Virginia Press, 2003. (See chapter 7 on *Libra*.)

10 DeLillo's Dedalian artists

Barrett, Laura. "'Here But Also There': Subjectivity and Postmodern Space in *Mao II*." *Modern Fiction Studies* 45.3 (1999), pp. 788–810.
Clippinger, D. "'Only Half Here': Don DeLillo's Image of the Writer in the Age of Mechanical Reproduction." In M. J. Meyer, ed., *Literature and the Writer*. Amsterdam and New York: Rodopi, 2004, pp. 135–53.
DiPrete, L. "Don DeLillo's *The Body Artist*: Performing the Body, Narrating Trauma." *Contemporary Literature* 46 (2005), pp. 483–510.
Lentricchia, Frank, and J. McAuliffe. *Crimes of Art and Terror*. Chicago: University of Chicago Press, 2003.
Osteen, Mark. "Echo Chamber: Undertaking *The Body Artist*." *Studies in the Novel* 37 (2005), pp. 64–81.
Simmons, Ryan. "What Is a Terrorist? Contemporary Authorship, The Unabomber, and *Mao II*." *Modern Fiction Studies* 45.3 (1999), pp. 675–95.

11 DeLillo and the power of language

Bonca, Cornel. "Don DeLillo's *White Noise*: The Natural Language of the Species." *College Literature* 23.2 (1996), pp. 25–44.
Cowart, David. *Don DeLillo: The Physics of Language*. Athens: University of Georgia Press, 2002. 2nd revd. edn 2003.
Foster, Dennis A. "Alphabetic Pleasures: *The Names*." In Frank Lentricchia, ed., *Introducing Don DeLillo*. Durham: Duke University Press, 1991, pp. 157–73.

12 DeLillo and mystery

Maltby, Paul. "The Romantic Metaphysics of Don DeLillo." *Contemporary Literature* 37 (1996), pp. 258–77.

Noya, José Liste. "Naming the Secret: Don DeLillo's *Libra*." *Contemporary Literature* 45 (2004), pp. 239–75.
Packer, Matthew J. "'At the Dead Center of Things' in Don DeLillo's *White Noise*." *Modern Fiction Studies* 51 (2005), pp. 648–66.

Conclusion: Writing amid the ruins: 9/11 and Cosmopolis

Baudrillard, Jean. *The Spirit of Terrorism and Other Essays*. Trans. Chris Turner. New York and London: Verso, 2002.
DeLillo, Don. "Baader-Meinhof." *New Yorker*, April 1, 2002, pp. 78–82.
Foer, Jonathan Safran. *Extremely Loud and Incredibly Close*. New York: Houghton Mifflin, 2005.
Kunkel, Benjamin. "Dangerous Characters." *New York Times*, September 11, 2005.
Spiegelman, Art. *In the Shadows of No Towers*. New York: Random House, 2004.
West, Paul. *The Immensity of the Here and Now: A Novel of 9.11*. Rutherford, NJ: Voyant, 2003.

INDEX

Cambridge Companions to ...

AUTHORS

Edward Albee edited by Stephen J. Bottoms

Margaret Atwood edited by Coral Ann Howells

W. H. Auden edited by Stan Smith

Jane Austen edited by Edward Copeland and
Juliet McMaster

Beckett edited by John Pilling

Aphra Behn edited by Derek Hughes and
Janet Todd

Walter Benjamin edited by David S. Ferris

William Blake edited by Morris Eaves

Brecht edited by Peter Thomson and Glendyr
Sacks (second edition)

The Brontës edited by Heather Glen

Frances Burney edited by Peter Sabor

Byron edited by Drummond Bone

Albert Camus edited by Edward J. Hughes

Willa Cather edited by Marilee Lindemann

Cervantes edited by Anthony J. Cascardi

Chaucer edited by Piero Boitani and
Jill Mann (second edition)

Chekhov edited by Vera Gottlieb and Paul Allain

Coleridge edited by Lucy Newlyn

Wilkie Collins edited by Jenny Bourne Taylor

Joseph Conrad edited by J. H. Stape

Dante edited by Rachel Jacoff (second edition)

Don DeLillo edited by John N. Duvall

Charles Dickens edited by John O. Jordan

Emily Dickinson edited by Wendy Martin

John Donne edited by Achsah Guibbory

Dostoevskii edited by W. J. Leatherbarrow

Theodore Dreiser edited by Leonard Cassuto and
Claire Virginia Eby

John Dryden edited by Steven N. Zwicker

W. E. B. Du Bois edited by Shamoon Zamir

George Eliot edited by George Levine

T. S. Eliot edited by A. David Moody

Ralph Ellison edited by Ross Posnock

Ralph Waldo Emerson edited by Joel Porte and
Saundra Morris

William Faulkner edited by Philip M. Weinstein

Henry Fielding edited by Claude Rawson

F. Scott Fitzgerald edited by Ruth Prigozy

Flaubert edited by Timothy Unwin

E. M. Forster edited by David Bradshaw

Brian Friel edited by Anthony Roche

Robert Frost edited by Robert Faggen

Elizabeth Gaskell edited by Jill L. Matus

Goethe edited by Lesley Sharpe

Thomas Hardy edited by Dale Kramer

David Hare edited by Richard Boon

Nathaniel Hawthorne edited by Richard
Millington

Ernest Hemingway edited by Scott Donaldson

Homer edited by Robert Fowler

Ibsen edited by James McFarlane

Henry James edited by Jonathan Freedman

Samuel Johnson edited by Greg Clingham

Ben Jonson edited by Richard Harp and
Stanley Stewart

James Joyce edited by Derek Attridge
(second edition)

Kafka edited by Julian Preece

Keats edited by Susan J. Wolfson

Lacan edited by Jean-Michel Rabaté

D. H. Lawrence edited by Anne Fernihough

Primo Levi edited by Robert Gordon

Lucretius edited by Stuart Gillespie and
Philip Hardie

David Mamet edited by Christopher Bigsby

Thomas Mann edited by Ritchie Robertson

Christopher Marlowe edited by Patrick Cheney

Herman Melville edited by Robert S. Levine

Arthur Miller edited by Christopher Bigsby

Milton edited by Dennis Danielson
(second edition)

Molière edited by David Bradby and
Andrew Calder

Toni Morrison edited by Justine Tally

Nabokov edited by Julian W. Connolly

Eugene O'Neill edited by Michael Manheim

George Orwell edited by John Rodden

Ovid edited by Philip Hardie

Harold Pinter edited by Peter Raby

Sylvia Plath edited by Jo Gill

Edgar Allan Poe edited by Kevin J. Hayes

Alexander Pope edited by Pat Rogers

Ezra Pound edited by Ira B. Nadel

Proust edited by Richard Bales

TOPICS

THE CAMBRIDGE COMPANION TO
DON DeLILLO

With the publication of his seminal novel *White Noise*, Don DeLillo was elevated into the pantheon of great American writers. His novels are admired and studied for their narrative technique, political themes, and prophetic commentary on the cultural crises affecting contemporary America. In an a␣␣ dominated by the image, DeLillo's fiction encourages the reader to think hi␣torically about such matters as the Cold War, the assassination of President Kennedy, threats to the environment, and terrorism. This *Companion* charts the shape of DeLillo's career, his relation to twentieth-century aesthetics, and his major themes. It also provides in-depth assessments of his best-known novels – *White Noise*, *Libra*, and *Underworld* – which have become required reading not only for students of American literature, but for everyone interested in the history and the future of American culture.

A complete list of books in the series is at the back of this book